IMAGES
of America

NORFOLK
NEBRASKA

Merry Christmas,
Doug!
from
"Bev"
Dec.
2002.

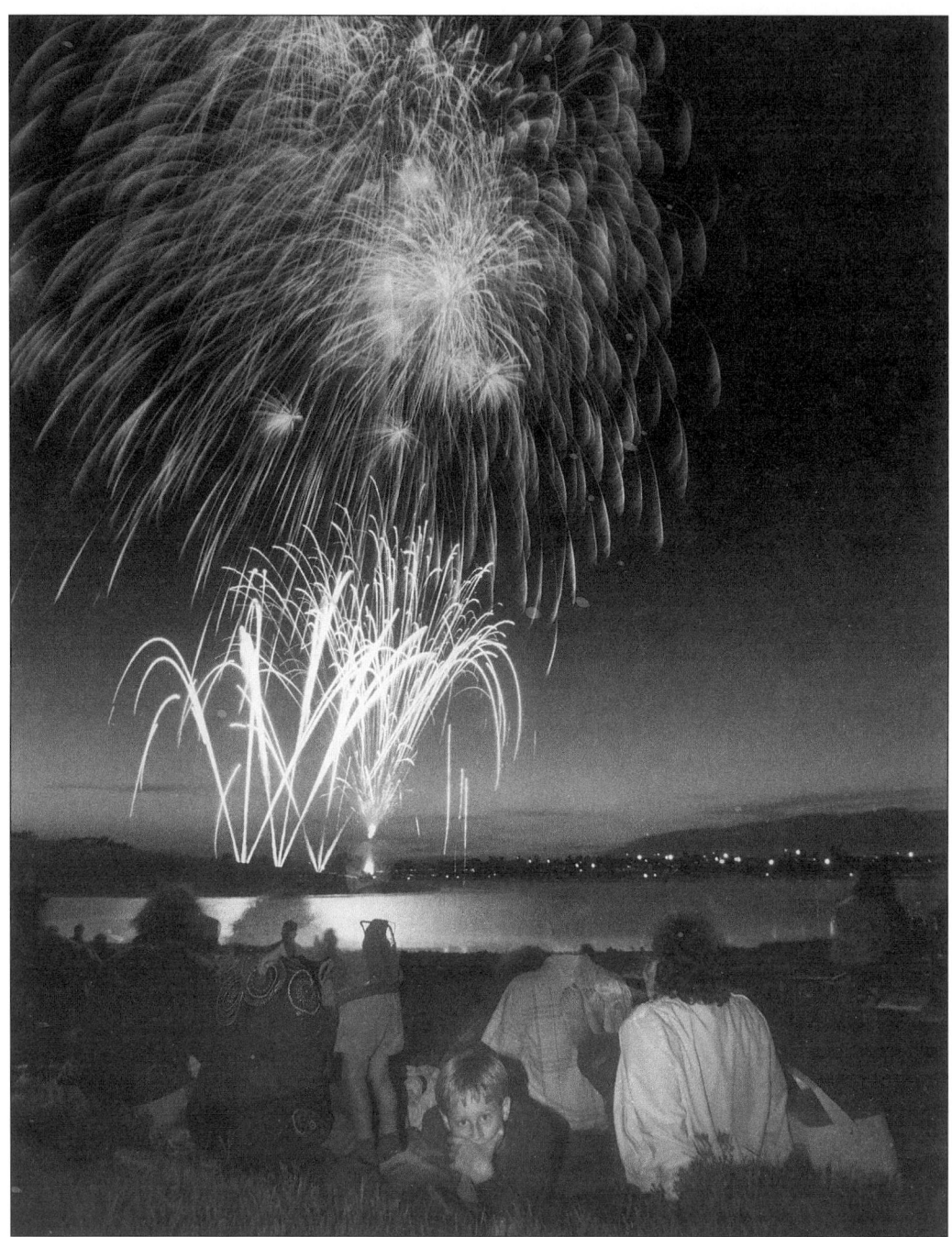

Fourth of July fireworks have been a tradition in Norfolk for many years. Orville Carlisle, who at one time owned Carlisle Shoes in Norfolk, was a fan of pyrotechnics and organized the first show with homemade rockets. Carlisle's first show at Skyview Lake was in 1976 in honor of the Bicentennial. Skyview Lake remains the site of the 4th of July celebration every year. Through the years, local businesses and civic organizations, including the Jaycees and later the Big Bang Boom Committee, have sponsored the event. The show itself is now produced by the Grucci Brothers, who have a long family history in pyrotechnics.

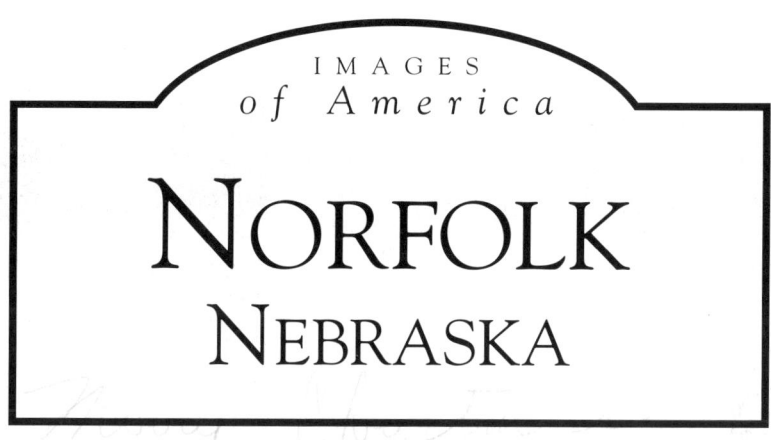

IMAGES
of America

NORFOLK
NEBRASKA

The Library Committee of the Elkhorn Valley Historical Society.

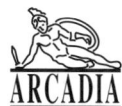

ARCADIA

Published by Arcadia Publishing,
an imprint of Tempus Publishing, Inc.
3047 N. Lincoln Ave., Suite 410
Chicago, IL 60657

Printed in Great Britain.

Library of Congress Catalog Card Number: Applied for.

For all general information contact Arcadia Publishing at:
Telephone 843-853-2070
Fax 843-853-0044
E-Mail sales@arcadiapublishing.com

For customer service and orders:
Toll-Free 1-888-313-2665

Visit us on the internet at http://www.arcadiapublishing.com

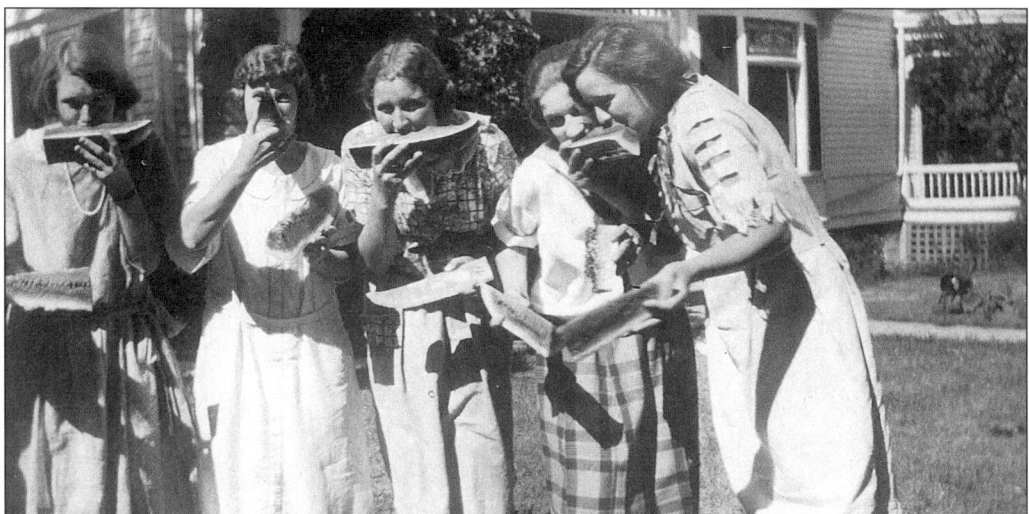

Norfolk is called "A slice of the good life" for a reason. The sandy soil in the area produces some of the best watermelons in the country. However, the rotund fruit wasn't introduced by early settlers; American Indians were growing watermelons here long before settlers came in the 1860s. Here a group of women eat watermelon the way they're supposed to—with their hands.

Cover Image: Farmers take a break from their threshing duties on a farm outside of Norfolk to enjoy a lunch delivered by the women and children.

CONTENTS

ACKNOWLEDGEMENTS

The story about to unfold before you takes place in a town that sprouted along the Elkhorn River in Northeast Nebraska in the late 1860s. While the book does include photographs of buildings, parks, and bridges, this book is about the people who made—and continue to make—Norfolk what it is today: an active, progressive community that entered the 21st century with a strong sense of its past and an eye on the future.

Putting together a history book is a little like putting together a puzzle. You find a piece here and a piece there, and hope, in the end, it all fits together. While it would be nice to include every building, event, and organization, that is impossible.

We do have many people to thank for helping us put the pieces of this book together. First, a hardy thank you to the committee members, Bernice Dewey, Joan Moody, Fred Stafford, and Nancy Zaruba, without whom this book would still be on the drawing board. These people sacrificed hours and hours of their time, often working late into the night to make this book the best it could be. We would also like to thank Mickie Ryan for proofreading our text.

Most of the photographs in this volume are from the Elkhorn Valley Museum and Research Center's permanent collection. The donors to this collection are too numerous to mention here, but we would like to thank them all for their contributions. We would also like to thank Jerry Huse and the *Norfolk Daily News* for giving us unlimited access to their photograph files, and to Dennis Meyer and Denny Fleming of the *Norfolk Daily News* for scanning and reproducing photographs. Thanks to American Legion Post 16, the Missionary Benedictine Sisters, Mary's Café, Nebraska Christian College, Northeast Community College, Prenger's, Radio Station WJAG, Senior Citizens Center, Tastee Treet, and VFW Post 1644 for loaning photographs and providing information.

Thank you to the Nebraska State Historical Society who gave us permission to reprint photographs from their collection. The Norfolk Public Library allowed us to use the Cora Beels collection and provided research assistance. Many, many other businesses and individuals dug up elusive facts, dates, and names.

And last but not least, thanks to the citizens of Norfolk for providing us with such a colorful history.

—Sheryl Schmeckpeper and Amy Mancini-Marshall, project chairpersons.

INTRODUCTION

A group of German immigrants left their homesteads in Ixonia, Wisconsin, leaving behind cold wet winters and expensive farmland, to settle at the confluence of the Elkhorn and the Northfork of the Elkhorn rivers in Northeast Nebraska. The year was 1866. The immigrants had come to America seeking relief from political repression and crop failures in Germany. They had originally been lured to Wisconsin with the promise of religious freedom, inexpensive farmland, low taxes, and the opportunity to become a citizen within a year.

What they found, however, was farmland selling for $35 to $40 an acre and less than fertile soil. So during the summer of 1865, three of the immigrants—Ferdinand Wagner, Herman Braasch, and John Gensmer—left Wisconsin to investigate portions of Northeast Nebraska as a possible settlement site.

Impressed with the area's rich prairie, trees, and streams, the group returned to Wisconsin and prepared to bring 42 families consisting of about 125 people to Nebraska. They arrived on July 17, 1866—each family bringing two cows, some sheep, and a wagon drawn by oxen—and quickly divided the area into 160-acre plots and proceeded to build their log and sod houses.

They were met by tribes of the Pawnee, Omaha, and Ponca Indians, who had lived in the area for many years. The Indians, and later fur trappers and traders, were Northeast Nebraska's first inhabitants.

The immigrants from Wisconsin plowed and planted the fields, spun their own cloth on handlooms, and made their own wooden shoes. Famine, disease, fire, floods, and blizzards tested their spirits, but they survived.

In 1868, the German farmers asked that a post office be established for their town of "Norfork." However, government officials, thinking the word had been misspelled, changed it to "Norfolk." On July 3, 1868, the first mail was delivered by Postmaster August Raasch.

Norfolk continued to attract settlers and by 1879 had a population of five hundred. Local businesses included five general stores, a land office, two hotels, two furniture stores, a bank, drug store, and many others. The first train, part of the Fremont, Elkhorn, & Missouri Valley Railroad, arrived in Norfolk on September 15, 1879. By 1885, the Union Pacific Railroad was providing daily service from Norfolk to Omaha. With the railroads came more new businesses, the need for village incorporation, and other community improvements, such as a police force, electric lights, and a telephone system.

On September 24, 1881, Charles Mathewson, August Pilger, John Koenigstein, Frederick Lucas, and John C. Olney were sworn in as the first village trustees. City ordinances were established covering everything from the sale of alcohol to keeping livestock within the city limits, and from street repair to civic improvements.

By 1900, the town had a population of three thousand, a police force and fire department, a street railway, water and sewer systems, electricity and telephones, and a new sugar beet refining factory. The eighth mayor was in office and Norfolk's first high school class had graduated. Real estate prices were also on the rise. Lots that would have sold for $175 to $200 in 1880 sold for $400 to $450 in 1882.

Religion has always been important to Norfolk residents. The Germans who first settled in the area established St. Paul's Evangelical Lutheran Church in 1866. By 1900, Norfolk was also home to the First Congregational Church of Norfolk, which was organized in 1870; the Methodist Episcopal Church, which was organized in 1875; and a Catholic Church, which was organized in 1880.

In the past one hundred years, Norfolk has evolved from a cow town to the industrial and trade center of Northeast Nebraska. With a population of 22,000, Norfolk is home to four high schools, three colleges, a veterans' home, and the Norfolk Regional Center. Plus it has survived its share of natural disasters, including the floods of 1944 and 1962 and the blizzard of 1948–49.

Other notable dates in Norfolk's history are: 1877—Norfolk's first weekly newspaper is published; 1913—A.J. Colwell received a patent for his Square Turn Tractor, which was manufactured in Norfolk during the early 20th century; 1916—Verges Park is dedicated; 1919—the Norfolk Livestock Market is founded; 1922—radio station WJAG receives its broadcast license; 1923—the Lutheran Community Hospital opens; 1929—the old mill wheel at the Norfolk Mill is replaced with a hydroelectric power plant; 1934—the DeLay National Bank is robbed; 1935—Our Lady of Lourdes Hospital is opened; 1944—Norfolk is covered in floodwaters; 1948—fire destroys Chicago Lumber Company and most of the buildings on that block; 1948–49—the winter of the great blizzards that killed people and livestock throughout the Midwest; 1968—the Northfork of the Elkhorn River flood control project was completed to protect the city from the type of floods that occurred in 1944 and 1962; 1992—Johnny Carson Theatre is opened; 1997—the Elkhorn Valley Museum and Research Center opens; 1998—the Lifelong Learning Center opens; 1998—Norfolk hosts its first Holiday Rhapsody of Lights Festival.

The new millennium will present as many challenges and opportunities as the one just passed. The battles may not be easy. There will probably always be fires, droughts, and floods, but Norfolkans have proven that they are a determined bunch. Years from now, when the next group of people gather to compile a history book, they will understand why Norfolk really is a "slice of the good life."

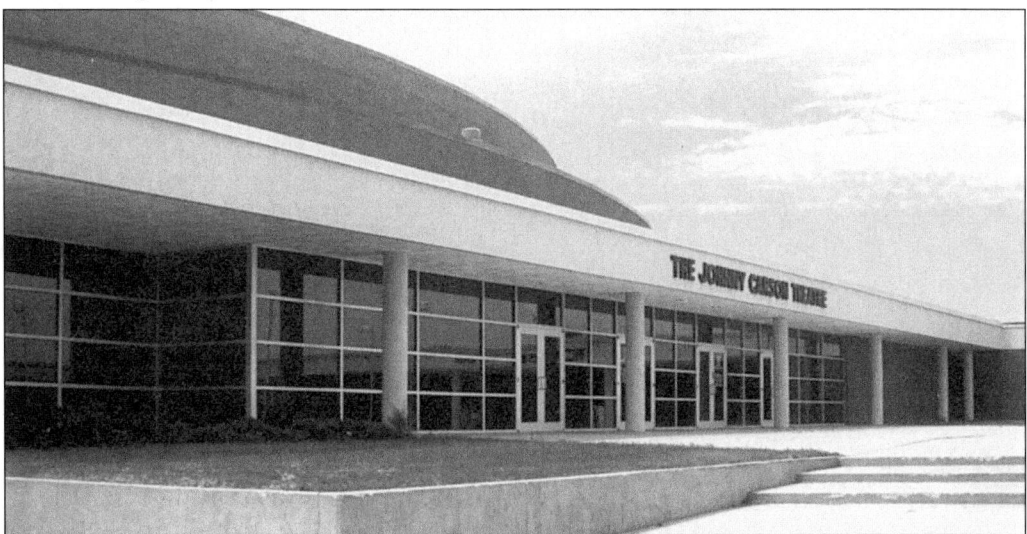

Since opening in 1992, Johnny Carson Theatre has hosted any number of activities, including concerts, plays, debates, and school programs. The 1,234-seat theater was funded, in part, with private donations, including a generous gift from its namesake, Johnny Carson.

One
EARLY DAYS
1866–1889

"Once you have heard the meadow lark and caught the scent of fresh plowed earth, peace cannot escape you."

—Sequiche

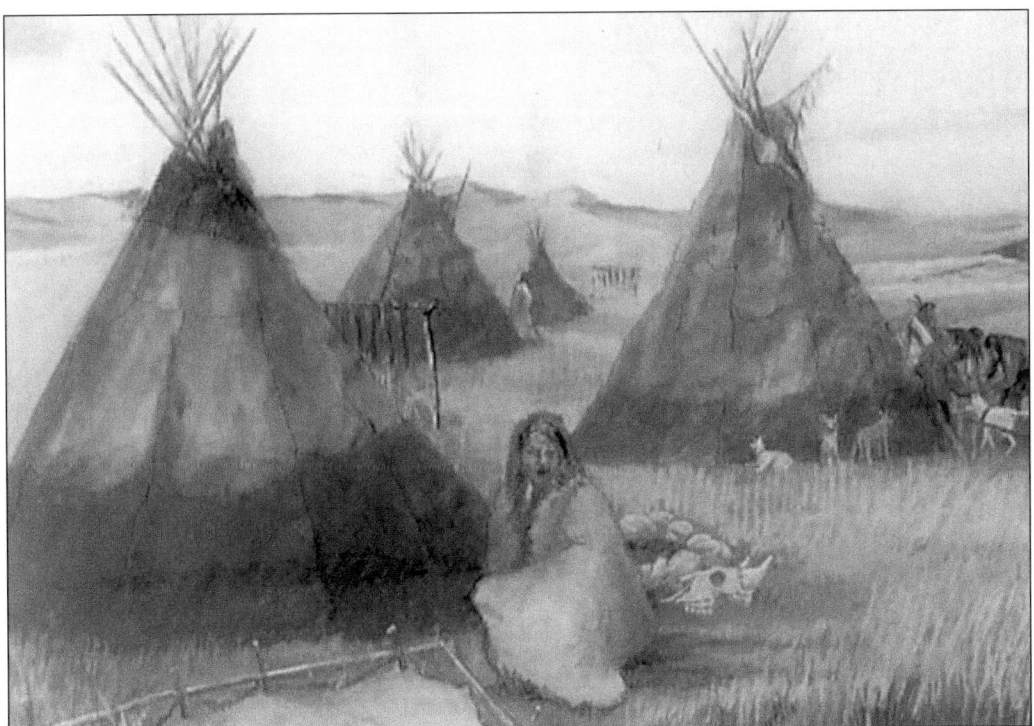

Evidence of American Indian settlement in Northeast Nebraska dates back to 400 A.D. It is believed that the first European contact was made in 1541 by Spanish explorers who met the Pawnee in this area. The Pawnee were farmers who relied on buffalo for their meat. They camped in tipis, like the ones depicted here, while on buffalo hunts.

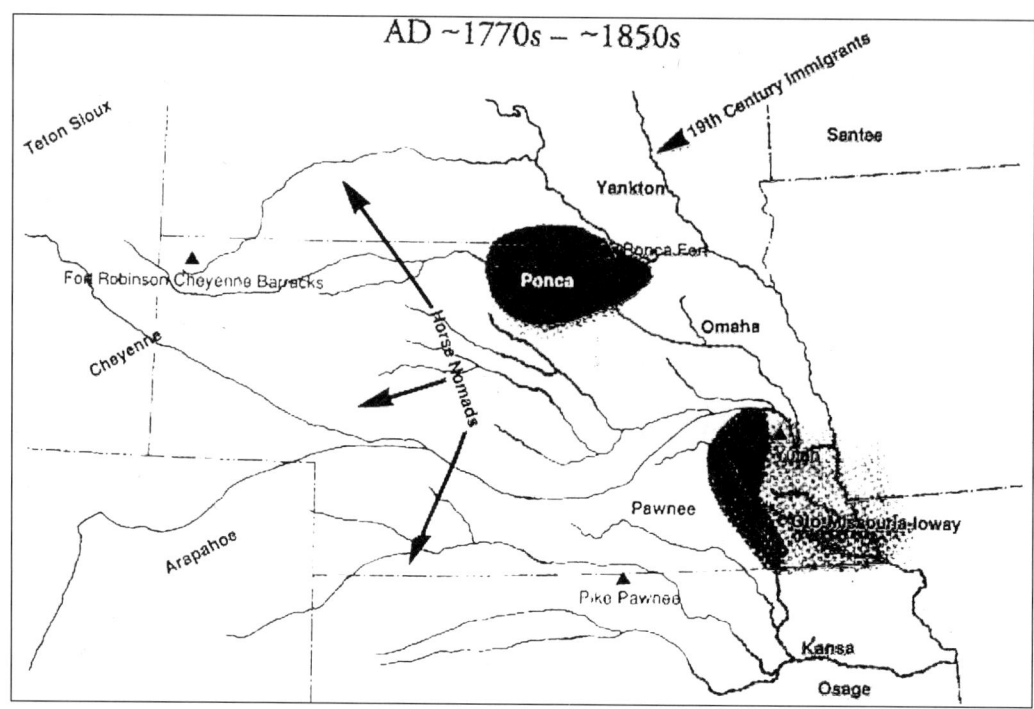

Eastern Nebraska has been blessed with an adequate water supply, rich farmland, rolling hills, and numerous animals. Farming combined with buffalo hunting met the needs of the many tribes in the region for hundreds of years.

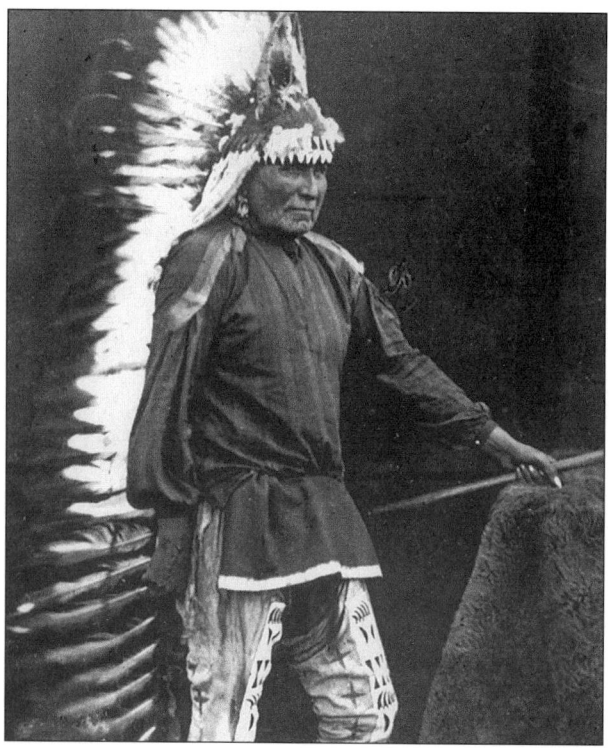

Pawnee Chief Peta-le-sharu led a band of eight hundred Pawnee from Fontanelle to West Point stealing one hundred head of cattle. The men were trapped in a house and ordered to surrender. Gunshots broke out; one white man and four Pawnee men were killed. U.S. troops were deployed, and they tracked the Pawnee to a camp ten miles above the fork of the Elkhorn River. Chief Peta-le-sharu unconditionally surrendered and agreed to pay for the property destroyed. The site of the meeting is present-day Battle Creek, so named to commemorate the battle that never was.

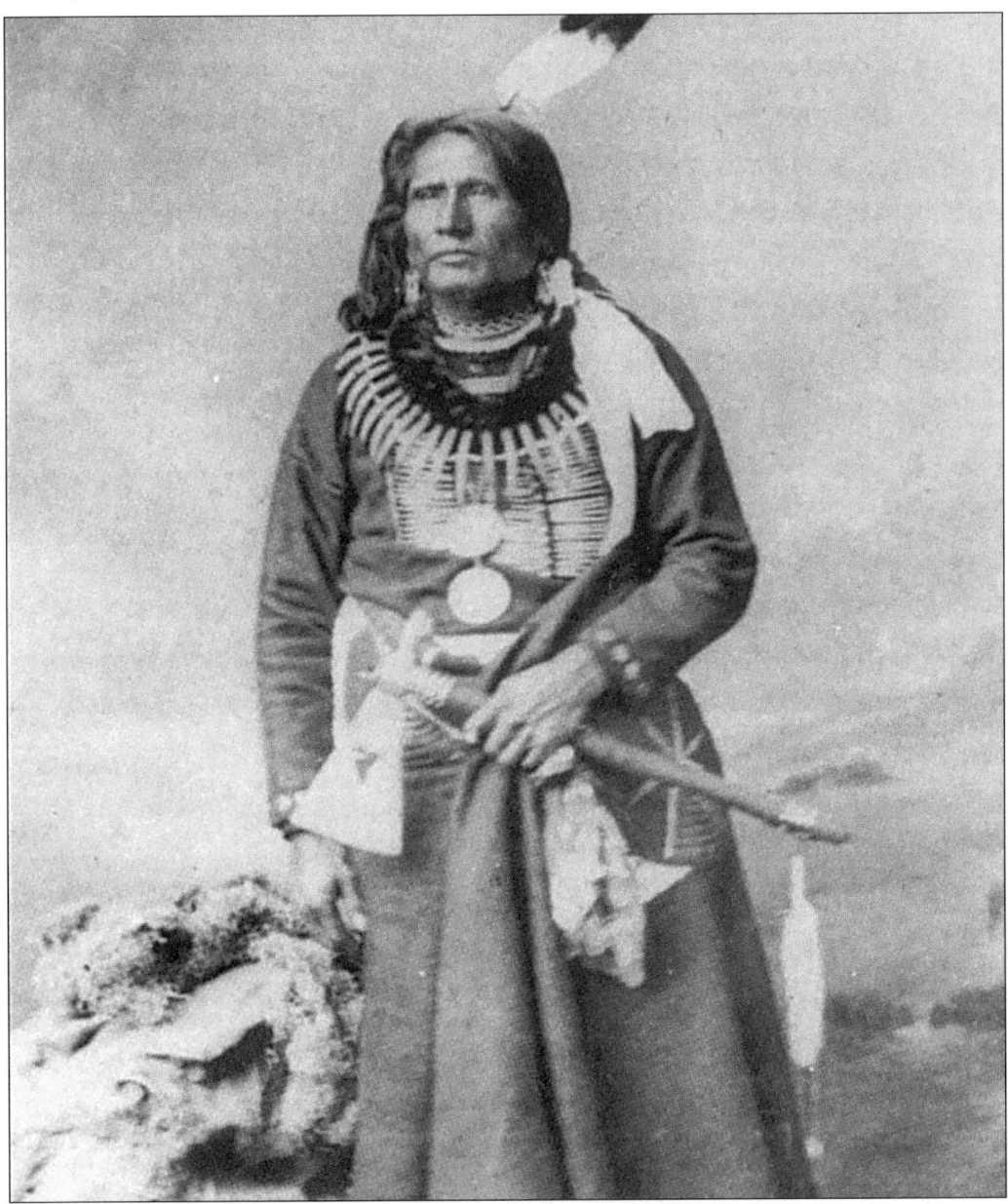

The Ponca Tribe was forced to move to Indian Territory in Oklahoma in 1878. Traveling in the winter, over one-third of the tribe died on the journey. Chief Standing Bear (pictured here) lost his son in Oklahoma, so several Ponca men set out for the burial grounds in Nebraska. They were arrested by the army and labeled renegades. The *Omaha World Herald* took up their cause, and two Omaha attorneys wrote a writ of *habeas corpus* to prevent the men from being removed to Oklahoma. The government argued that an Indian was not a person under the law and could not appeal to the courts. In the case of *Standing Bear v. Crook*, the court ruled on May 12, 1879, that "an Indian is a person within the meaning of the law" and free to live where he chooses. In 1881, the government stated "a great wrong" had been done to the Ponca people, and 26,236 acres in Knox County, Nebraska, were set aside for the tribe. Half of the tribe returned from Oklahoma to Nebraska.

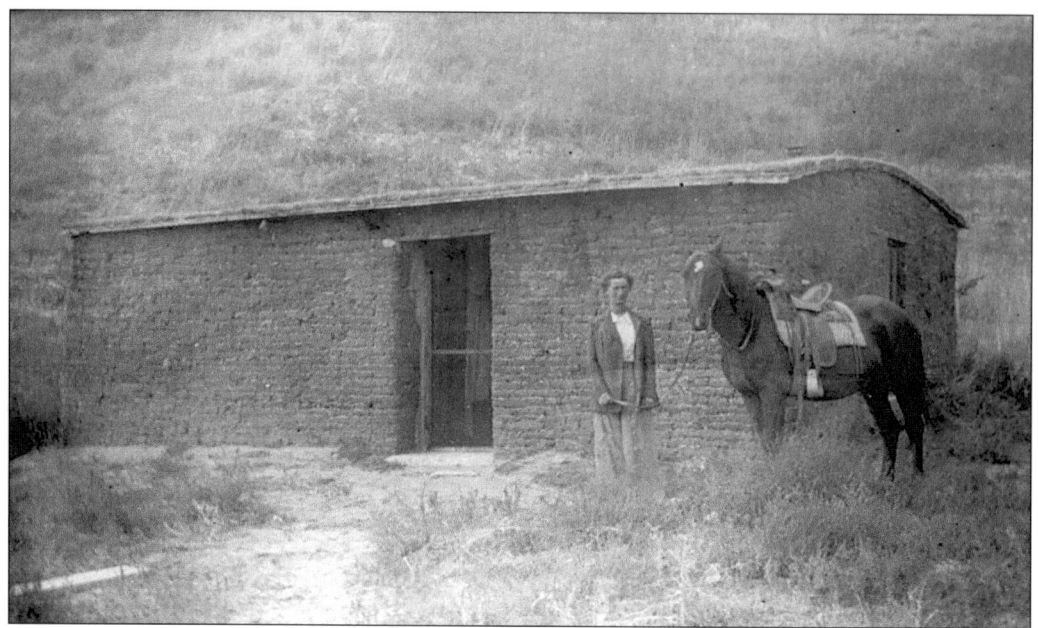

In the Great American Desert, an unidentified woman and her horse stand outside a "soddy," a typical first dwelling for many of the early settlers. Sod houses, constructed of 50-pound sod bricks and wooden poles, were inexpensive to build, cool in the summer, and warm in the winter. However, they were difficult to keep clean and were often home to mice, snakes, and bugs, in addition to people.

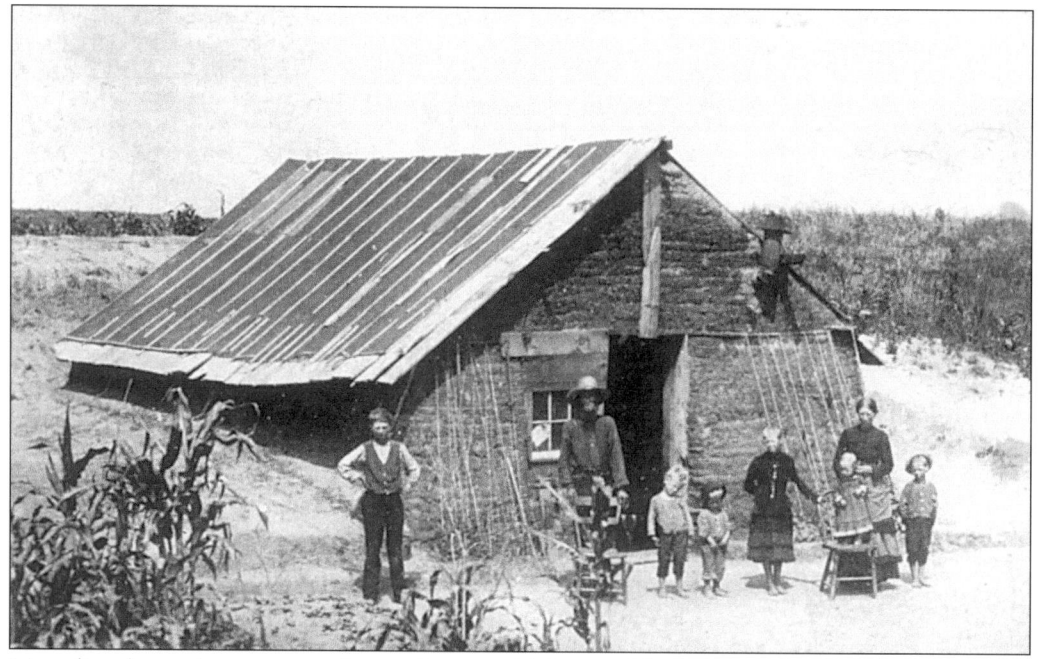

It's a dirty house but someone has to live in it! Many sod houses were built into the side of a hill for extra strength against the cold Nebraska wind. The Steele family homesteaded on a 40-acre tract one-fourth of a mile west of 1st Street, and three and one-fourth miles south of Norfolk Avenue in 1883.

John Frederick Dederman and Maria Heckman Dederman traveled with the original colony from Ixonia, Wisconsin, in 1866. The group of 125 German settlers established a small farming community along the banks of the Northfork of the Elkhorn River. Once there, the colonists drew lots for farms fronting on the river.

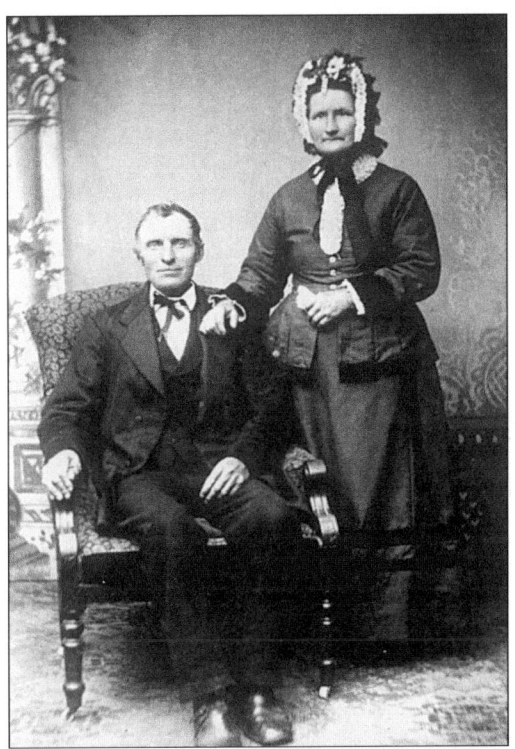

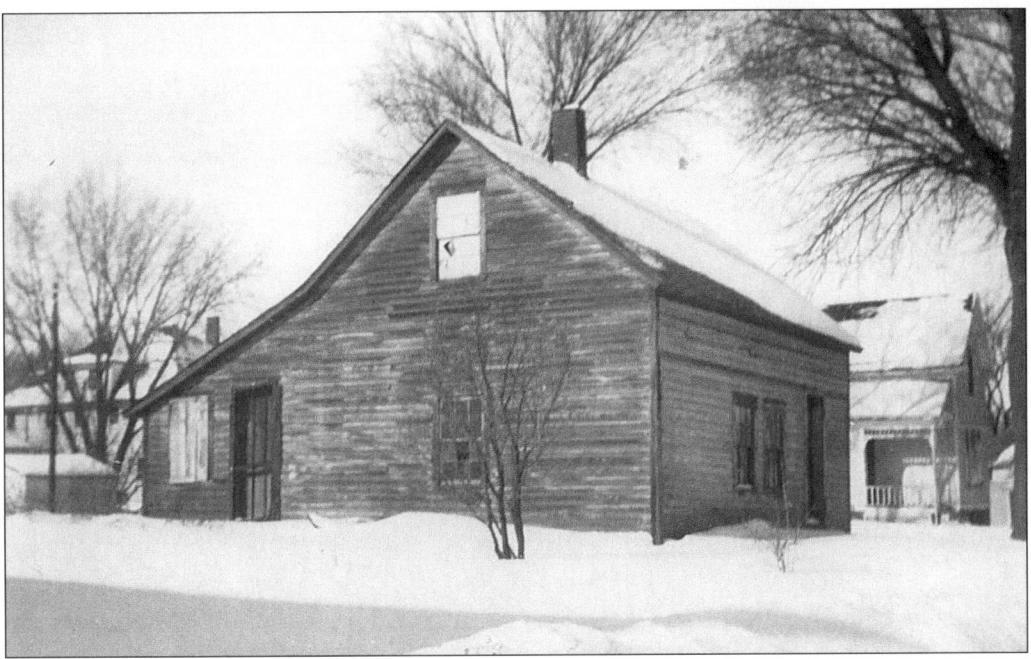

The Dederman family was fortunate to have enough wood to build this cabin on what is now North 8th Street. John and Maria built this home in 1869. The cabin is now Norfolk's oldest standing structure. It was moved to Johnson Park in 1941 and has undergone a number of transformations since this photo was taken, although the present cabin is part of the original structure.

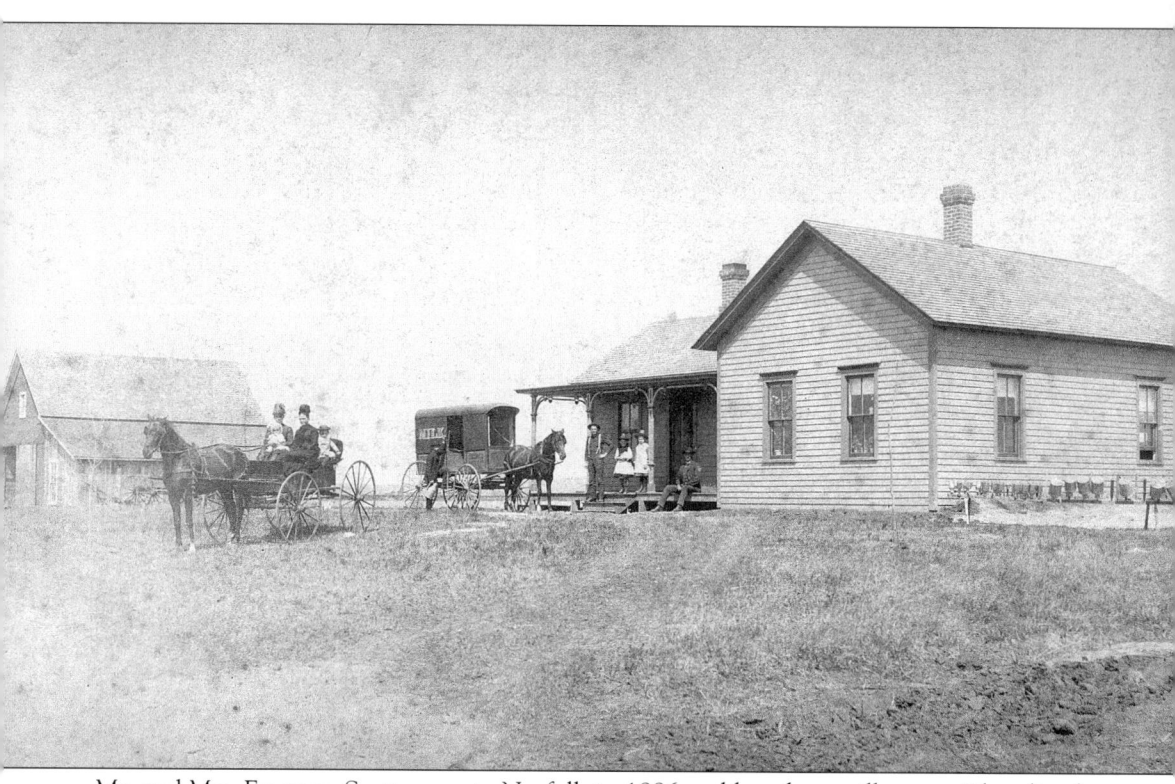

Mr. and Mrs. Freeman Scott came to Norfolk in 1886 and bought a milk route. They lived on a farm located at what is now the intersection of Omaha Avenue and 4th Street. In the wagon are Mrs. Scott holding Horace Leslie, Aunt Lucy Higley, and Arthur Wayne in the back seat. Behind them, by the milk wagon, is Mr. Scott (the horse is Jule), and on the steps are (from left to right) John C. Adams, Minnie Ann Scott, Minnie E. Higley, and Clark Higley. Note the milk cans hanging on the fence.

Cora Beels collected photographs of each of the original founders of Norfolk, including this image of Mrs. J.M. Machmueller. Mr. Machmuller would not have his picture taken as he thought it was wicked to do so.

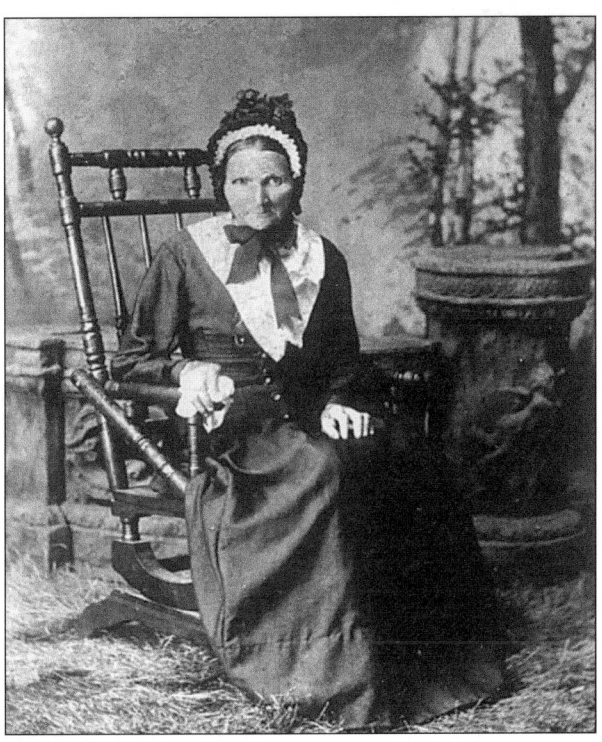

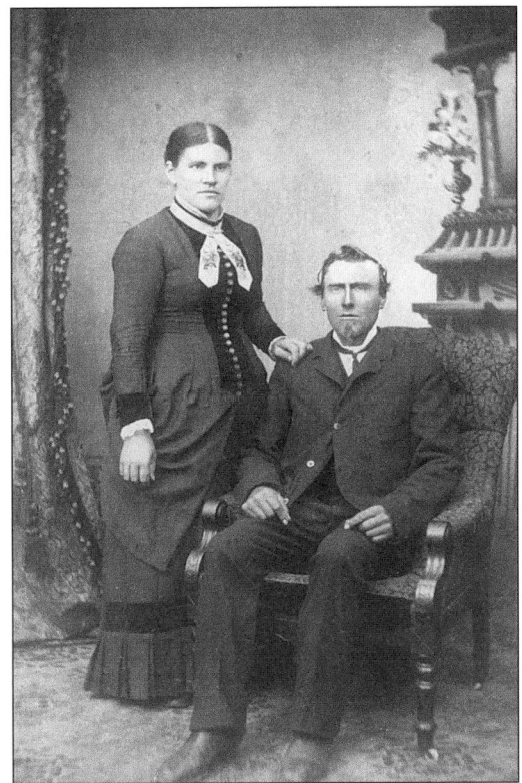

Maria (Rohrke) and August Raasch pose for their wedding photograph on June 6, 1872. The city selected August to be Norfolk's first postmaster on June 4, 1868, because of his excellent Civil War record. The first mail delivery consisted of three letters delivered to the Raasch home west of the village.

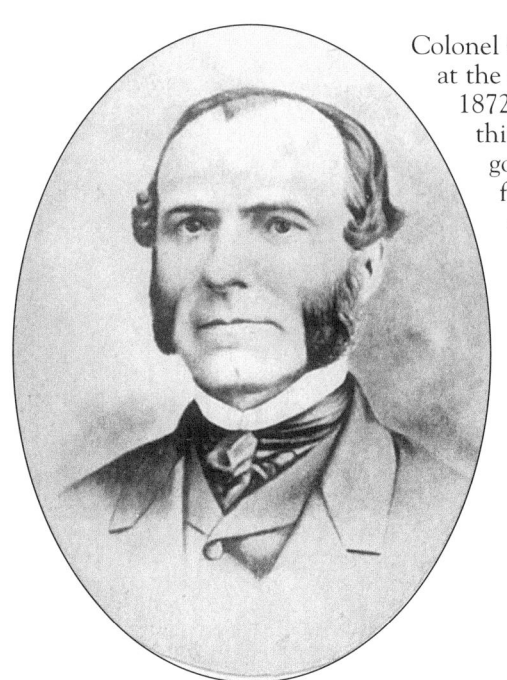

Colonel Charles Mathewson opened Norfolk's first bank at the corner of 2nd Street and Norfolk Avenue in 1872. The Norfolk National Bank hosted the town's third post office location, and was the site of city government meetings. Mathewson served as the first chairman of the village trustees beginning on September 24, 1881, the official date of Norfolk's incorporation.

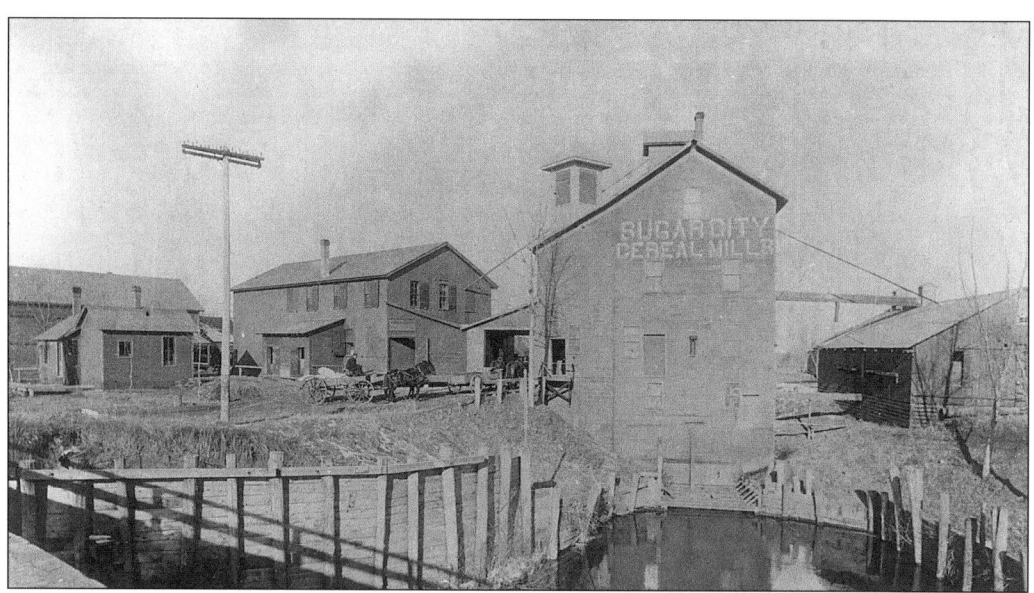

Built in 1870 at the corner of Norfolk Avenue and State Street (now 1st Street) by Col. Charles Mathewson and his two sons, Charles and Joseph, the Norfolk Mill served as both a sawmill and gristmill. The mill store operated an early general store and Norfolk's post office. By 1897, when this photograph was taken, the new owners had completely remodeled and added several additional buildings to the mill complex.

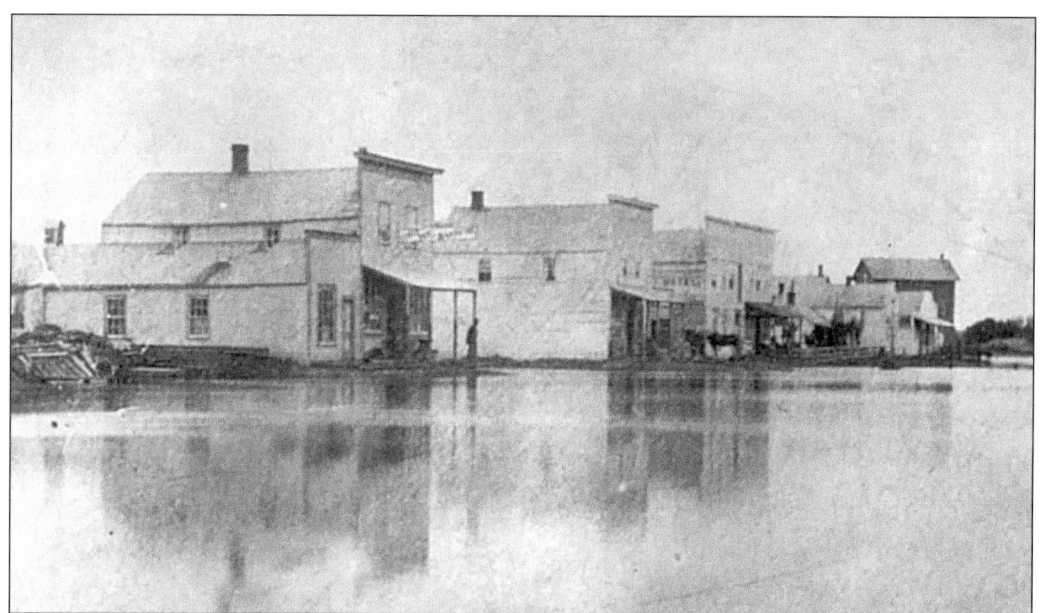

The raging waters look like peaceful, reflecting glass on this day during the 1877 flood. This photograph was taken from the steps of Pilger's Store looking to the northeast on Norfolk Avenue. The mill can be seen at the far end of the street. Flooding would prove to be an unfortunate trend for the city's next 90 years.

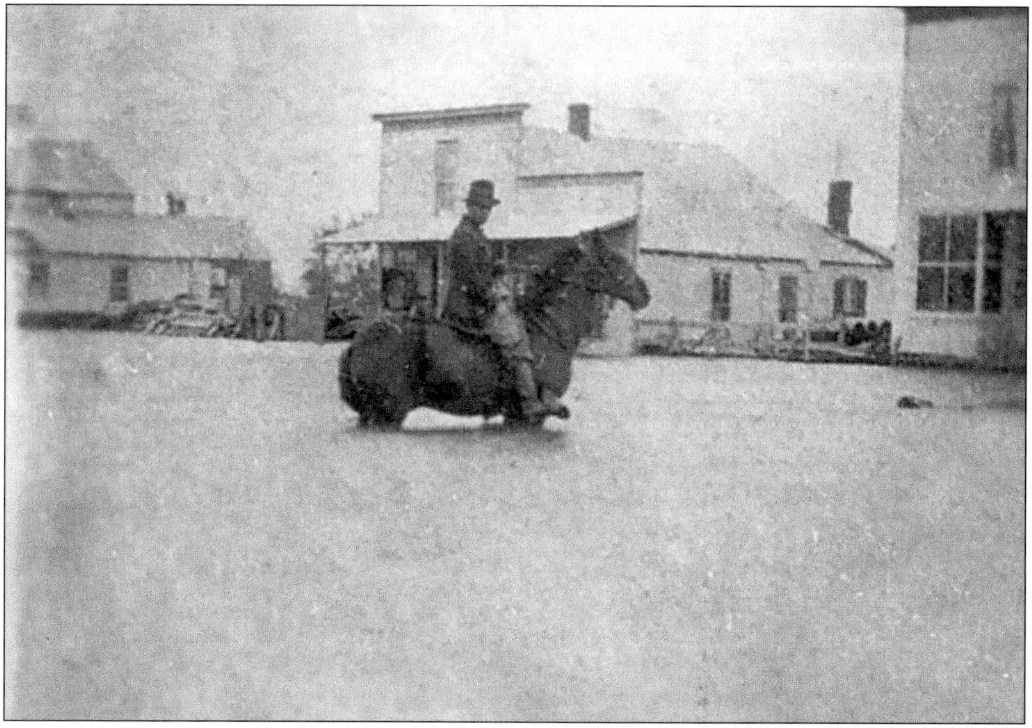

Stranded! This hapless rider and his horse have gotten themselves into some deep water during the flood of 1877. The buildings behind them are on the north side of the second block of Norfolk Avenue.

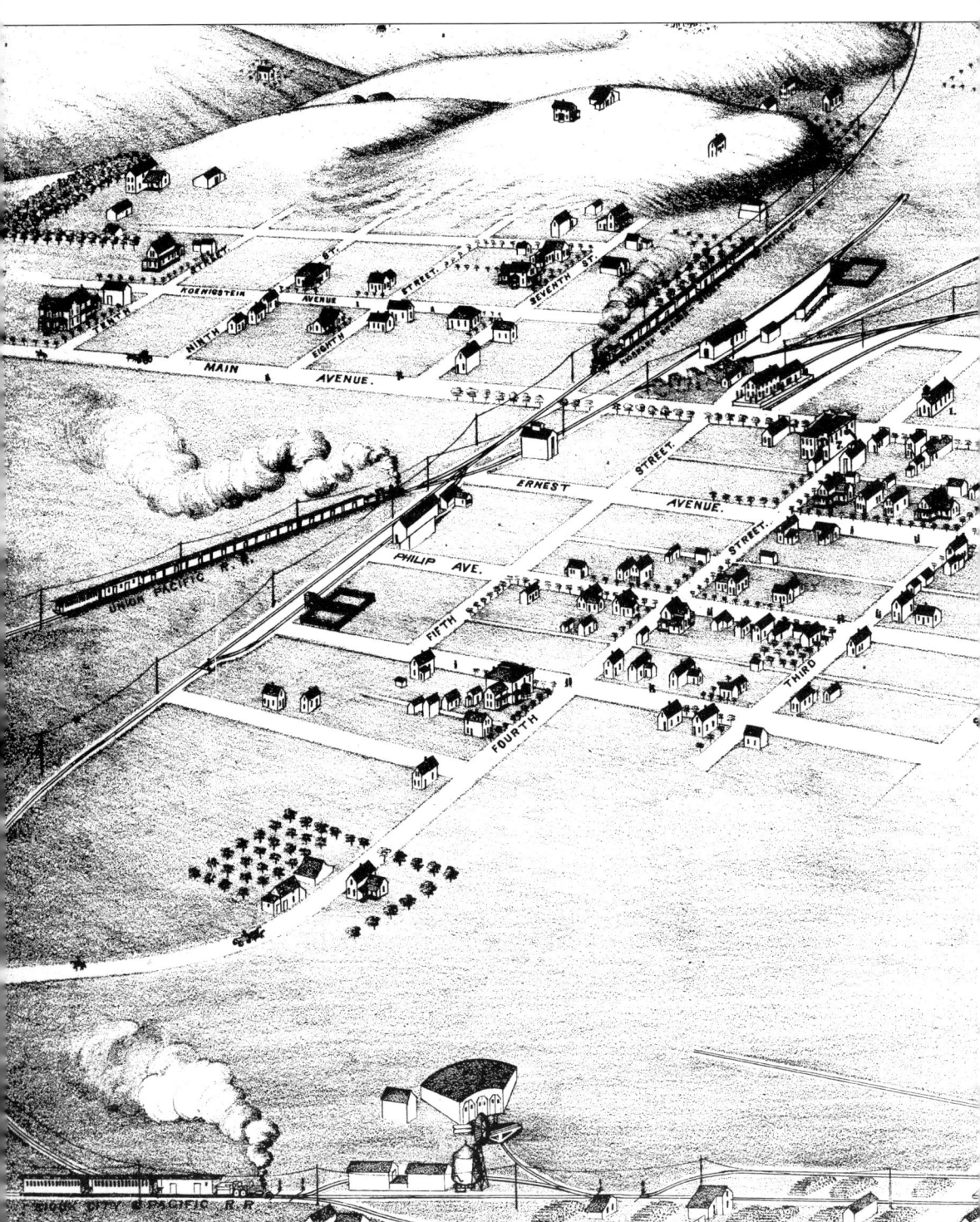

The first settlers arrived in Norfolk in 1866, and by 1881 Norfolk was home to more than five hundred people and a variety of businesses, including a mill, land office, hardware stores, railroads, several churches, and schools. Artist Augustus Koch created this sketch of Norfolk as

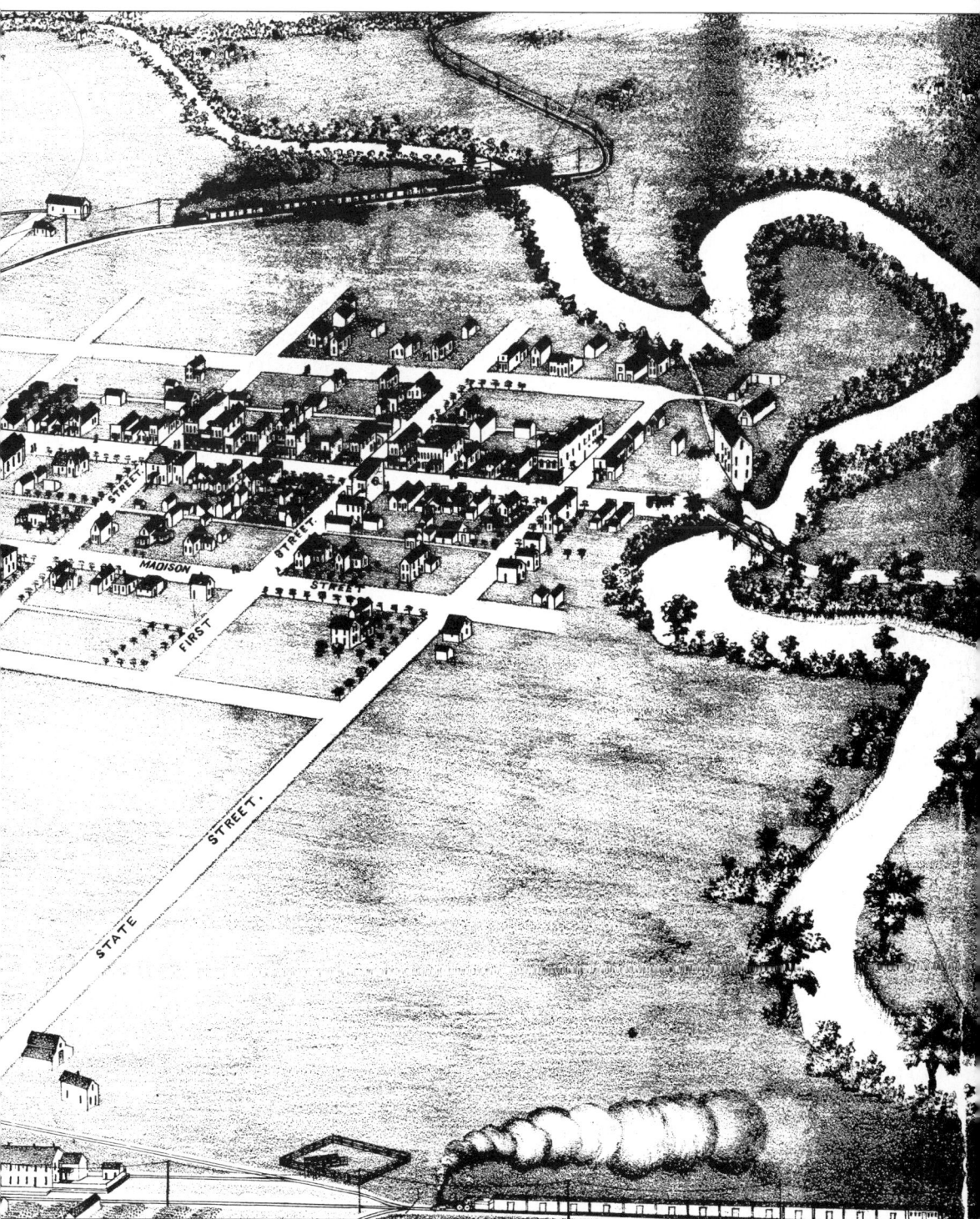

it appeared in 1881. The winding Elkhorn River served as Norfolk's eastern boundary for decades. Of considerable note are the three different railroad lines entering the village: the Union Pacific, the Sioux City & Pacific, and the St. Paul & Sioux City.

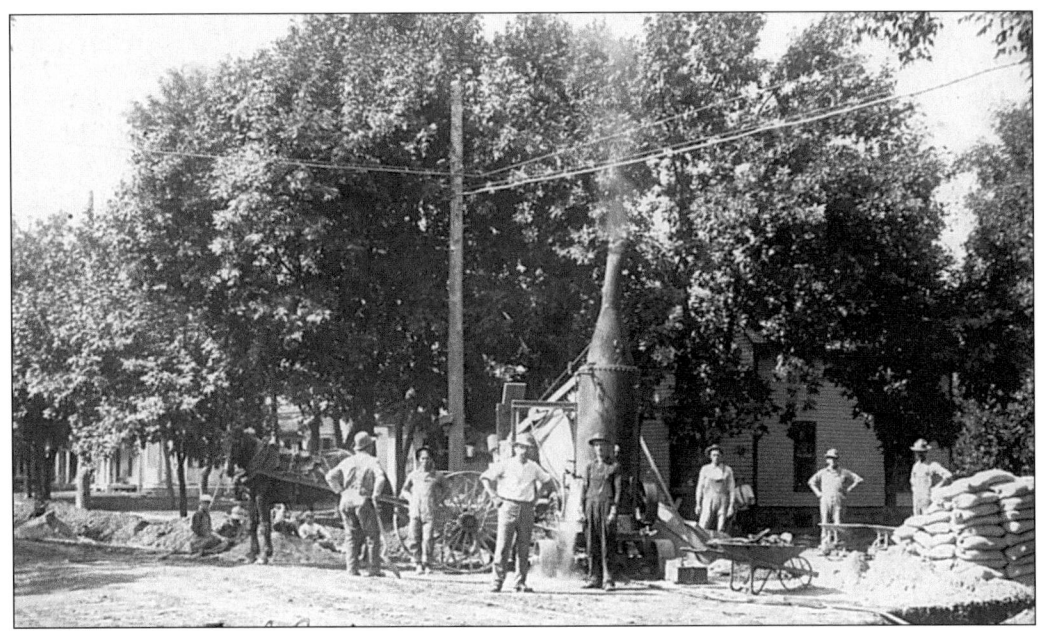

These street workers are taking a break after a hard day's work, in 1883. By city ordinance, all able-bodied men between the ages of 21 and 50 had to perform two days' labor on the streets each year beginning in 1882. The men would mow and grade streets, build crossings, and widen roads. Apparently, this corner was "the place to be" for the small boys in the neighborhood who watch from the edge of the road.

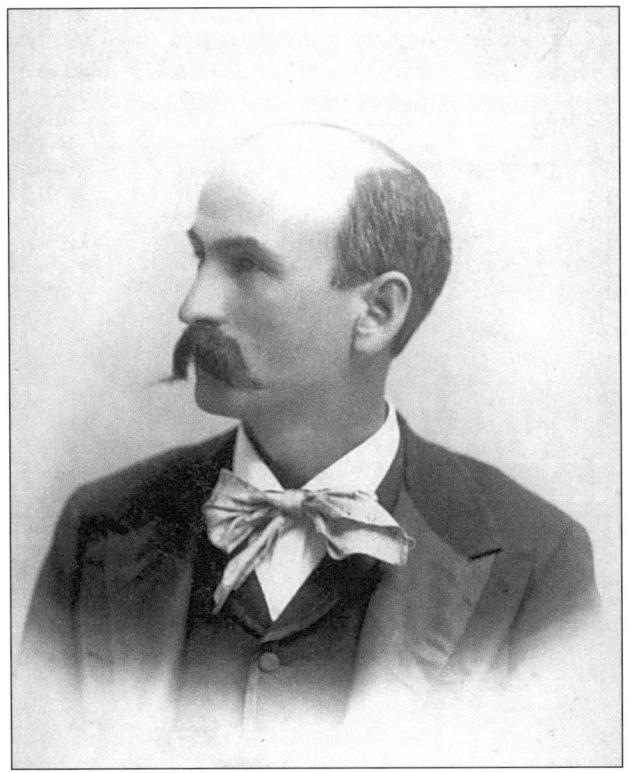

George A. Latimer came to Norfolk in 1884 and was elected Madison County's surveyor just two years later. Latimer also served as Norfolk's city engineer between 1884 and 1890. During these years, the city grew tremendously, adding 23 new housing additions.

Modeling the "Little Lord Fauntleroy" fashion, if not the hair, is Darius Raasch, far left. Darius and his sisters Leona, center, and Hedwig were the children of August and Maria Raasch.

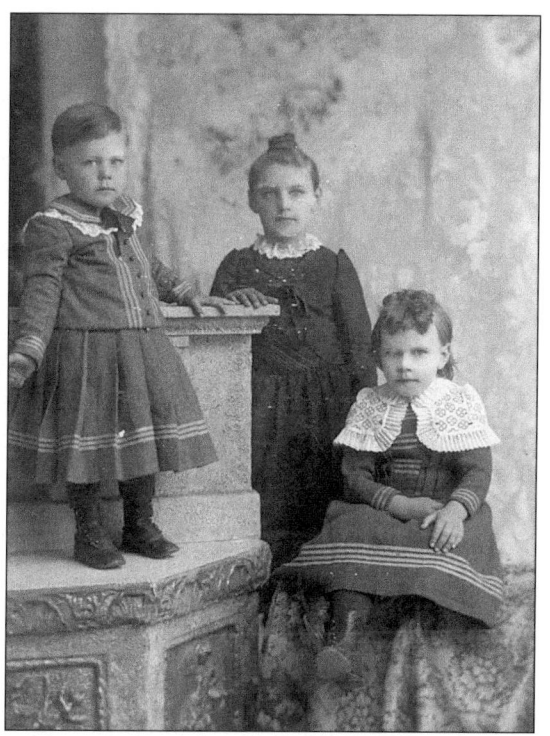

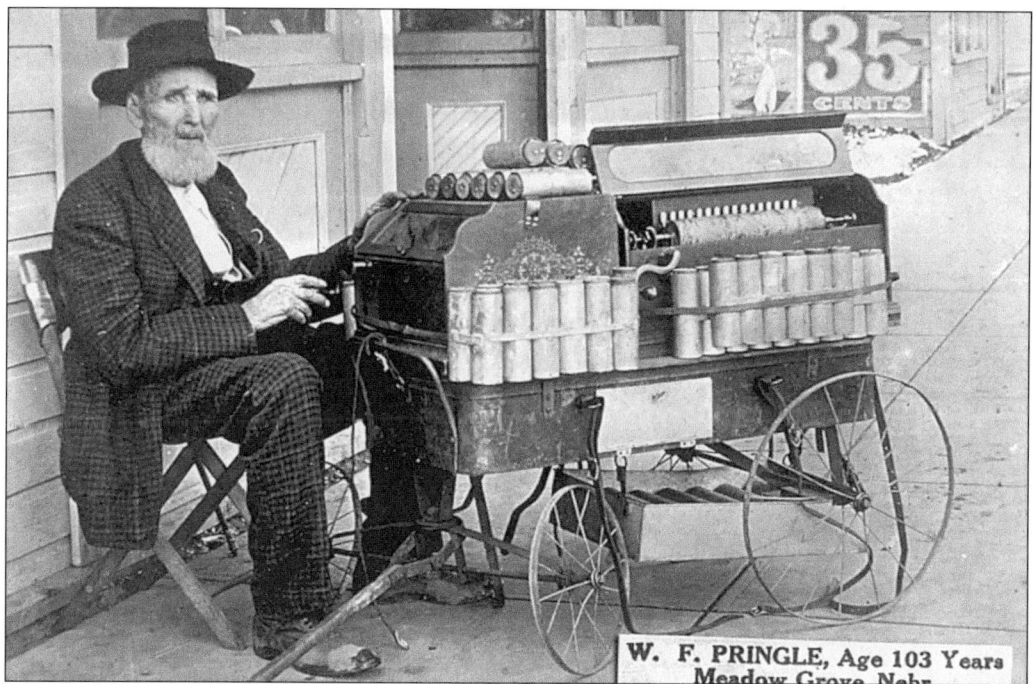

W. F. PRINGLE, Age 103 Years
Meadow Grove, Nebr.

William Forest "Grandpa" Pringle played his hand-cranked music box on the streets of Norfolk for many years. Grandpa died in 1913 at the age of 107; he was the oldest Nebraskan at the time. While living on the Madison County Poor Farm, Grandpa would meet the passenger trains in various towns to panhandle for money by playing his hurdy gurdy.

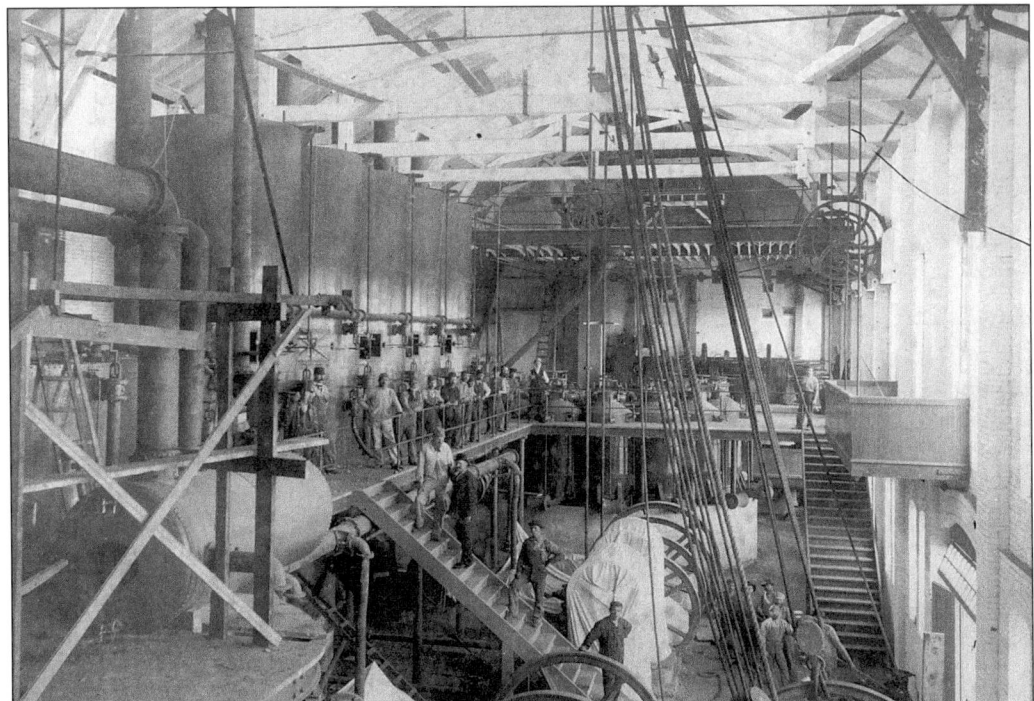

Norfolk became home to the Oxnard Company Sugar Beet Factory after defeating 21 other communities. Opened October 15, 1891, the factory refined 2,500 acres of sugar beet crops grown around Norfolk. The company offered prizes for the best three acres of beet crops; first prize was $200 and a silver medal.

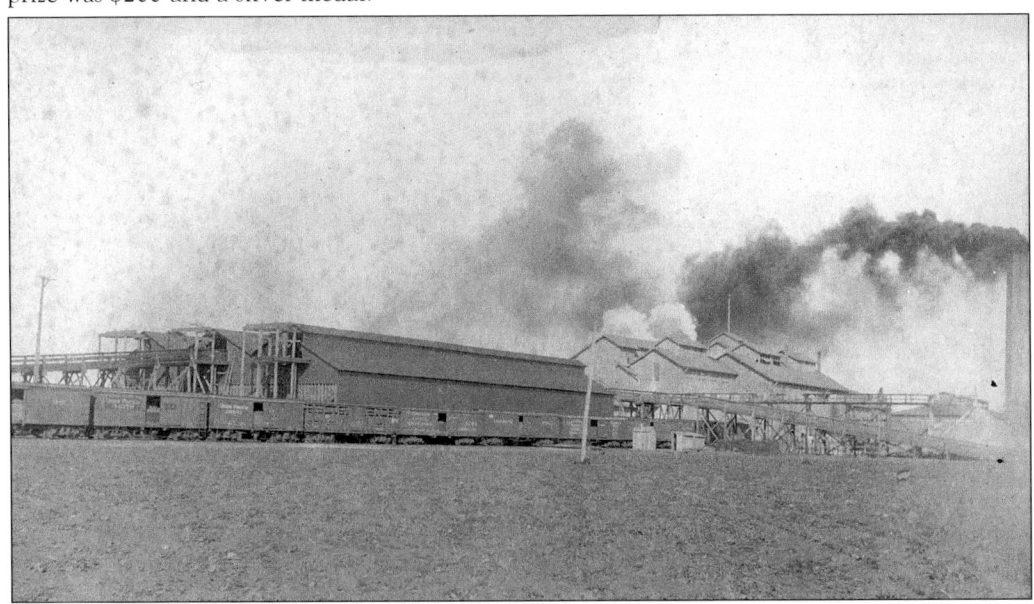

In 1881, Nebraska implemented a one-penny bounty for each pound of sugar produced from Nebraska sugar beets or sorghum. This bounty plus the two-cent per pound bonus given by the federal government made sugar refining very lucrative. In 1893, the Norfolk factory operated for three months and produced 5,590,000 pounds of sugar.

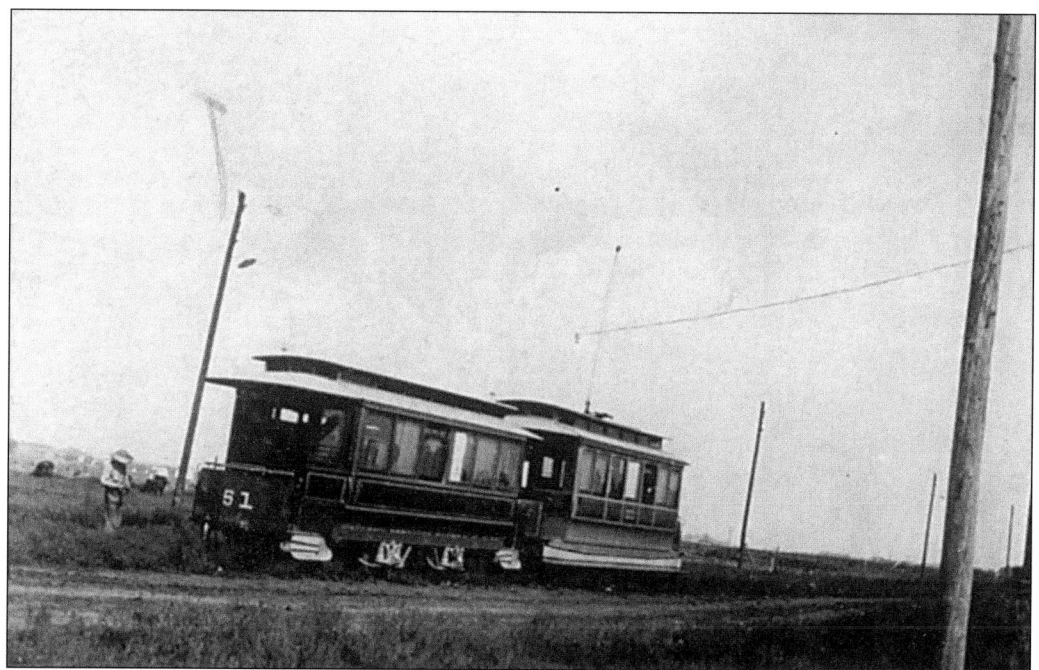

Now people could live in town and work in the country; an electric street railway transported workers from Norfolk Avenue to the factory located in the 1900 block of Riverside Boulevard. Three passenger trains also brought laborers from Omaha for the harvest. The factory spurred a housing boom; in 1892, all houses in Norfolk, including 175 new ones, were occupied.

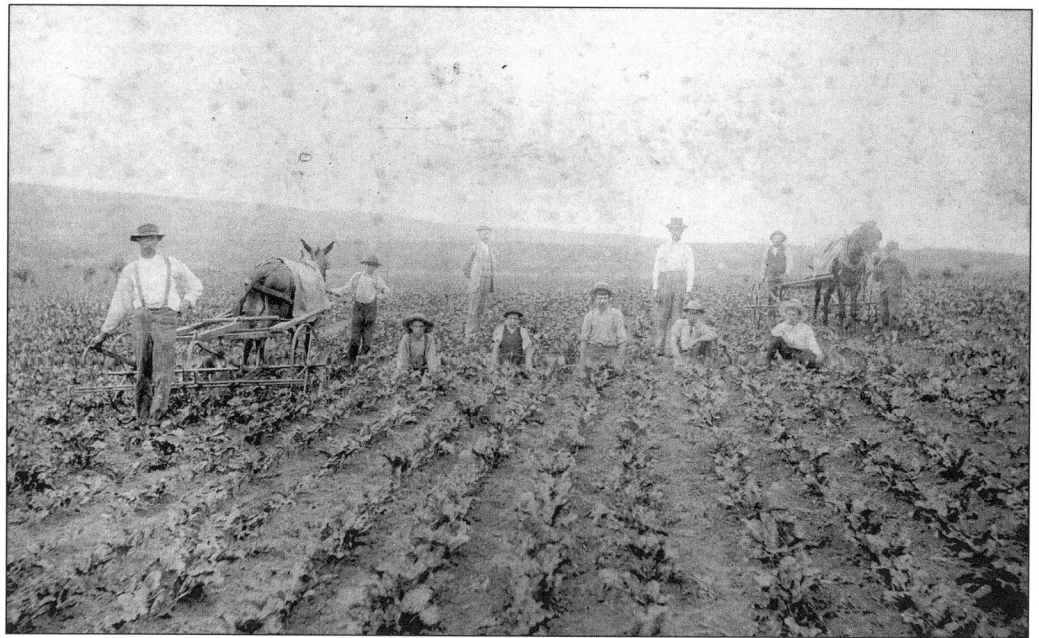

Sugar beets were a very labor-intensive crop, with all planting and harvesting done by hand. The factory closed in 1895 following a financial panic, two years of drought, and repeal of the state per-pound bonus. However, the factory left a lasting mark on the town. The population had doubled, a high school was built, and many new businesses were opened.

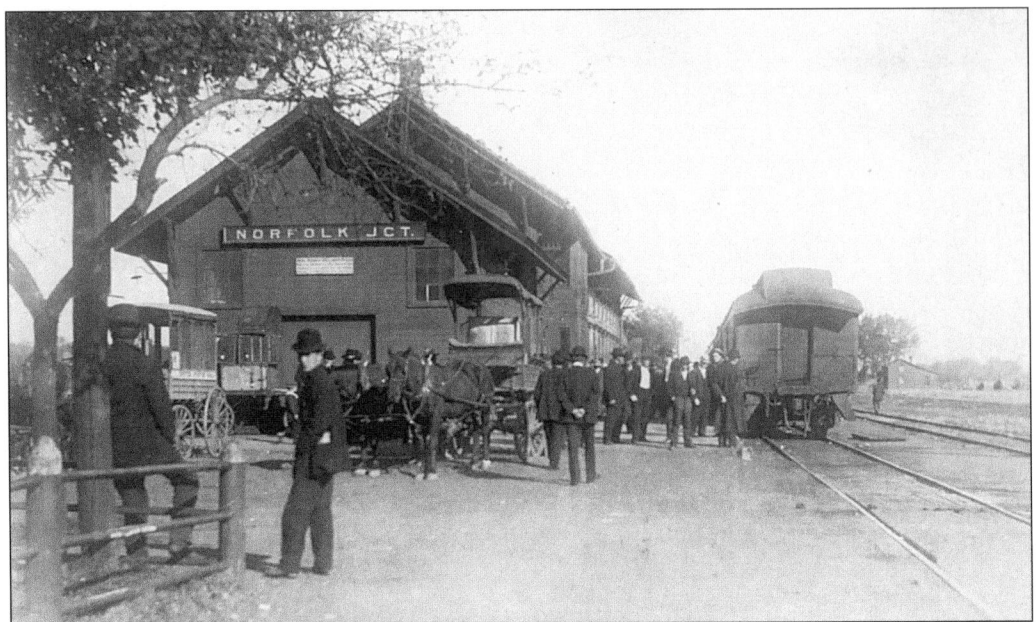

The Fremont, Elkhorn, and Missouri Valley Railroad expanded into Northeast Nebraska after 1874 when gold was discovered in the Black Hills. When Norfolk refused to grant a right-of-way, the railroad built a major terminal on the south side of the city. The train pulled into the depot in Norfolk Junction on September 15, 1879 to the cheers of Norfolk's five hundred residents. Soon Norfolk Junction was a separate town with its own hotels and businesses.

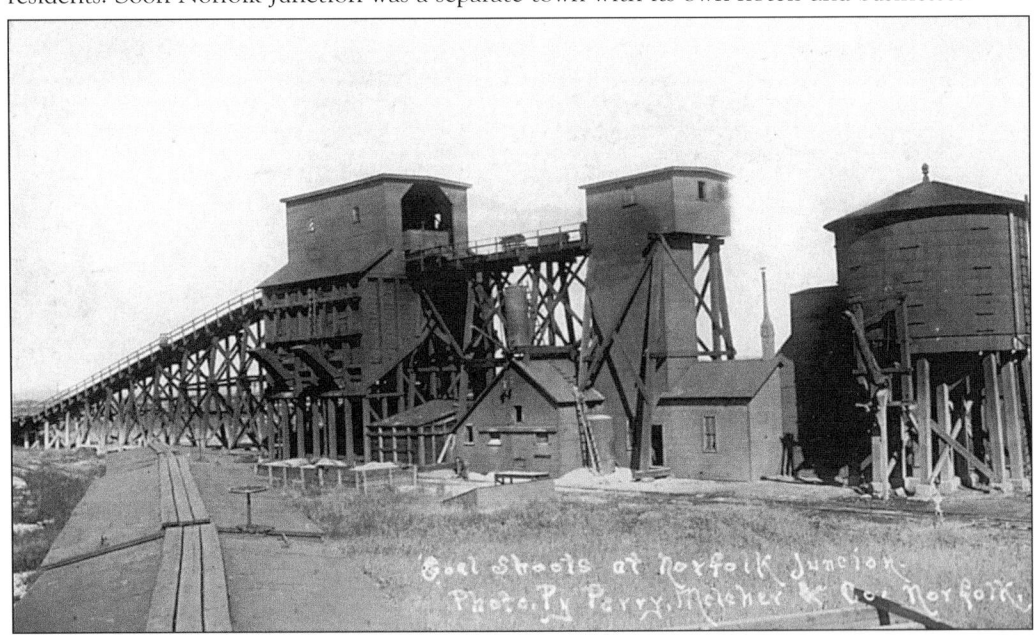

In early days when engines used coal, it was necessary to stop often for water, so stops were made at smaller villages where no passengers were accommodated. The stop was only to jerk water up into the tank. Thus the expression, "jerk water town." Norfolk and Norfolk Junction did not fit this description, as five incoming and outgoing trains stopped daily for passenger and freight service.

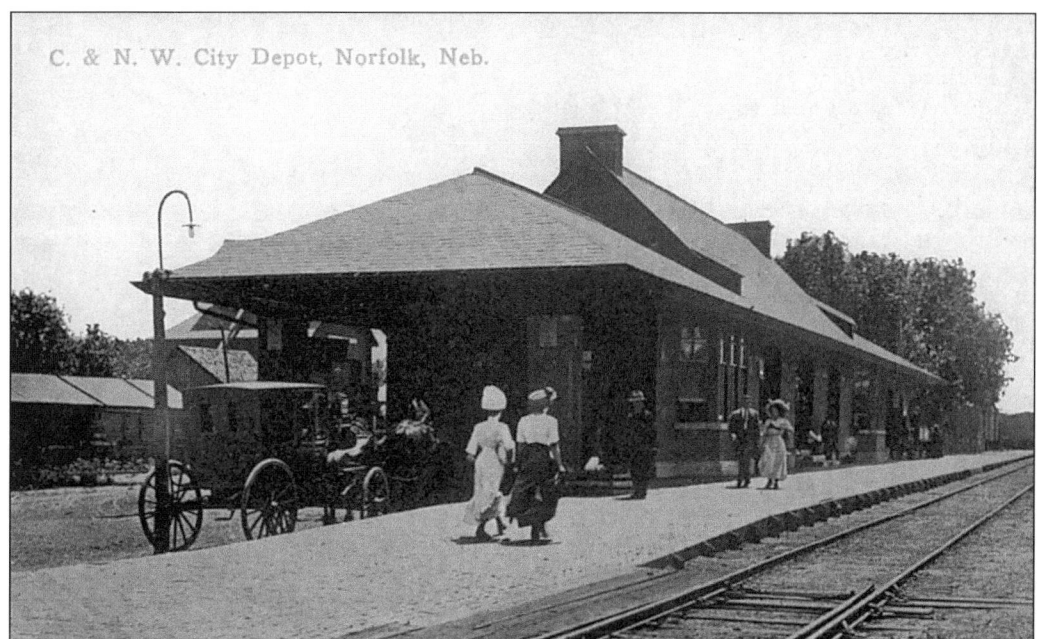

C. & N. W. City Depot, Norfolk, Neb.

In 1880, the Chicago and North Western Railroad built a "city" depot in Norfolk on 7th Street between Madison and Phillip Avenues. Eventually, the C. & N. W. operated both the Norfolk Junction depot and the city depot.

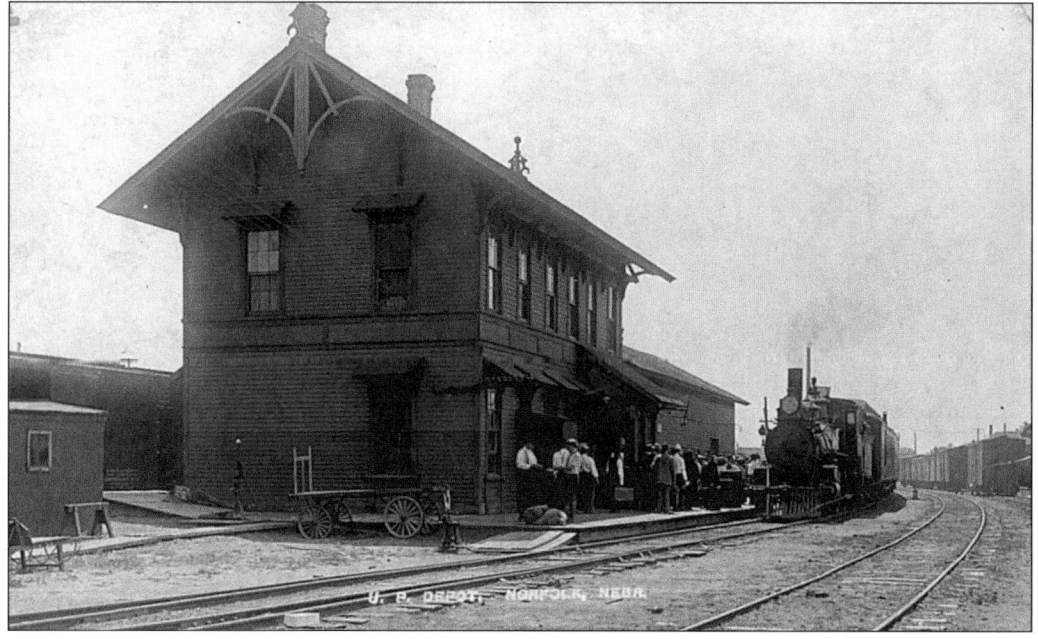

U. P. DEPOT, NORFOLK, NEBR.

The Omaha, Niobrara, and Black Hills branch of the Union Pacific opened this depot and line in 1880, at the northwest corner of 5th Street and Braasch Avenue. The railroad was the most important factor in the settlement of Nebraska from the 1860s–1880s. It made settlement away from the Missouri River possible.

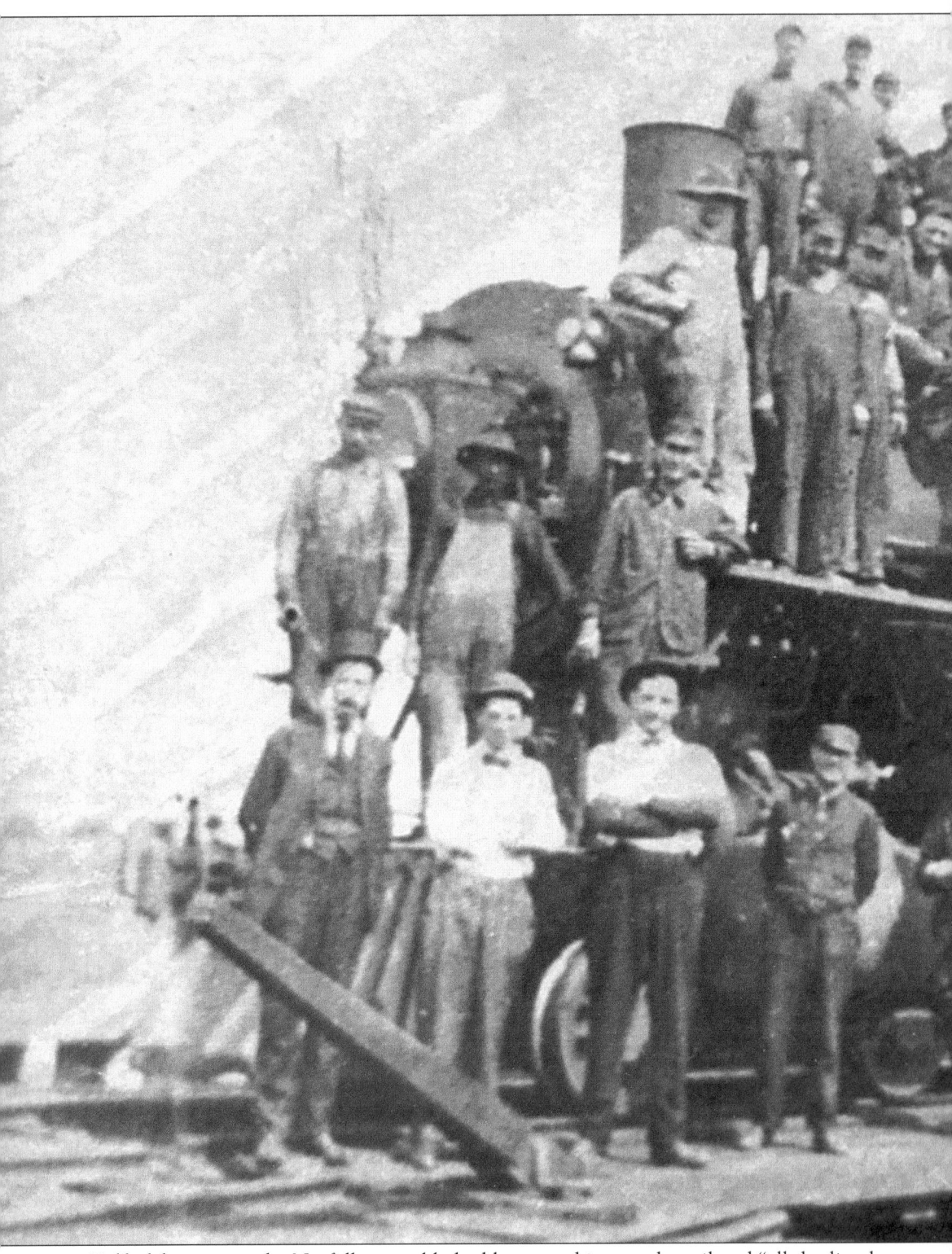

Half of the crew at the Norfolk turntable had been working on the railroad "all the live-long

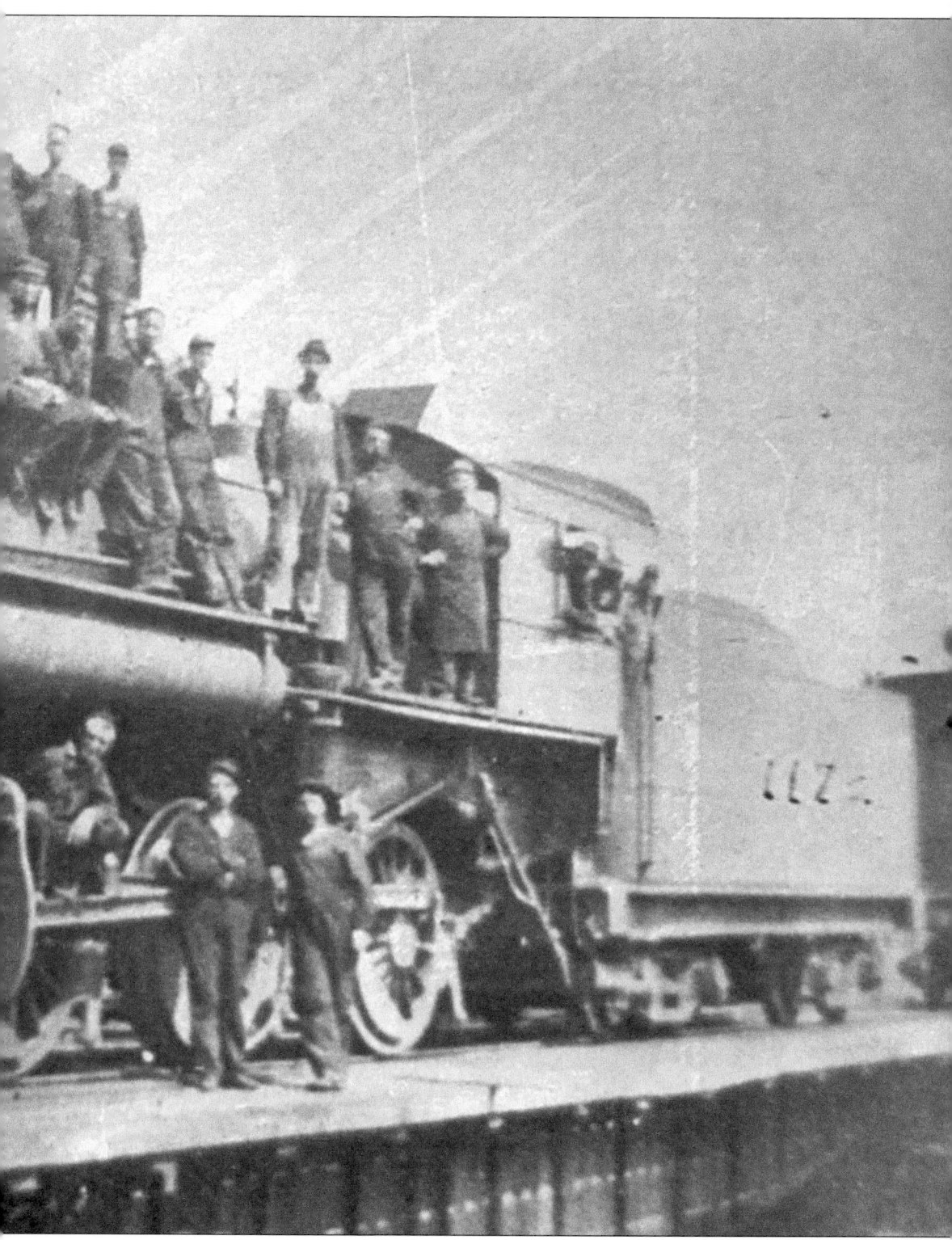

day" in this photograph taken c. 1910.

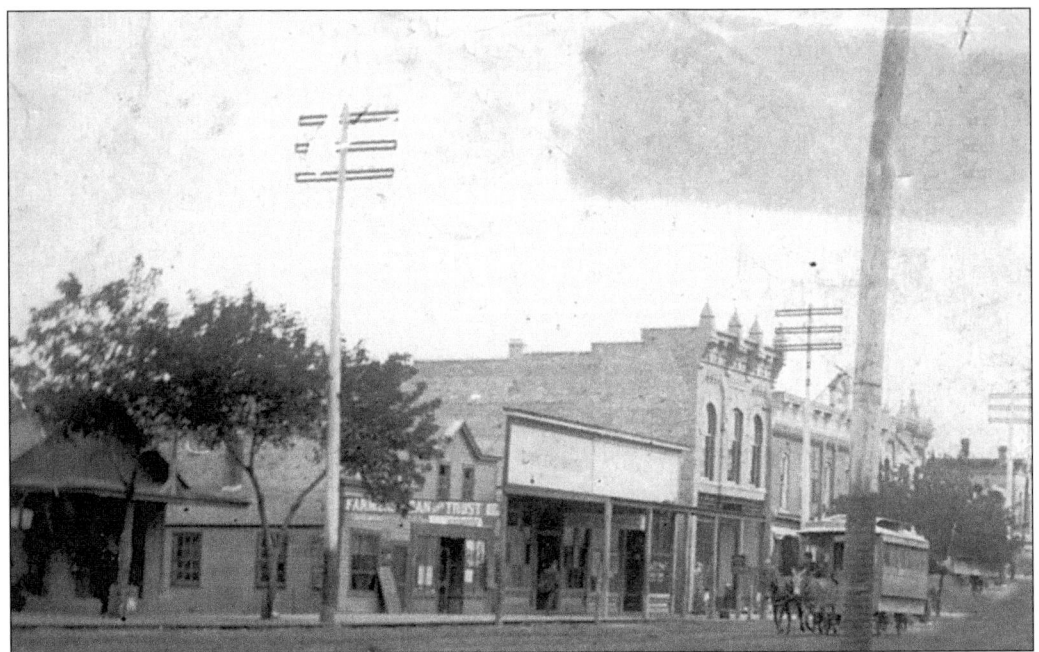

More than a one-horse town, Norfolk used two mules to pull the streetcar in the downtown area This view is of the north side of Norfolk Avenue between 3rd and 4th Streets. The lucky pedestrians could get out of the mud and "mule mess" on the street by using the elevated boardwalks.

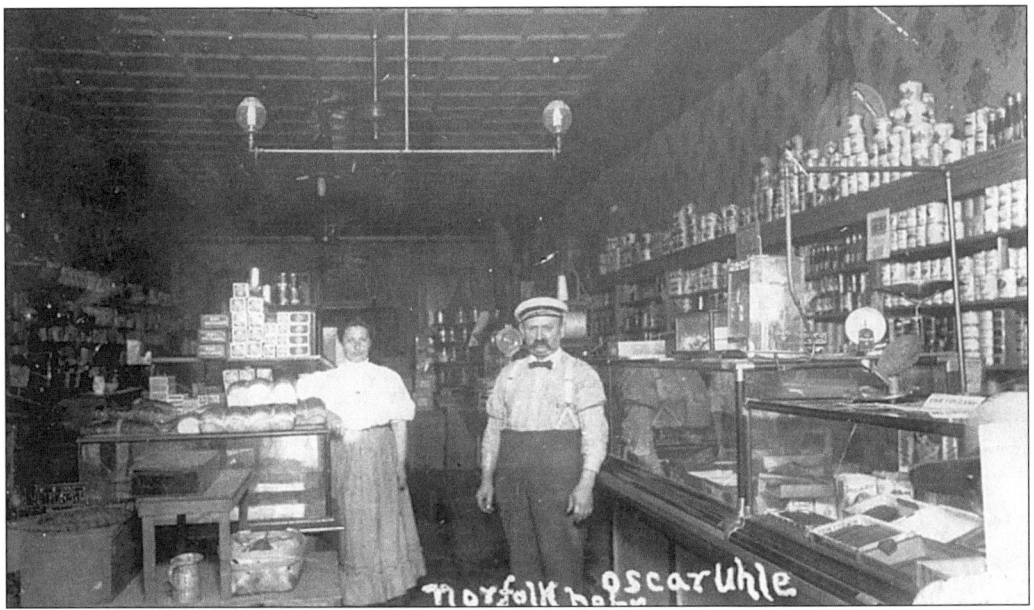

While early settlers were largely self-sufficient, most were unable to produce everything they needed. People needed a place to purchase dry goods, food, and such pleasantries as candy and cigars. General stores, such as this one owned by Oscar Uhle at 217 Norfolk Avenue in the 1890s, filled that need. The store offered groceries, canned goods, fruits, flours, and feed. It is said Uhle was a "courteous businessman" who was a "pleasure to deal with."

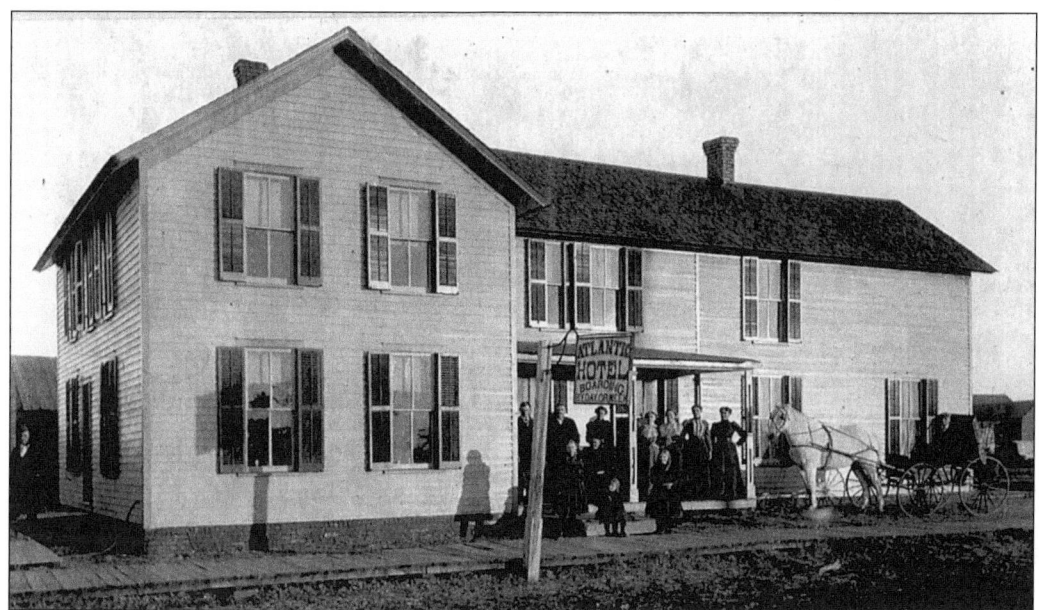

The long shadows of late afternoon show it's time for the staff of the Atlantic Hotel to take a break, at least long enough to pose for a picture. Beginning in the 1880s, travelers who came in on the railroad would often stay at the Atlantic Hotel located at 111 South 6th Street. The Hotel was erected by John Koenigstein and operated for over 60 years.

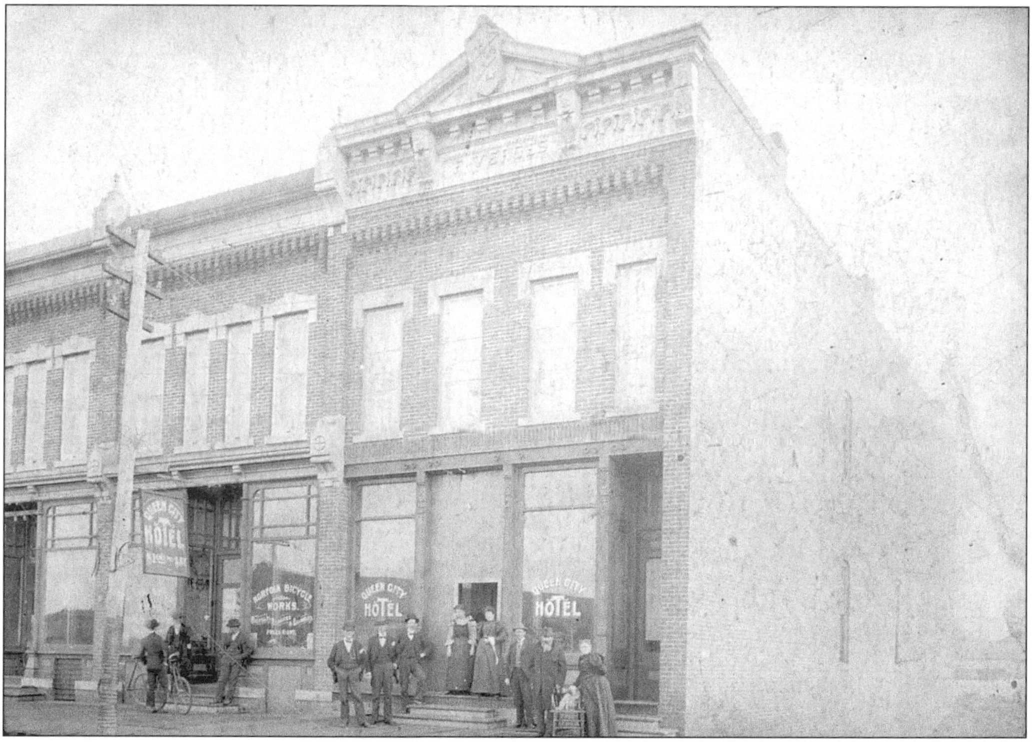

Visitors to Norfolk could also stay uptown at the Queen City Hotel, located at 511 Norfolk Avenue.

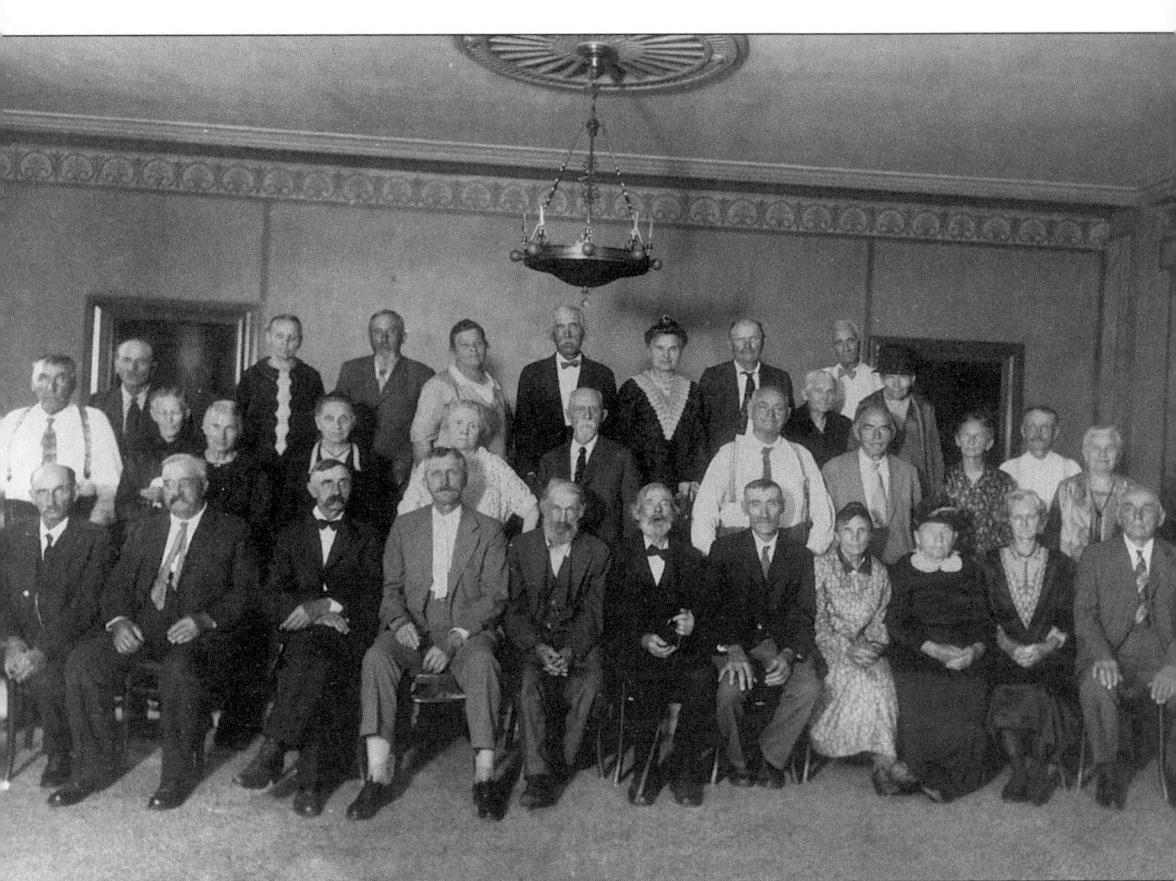

Members of the original Wisconsin colony who settled in what was to become Norfolk pose for this 1929 photograph taken at Hotel Norfolk. They are, first row, (from left to right) Herman Winter, Herman Braasch, August Braasch, Fred Dederman, August Melcher, Herman Rohrke, Henry Raasch, Mrs. Henry Raasch, Mrs. Henry Korth, Mrs. Sophia Faubel, and Herman Pasewalk. In the second row. from left to right, are Edward Wickman, Mrs. Amelia Lehman, Mrs. David Rohrke, Mrs. August Braasch, Mrs. George Beels, George Beels (the Beels, who were special guests, came about five years after the original colony), William Siefert, August Pasewalk, Mrs. Gottlieb Heckman, Edward Uecker, and Mrs. Adam Pilger. Pictured in the third row, from left to right, are Herman Boche, Mrs. John Raasch, John Raasch, Mrs. Frank Wichert, Frank Wichert, Minnie Nenow, Herman Nenow, Emilie Bergman, Herman Buettow, and Mrs. Herman Rohrke. Mrs. Frank Wichert became the last survivor of the original colony.

Two
MOVING ALONG
1890–1916

"We must welcome the future, remembering that soon it will be the past; and we must respect the past, knowing that once it was all that was humanly possible."

—George Santayana

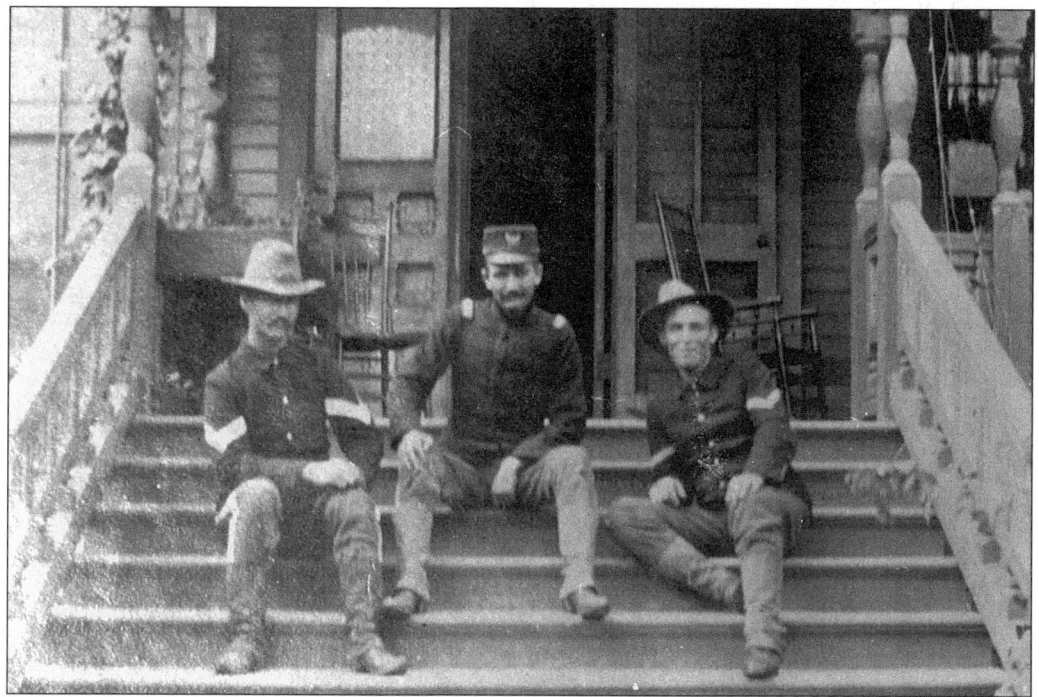

In this 1890 photograph, Civil War veterans sit on the steps of Herman Gerecke's home at 1202 Norfolk Avenue. Gerecke, sitting in the middle, enlisted in December of 1861, and his final discharge was in May of 1866. He came to Norfolk in April of 1869, and was elected mayor in 1886; he was re-elected in 1889 and 1890. Norfolk's first eight mayors were all Civil War veterans.

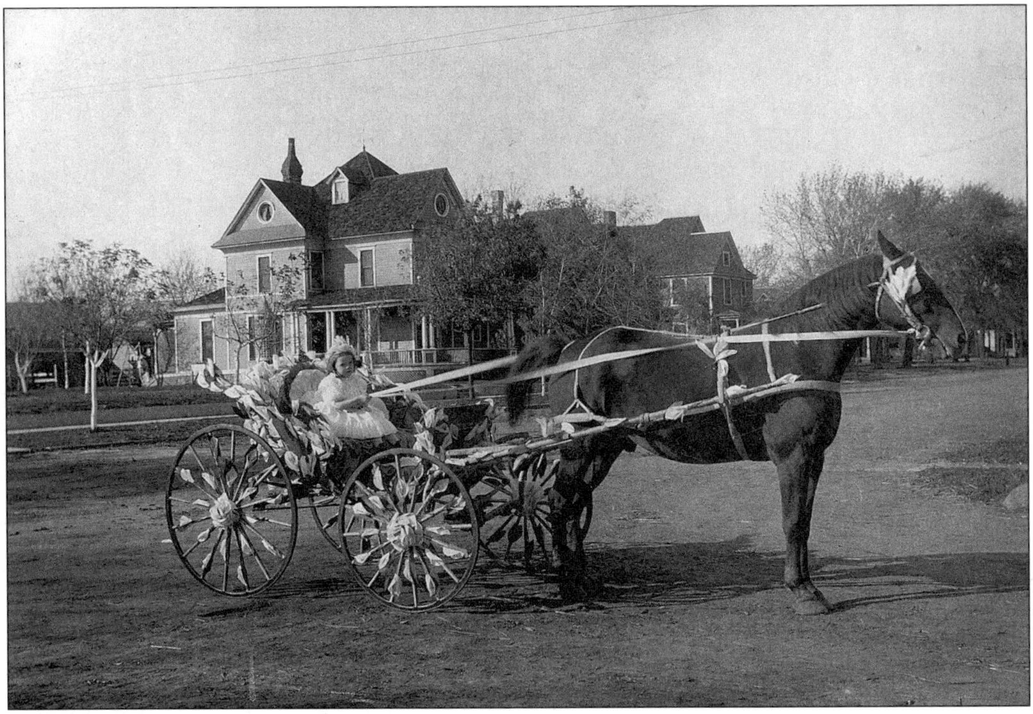

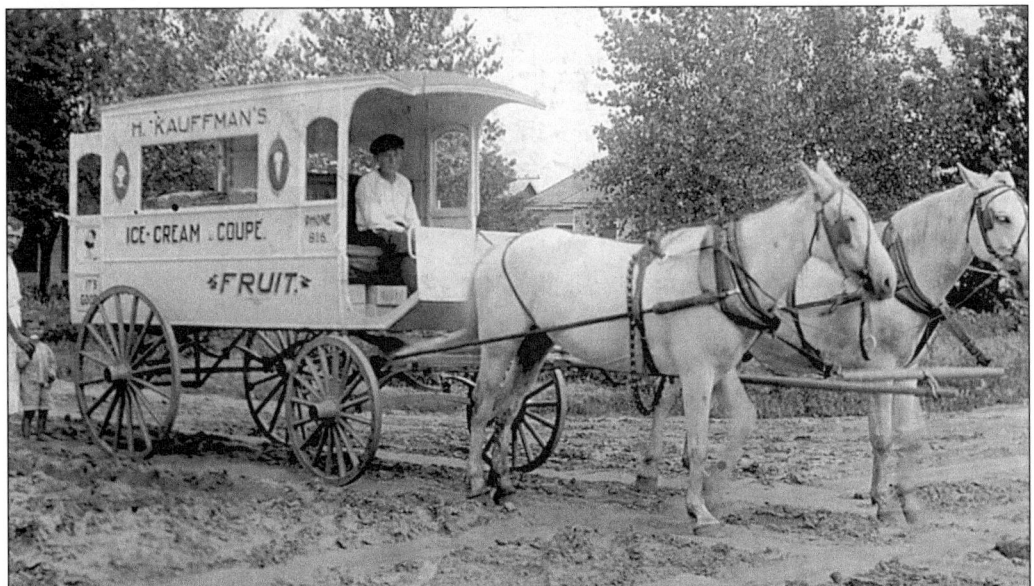

Dorothy Salter, the daughter of Dr. P. Harold and Edith Hays Salter, sits in a carriage that has been decorated for Easter at the northwest corner of 13th Street and Norfolk Avenue. Dorothy was born March 5, 1893. Her mother died shortly after, and her father later remarried. Dorothy's half-brother was Dr. George Salter. On October 5, 1916, Dorothy married Charles A. Durland, who was secretary of the Norfolk Building and Loan Association.

The gentle tinkle of bells on ice cream trucks has been music to the ears of children—and adults—for years. Those first trucks were actually wagons pulled by horses, like H. Kauffman's Ice Cream Coupe shown in this photo.

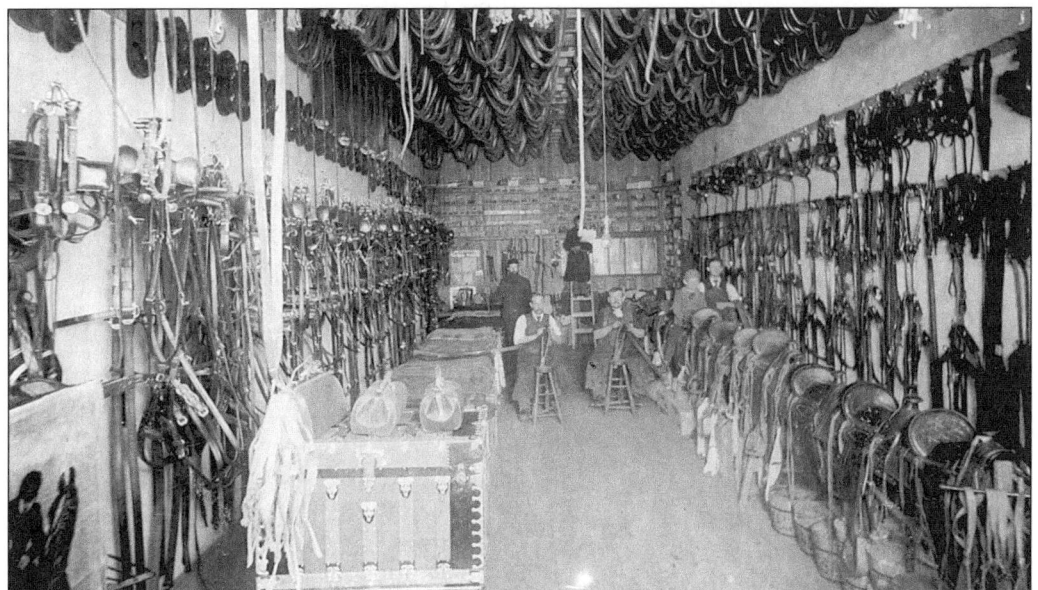

Before tractors and automobiles, horses were called on to pull plows and buggies and provided a means of transportation and power. Consequently, harnesses and saddles were needed, which were supplied by a variety of sources, including the Freeland and Winter Harness Shop in Norfolk. This 1896 photo shows the harnesses hanging from the ceiling to drip-dry after being soaked in oil to keep them pliable and moist.

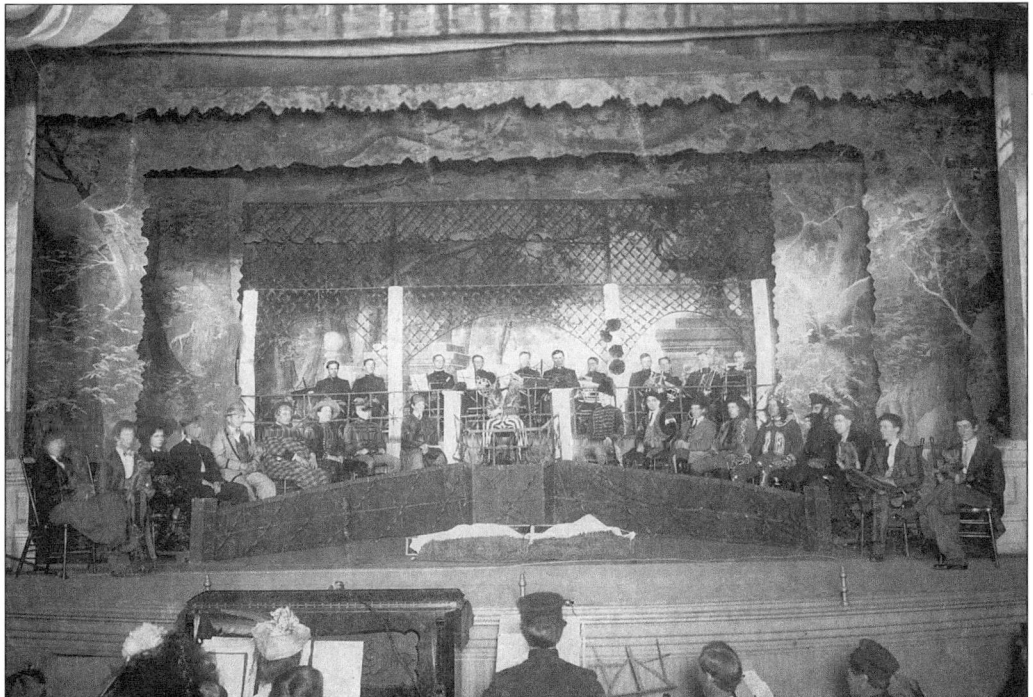

Norfolk's own Opera House was host to all kinds of entertainment. Located at 118 North 4th Street, the Opera House could seat 1,100 people. It even had an orchestra pit, as is shown in the foreground of the photograph.

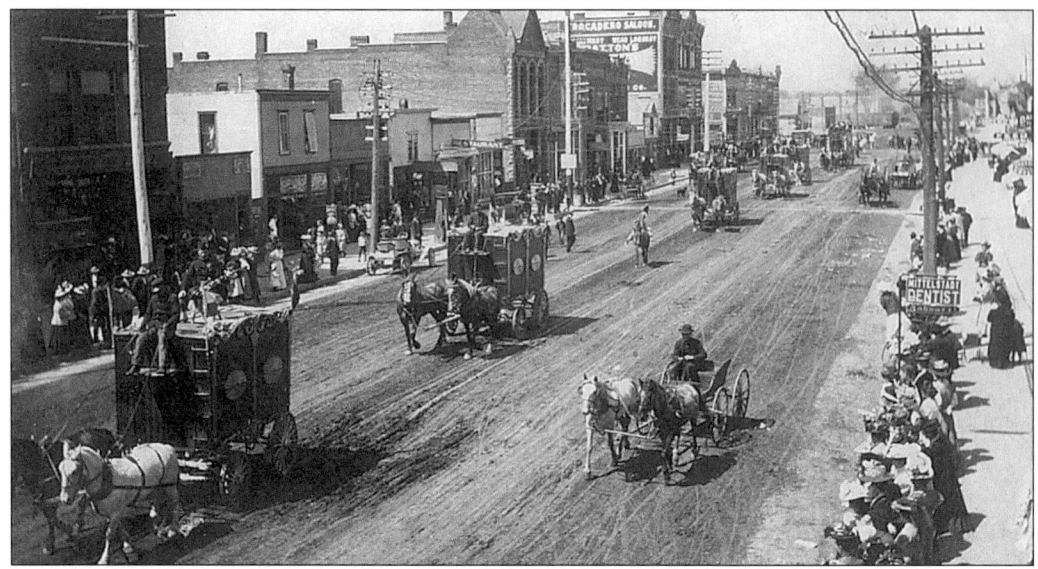

A circus parade makes its way down Norfolk Avenue. The circus was a popular form of entertainment during the latter years of the 19th century and the early years of the 20th century. In 1884, the city board imposed a license tax of $100 a day on circuses. The "Vons" traveled with the Walter Savage Carnival. They used a double trapeze and a revolving ladder in their act, often while dressed as clowns.

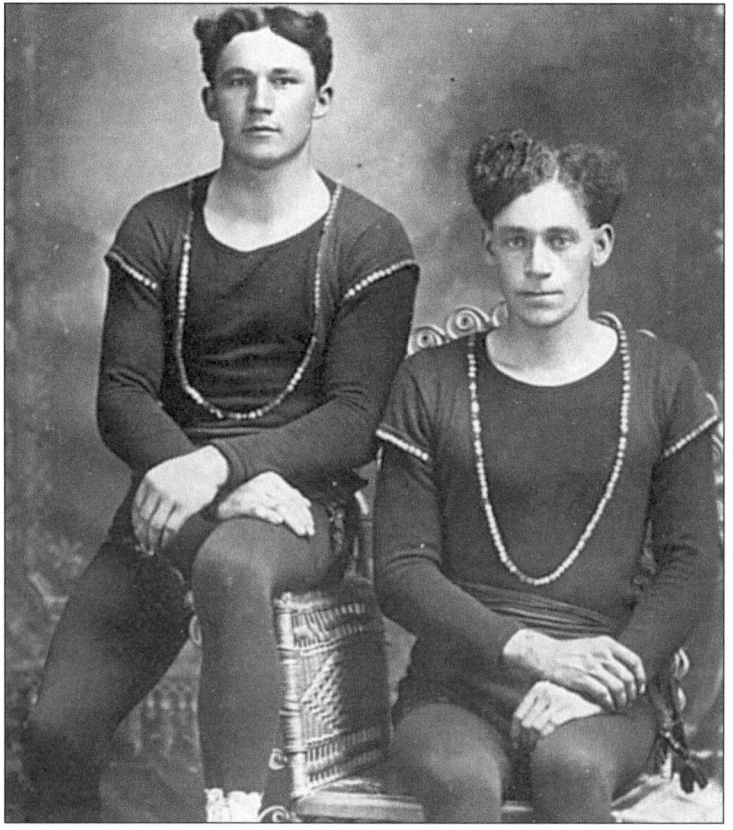

The "Aerial Vons" were popular circus performers who did most of their work on the "high wire." The daredevils are Fritz Von Seggern, on the left, and Ira A. Mallory, on the right.

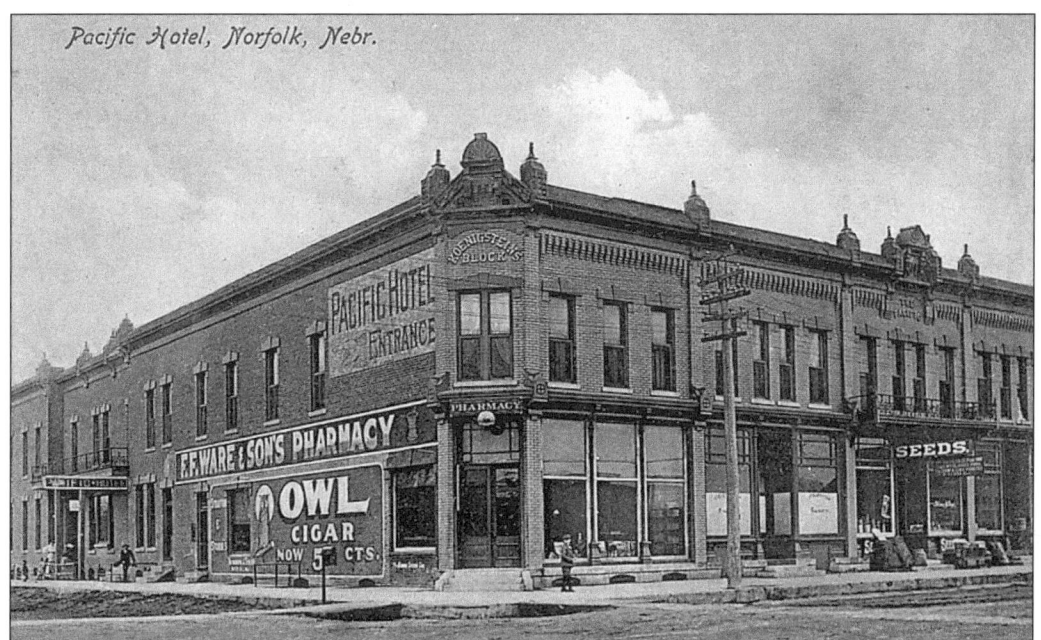

Pacific Hotel, Norfolk, Nebr.

Norfolk has always been a hub of activity, with several trains going in and out of the city during its early days. Consequently, the need for lodging was great, which is why several hotels sprang up around the city. John Koenigstein built the Pacific Hotel on South 5th Street in 1886. Forty years later, John's son, Jack, tore down the Pacific Hotel and built the Granada Theater.

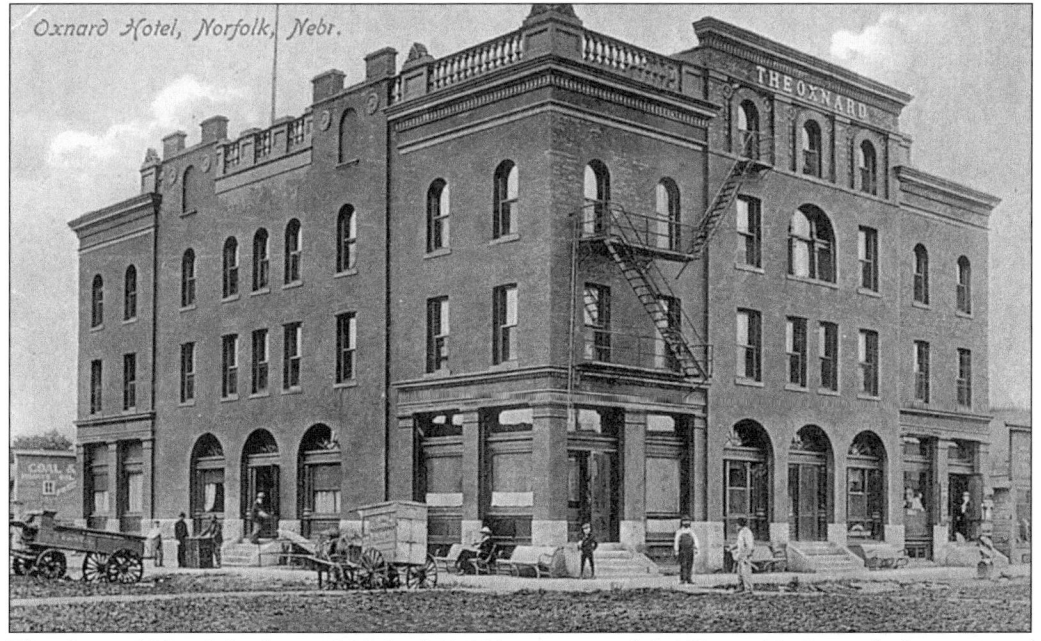

Oxnard Hotel, Norfolk, Nebr.

The Oxnard Hotel, built in 1892 for $40,000, was named for Henry T. Oxnard, the owner of Norfolk's Sugar Beet Factory. However, the Oxnard Hotel remained a Norfolk landmark until 1965, when it was torn down. The structure had a Norfolk Avenue entrance for men, a 3rd Street entrance for women, and an elevator to take women to their second floor parlor.

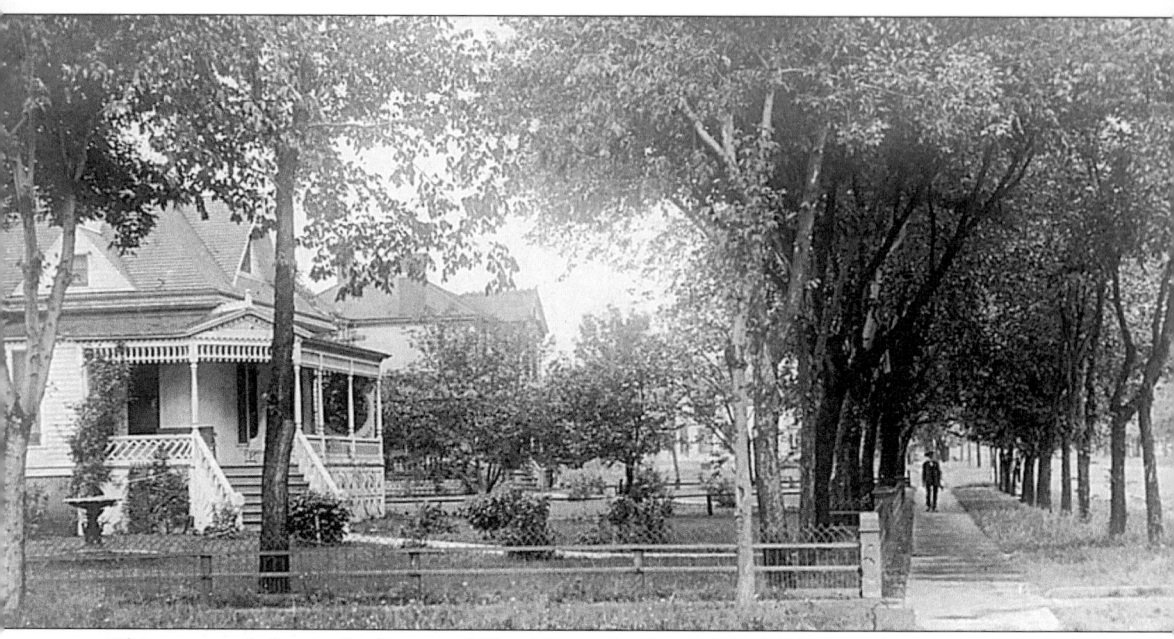

This postcard shows the house of Dr. Alexander Bear, Norfolk's first doctor, at the corner of Ninth Street and Norfolk Avenue. The postcard is unique because it was printed by the Norfolk Book and Stationery Company, which was the forerunner of Hallmark Cards, now located in Kansas City, Missouri. William Hall purchased the Norfolk Book and Stationery Company in 1905. He also owned Hall Smoke House, Hall's Gift and Card Shop, and one-third interest in the Norfolk Post Card Company. William's brother, Joyce, worked for him. Another brother, Rollie, was a salesman for Marshall Paper Company until postcards became popular in the early 1900s. That's when the three brothers decided to invest in the postcard business. In 1909, Joyce Hall moved to Kansas City. Rollie soon followed, and the pair founded Hall Brothers. When the postcard business began to wane, they started producing their own greeting cards, and Hall Brothers Engraving was born. William joined his brothers in 1921 after selling the Norfolk Book and Stationery Company to Huse Publishing. Hall Brothers Engraving was changed to Hallmark Cards in 1954.

Leo Spaulding and Joe Horskey clown around for the camera with what may be their first cigarettes. The young men, with their suits and hats, are dressed in styles that were so popular around the turn of the 20th century.

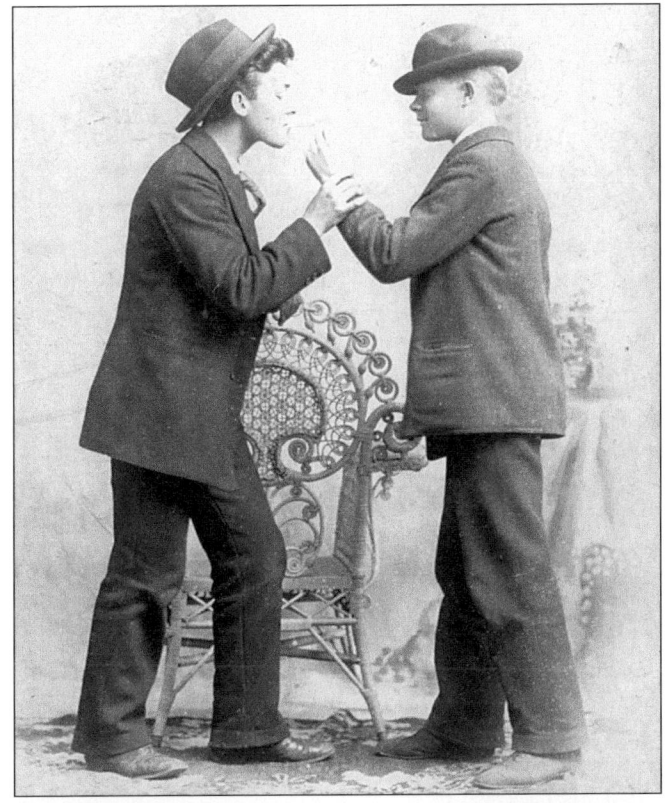

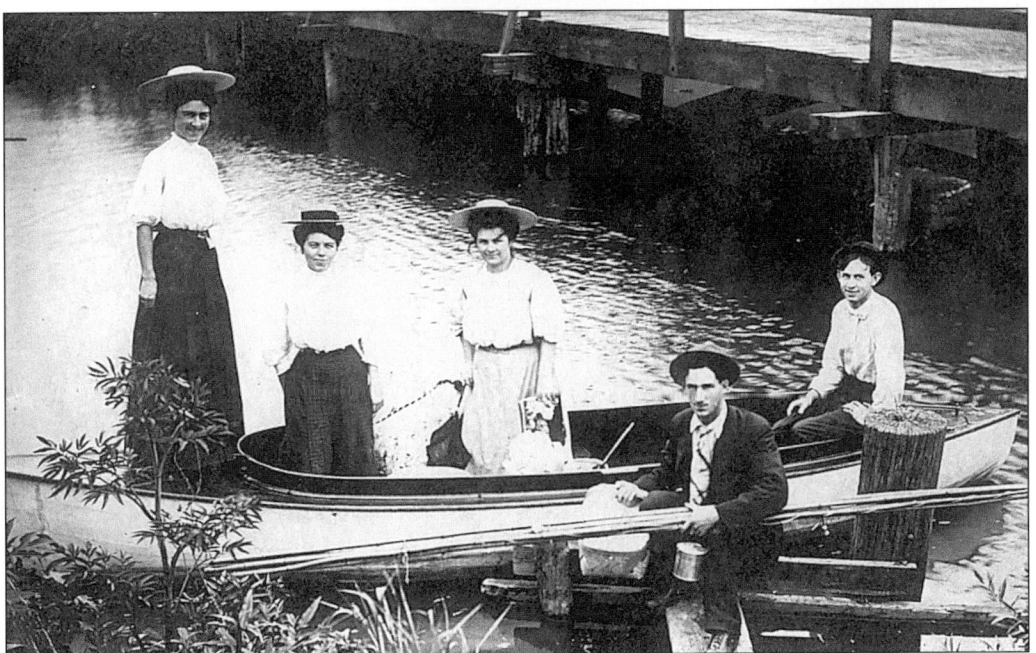

A Sunday afternoon outing? The boating party includes (second from left) Mrs. Bough, whose husband took the photograph; Nina and Bob Brashear; and Paul Wetzel. The first woman on the left is unidentified. The photo was probably taken in the early 1900s.

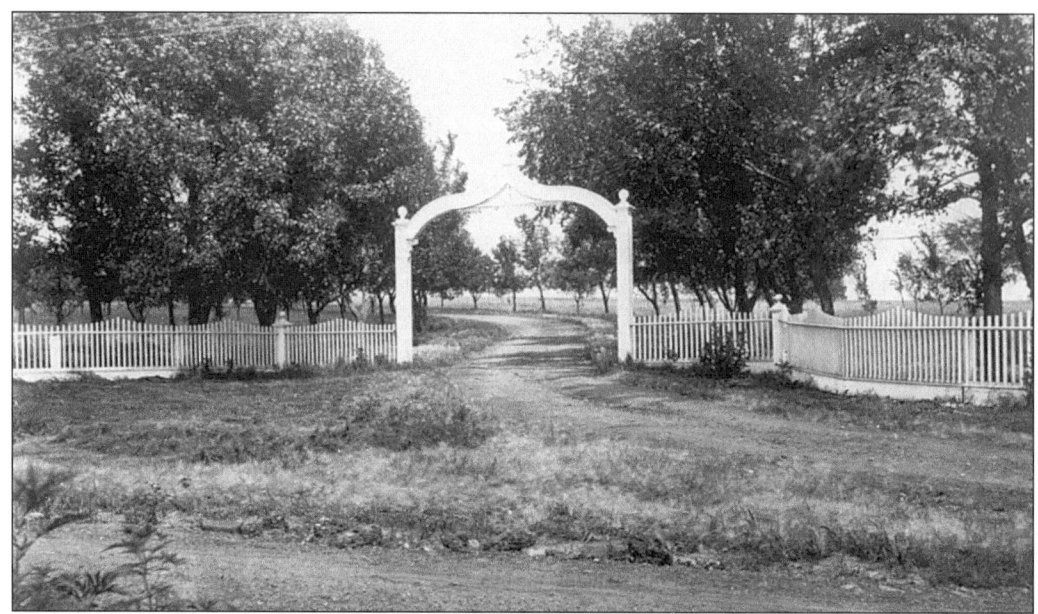

The Norfolk Hospital for the Insane, now the Norfolk Regional Center, began operations on February 15, 1888, with 97 patients. It was the second psychiatric facility in the state and was established in response to increased demand for that type of care. The first structure was 240 feet long and 50 feet wide. Within one year, an addition was built to the main structure, which doubled the size of the facility. Another wing was added in 1898 bringing capacity up to 300. For many years, the hospital was a self-sufficient community with a complete farm operation.

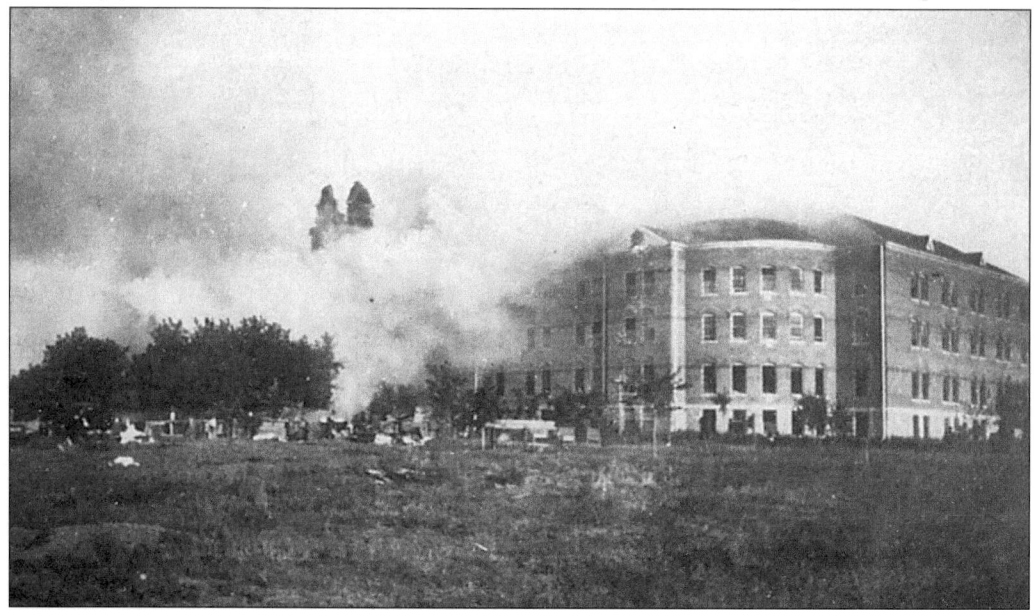

A fire in September of 1901 destroyed the hospital's main building and all but one of the additions. The patients were immediately moved to hospitals in Lincoln and Hastings. The slow-burning fire allowed staff to salvage furniture, fixtures, and personal property, which are shown on the lawn in this photo. One patient's life was lost in the blaze when he ran back into the building.

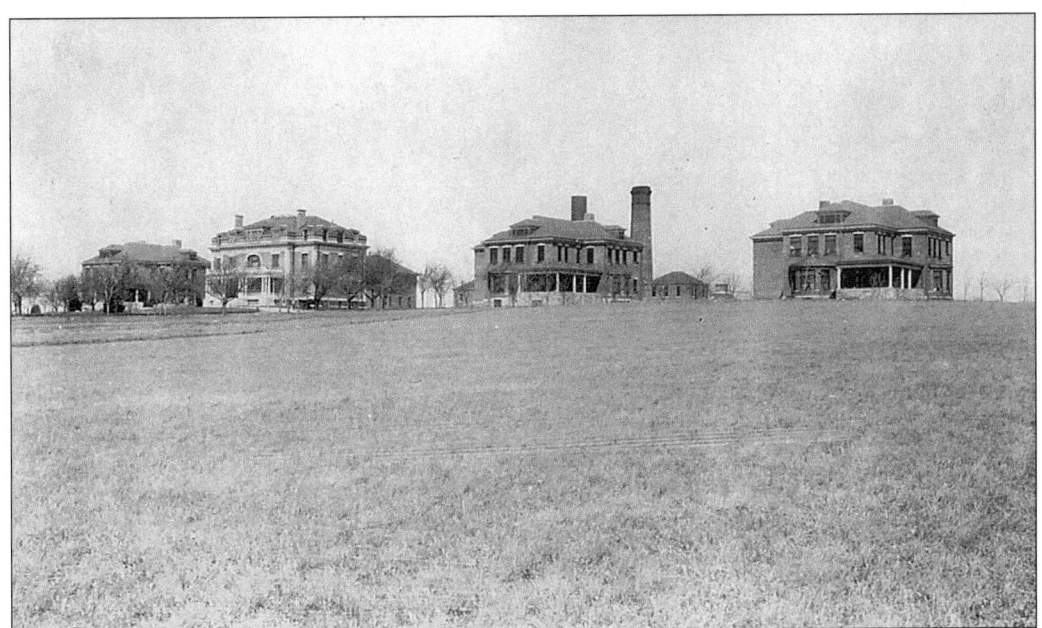

The hospital reopened in 1905 with three separate ward cottages and an administrative building. The state built more facilities as the patient population increased. The patients and staff produced their own food, clothing, and power. The hospital grounds were home to a prize-winning dairy herd; they butchered their own meat and preserved vegetables. On campus was a medical, surgical, and dental facility along with a church and cemetery.

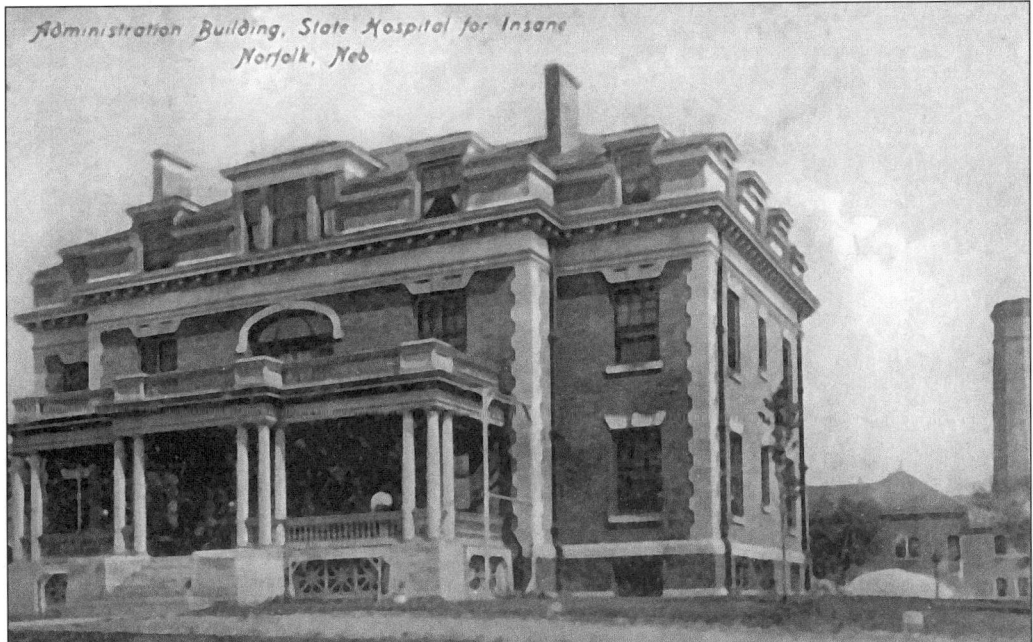

During its peak years, the hospital was home to more than 1,300 patients. The facility's name was changed to the Norfolk State Hospital in 1920. During this time recreational and occupational therapy were introduced. The hospital had a chorus and orchestra, showed movies, and held plays and dances.

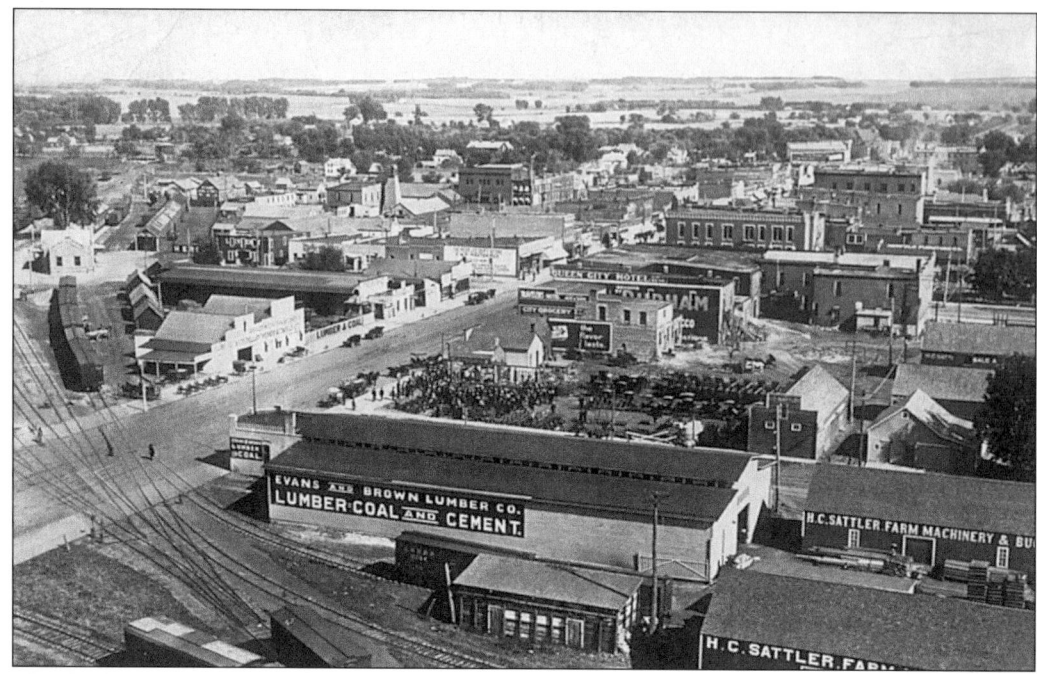

This bird's-eye view of Norfolk was taken in 1914, looking north and east from 7th Street. The rail tracks belong to the Union Pacific and the Chicago North Western Railroads. A large group of people with their cars and buggies have gathered just to the east of Evans and Brown Lumber Co. for a performance of the play, *Uncle Tom's Cabin*.

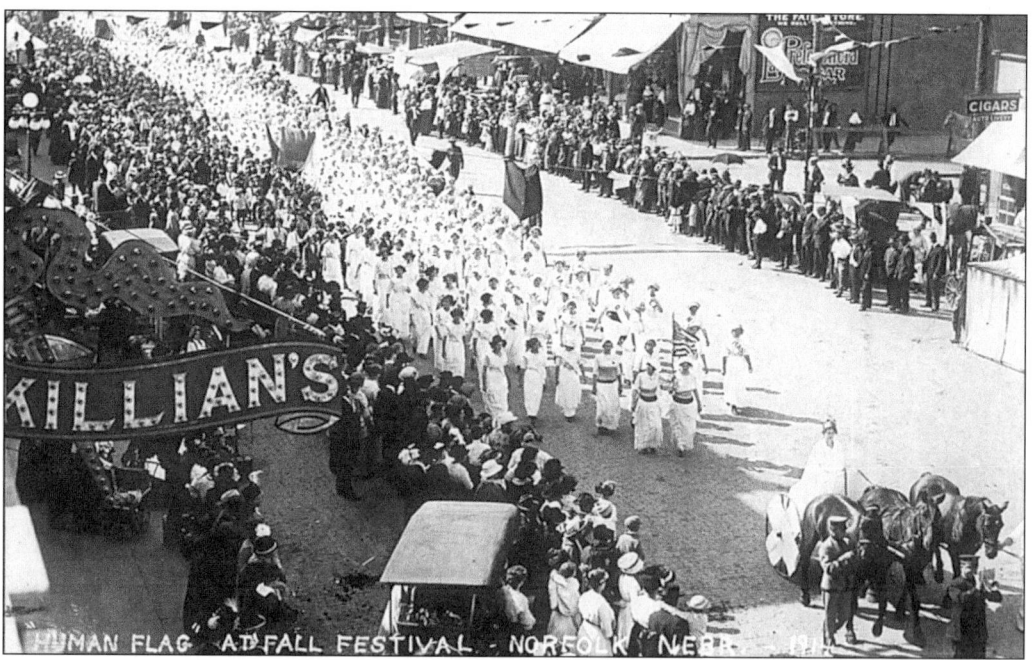

Women form a "Human Flag" that parades down Norfolk Avenue in 1914 during the Fall Festival. The tradition of a fall festival continues in Norfolk with the Hallow'esta Festival and now with LaVitsef Time.

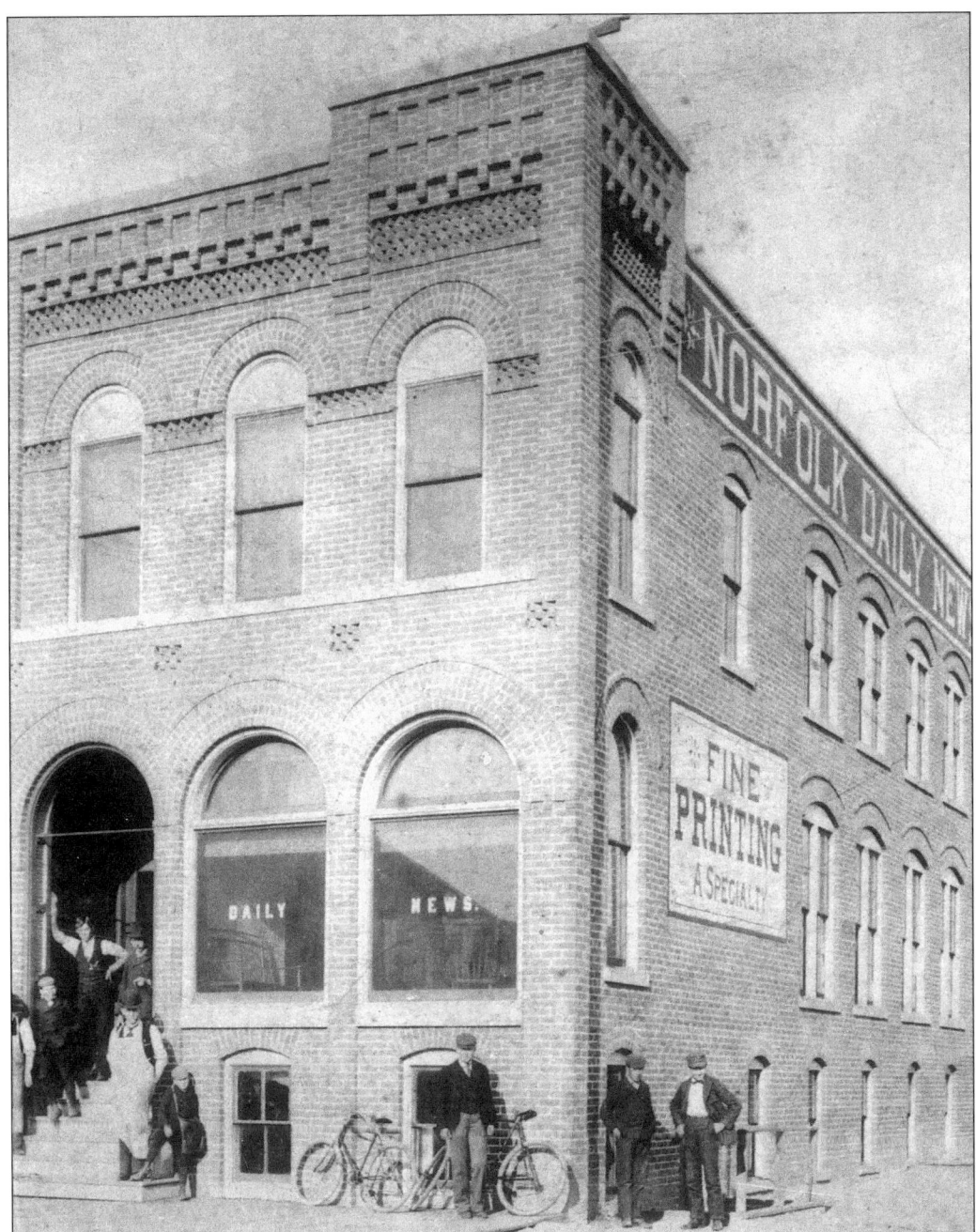

The *Norfolk Daily News* began publication in 1877, and William Huse and his son, W. N. Huse, purchased it in 1888. At the time, the circulation was four hundred. W.N. Huse served as publisher until his death in 1913. He was succeeded by his son, Gene Huse, who was publisher until 1956 and president of the firm until his death in 1961. Jerry Huse, son of Gene Huse, is the present publisher. The *News* wasn't Norfolk's first newspaper. *The Pioneer* was published in 1872. Written by hand, this first paper was published only twice. It was edited by Charles Mathewson and Mary Fish. The subscription price for a year was three bushels of wheat or one-half cord of wood.

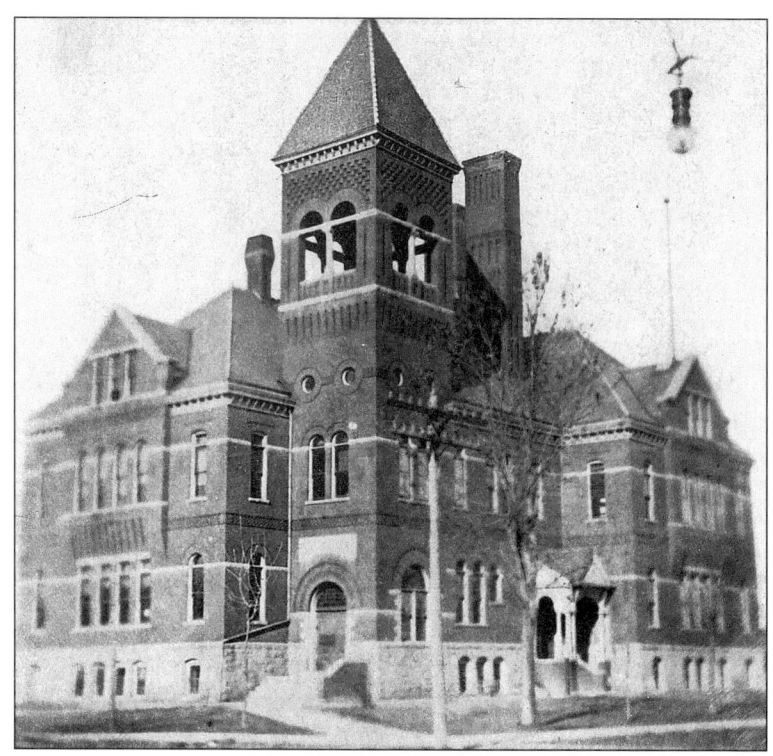

Norfolk High School, built in 1891 for $22,500 at the corner of 6th Street and Phillip Avenue, had only two teachers when it opened. Yet the 104-foot by 84-foot structure could seat five hundred students. The first superintendent of schools was Joe Grimstead, who began his duties in 1888.

The high school building was completely destroyed by fire in 1907. However, the structure was rebuilt and remodeled several times during the next few years. In 1922, a new high school was built between 5th and 6th Streets on Pasewalk Avenue. Currently, that building functions as Norfolk Junior High School. High school students moved into another new facility in 1968.

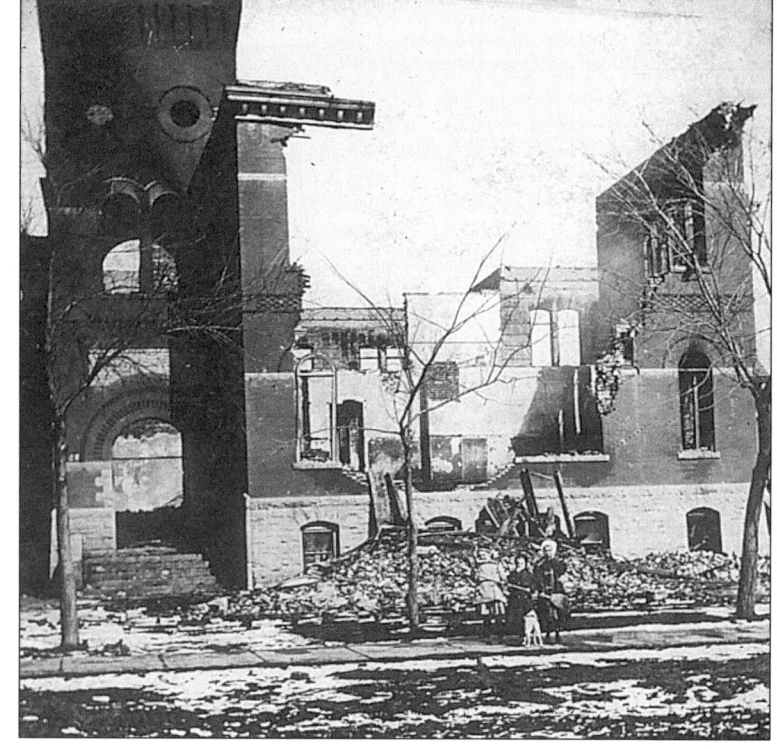

42

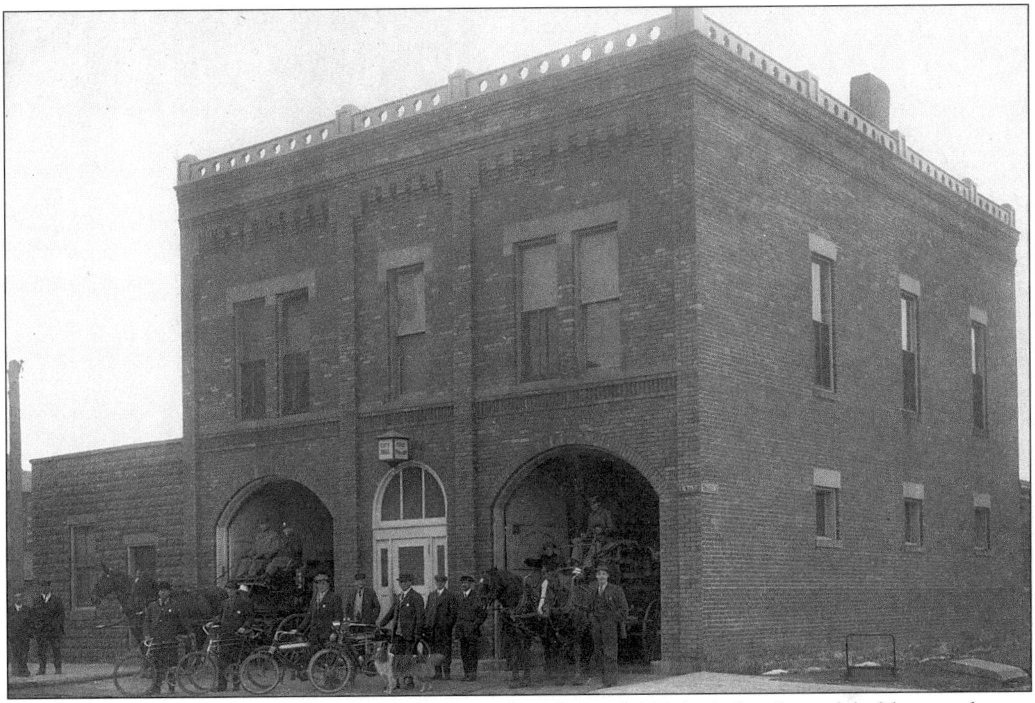

Norfolk's Fire Department was organized in October of 1884. A hook and ladder truck was purchased in 1886 for $450. More equipment was purchased in 1887, and in 1888 a fire station was built at a cost of $3,975. Located on the southwest corner of 4th Street and Braasch Avenue, the station also housed the City Hall.

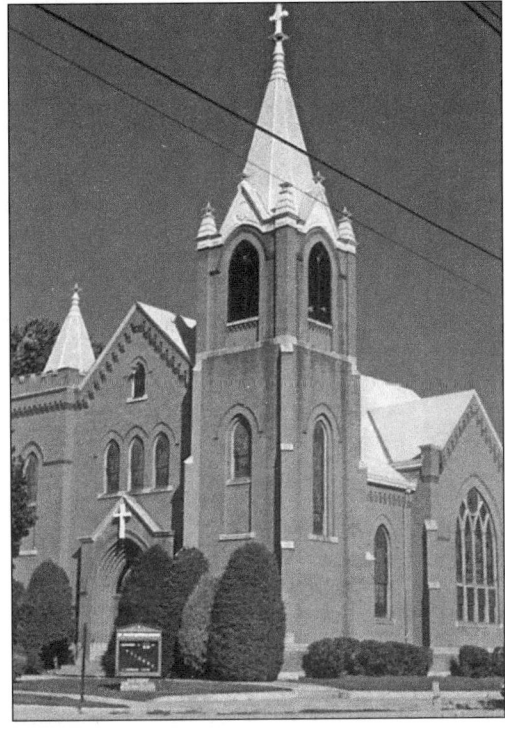

This is St. Paul's Evangelical Lutheran Church, 1100 Georgia Avenue, as it appeared in 1966, during its centennial. St. Paul's Lutheran is the oldest congregation in Norfolk, founded by pioneers from Ixonia, Wisconsin. Its first church was a log cabin, with Reverend John Heckendorf as the first minister. He was also the teacher of the first school in Madison County, which was established in 1867. The congregation built a wood frame church in 1878. The church in this photograph was dedicated on May 3, 1908.

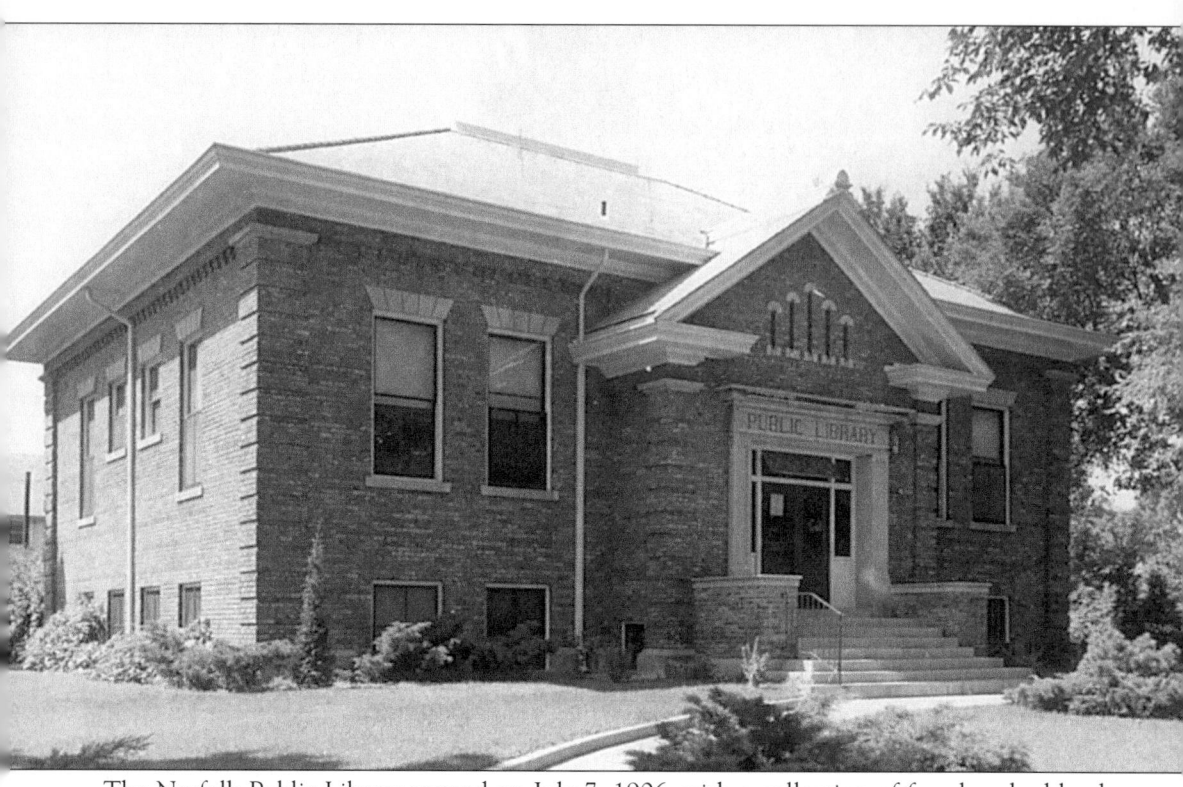

The Norfolk Public Library opened on July 7, 1906, with a collection of four hundred books. The Norfolk Woman's Club began planning for a library nearly ten years earlier. During its first six months, librarian Mrs. Robert Utter reported loaning 3,694 books, even though the facility was only open on Saturdays. In 1908, the Woman's Club transferred ownership to the City of Norfolk, making it a free public facility. In 1908, the city applied for funds from the Andrew Carnegie Foundation, and construction began in 1909, with completion in September of 1910. Carnegie made a grant of $10,000 with the stipulation that the city must provide ten percent of the amount annually to maintain the facility. The building served as a library until 1977. It currently is home to an architectural firm and has been placed on the National Register of Historic Places.

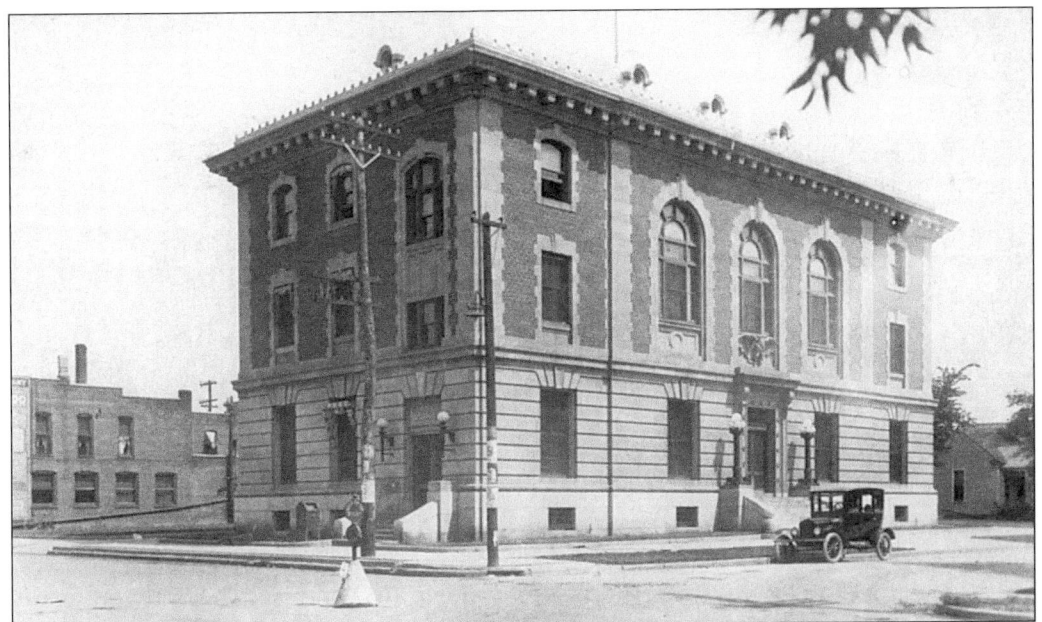

The U.S. Post Office and Courthouse in Norfolk, which was completed in 1904, was built after Congress appropriated $100,000 for its construction. The three-story stone and brick structure was designed under plans attributed to James Knox Taylor, supervising architect of the U.S. Treasury. An addition in 1930 expanded the size of the building.

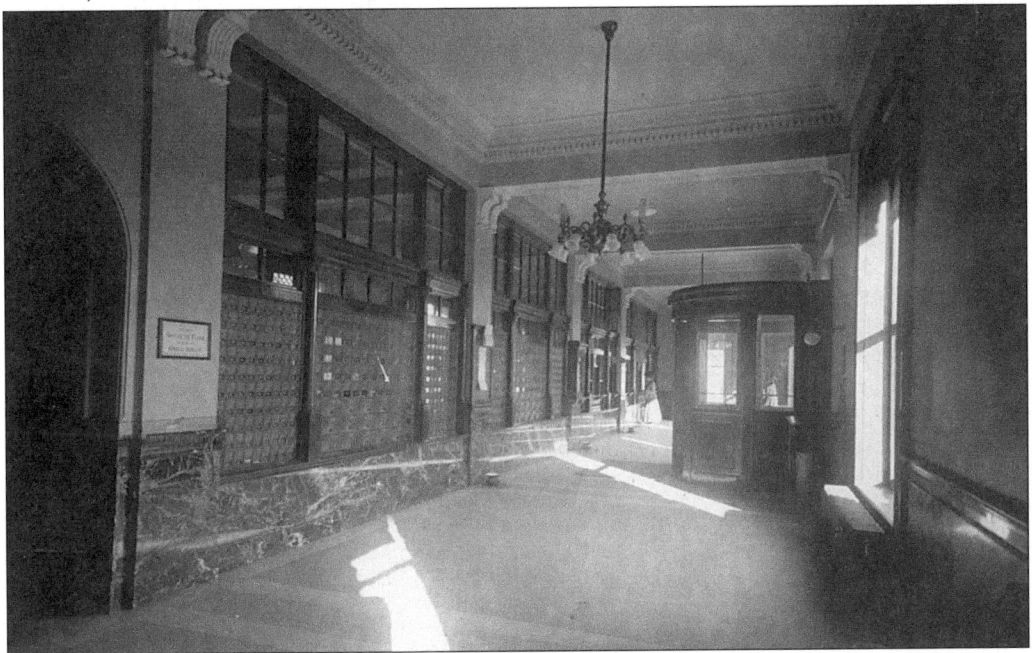

Pictured here is the interior of the new post office shortly after opening. Please note the sign warning against spitting on the floor, and the brass spittoons. This building, now privately owned, is called the McMill Building, a name derived from the date of its construction in Roman numerals, MCMIII. The McMill Building is now listed on the National Register of Historic Places.

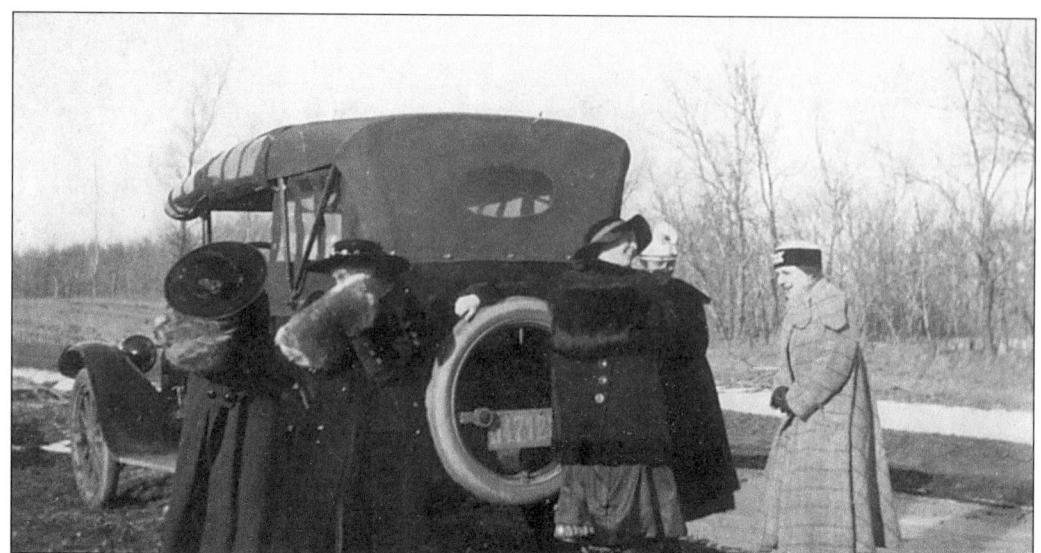

These five friends decided to take a spin in the car on a cold winter day. The women on the left are either covering their laughter, or they have decided that the best way to keep warm is to bury their heads in their fur muffs. Despite the snow and ice on the ground, they seem to be enjoying themselves.

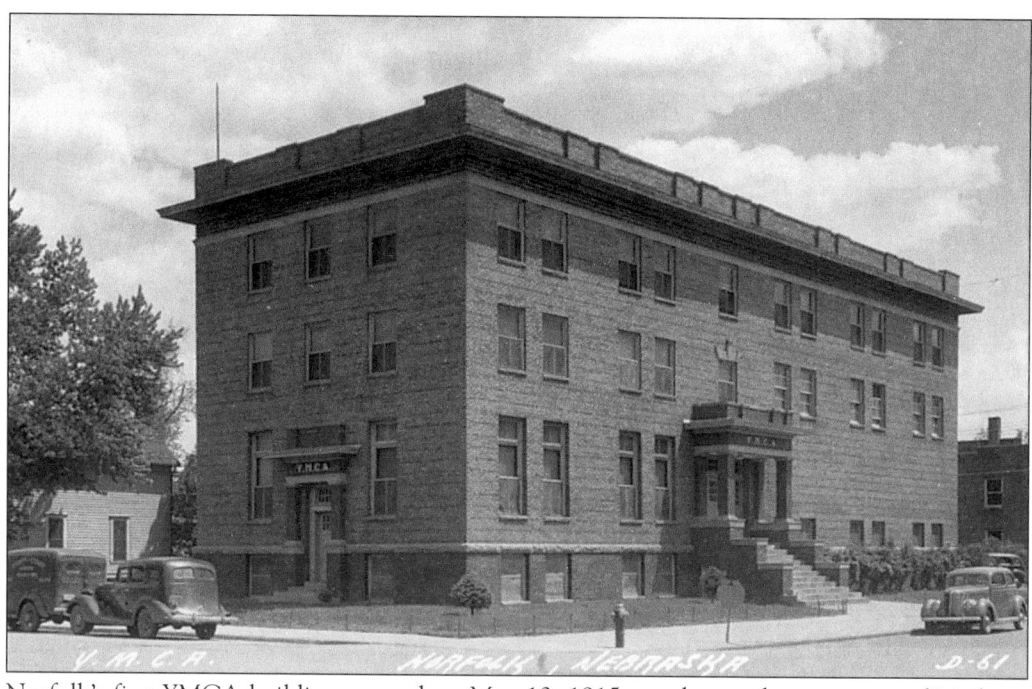

Norfolk's first YMCA building opened on May 13, 1915, on the southeast corner of Madison Avenue and 4th Street. However, the Norfolk Young Men's Christian Association had its inception in Norfolk back in 1899. In 1902, it became an official YMCA. A swimming pool was added to this structure in 1959.

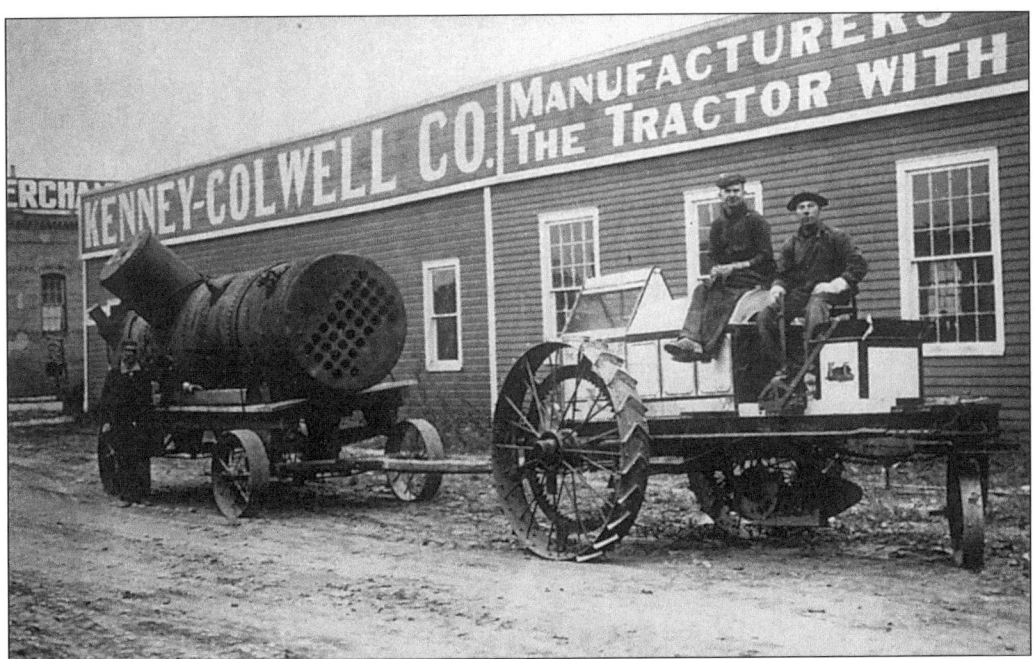

Norfolk was the birthplace of the Square Turn Tractor Factory, the only facility in the nation that produced a tractor that could do exactly what the name implies—make square turns. Two Norfolk residents, Albert Kenney and A.J. Colwell, masterminded the design, and by 1915 had developed a prototype, which was advertised in newspapers and at fairs throughout the country.

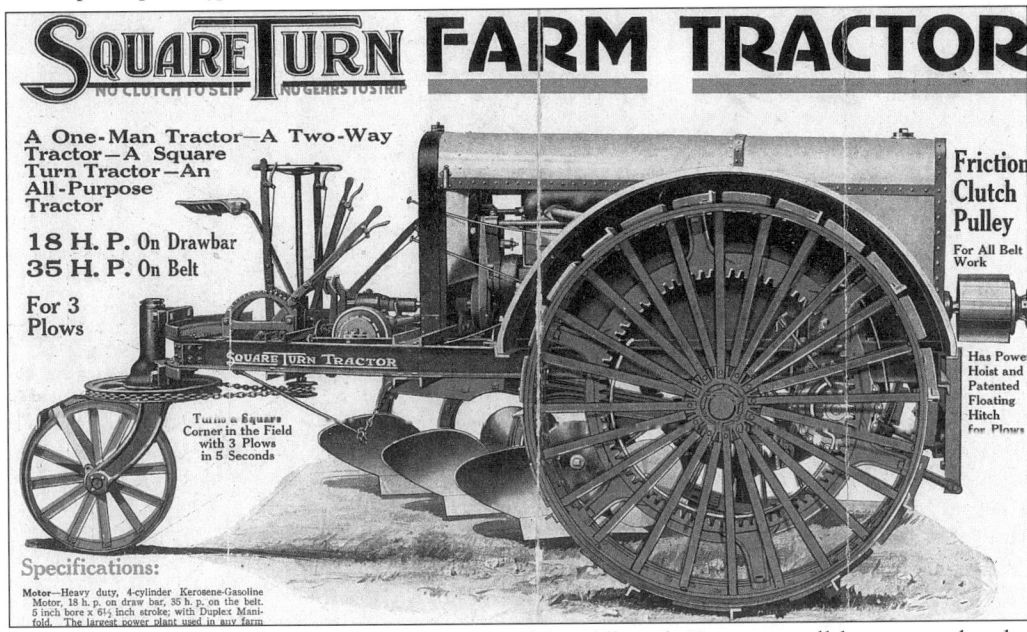

In 1916, the Square Turn Tractor Factory was sold to Albough-Dover, a well-known mail-order firm, who moved the factory into a new, state-of-the-art plant north of Norfolk. The tractors were manufactured until 1925 when the declining economy caused by the effects of World War I forced the company to close. In 1991, the Elkhorn Valley Historical Society purchased the last operable Square Turn Tractor in the country.

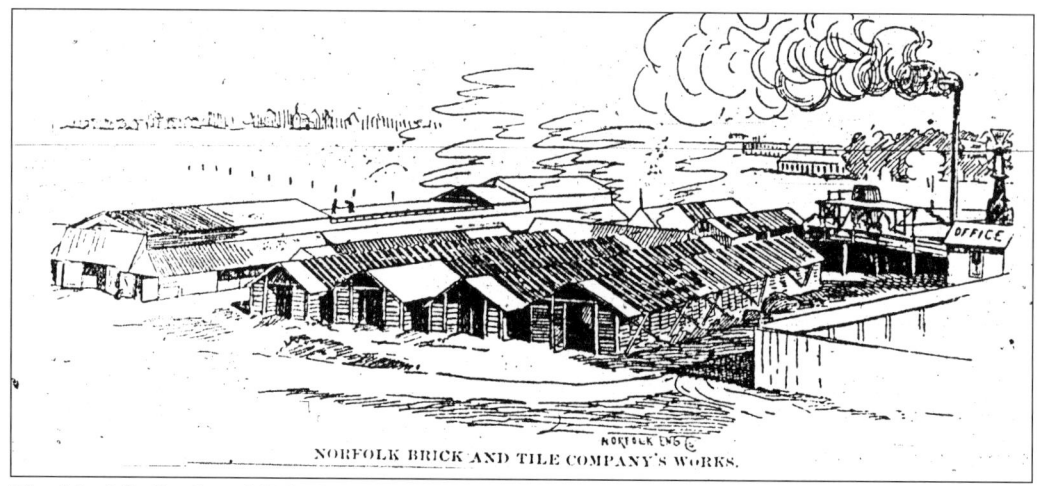

NORFOLK BRICK AND TILE COMPANY'S WORKS.

The Norfolk Brick and Tile Company was built in 1883 and produced 30,000 bricks a day until it closed in 1907. Many of the buildings on Norfolk Avenue were built with bricks produced here. After the Norfolk Brick and Tile Company closed, the land was purchased by Dr. Carl Verges, son of Norfolk doctor Ferdinand Verges.

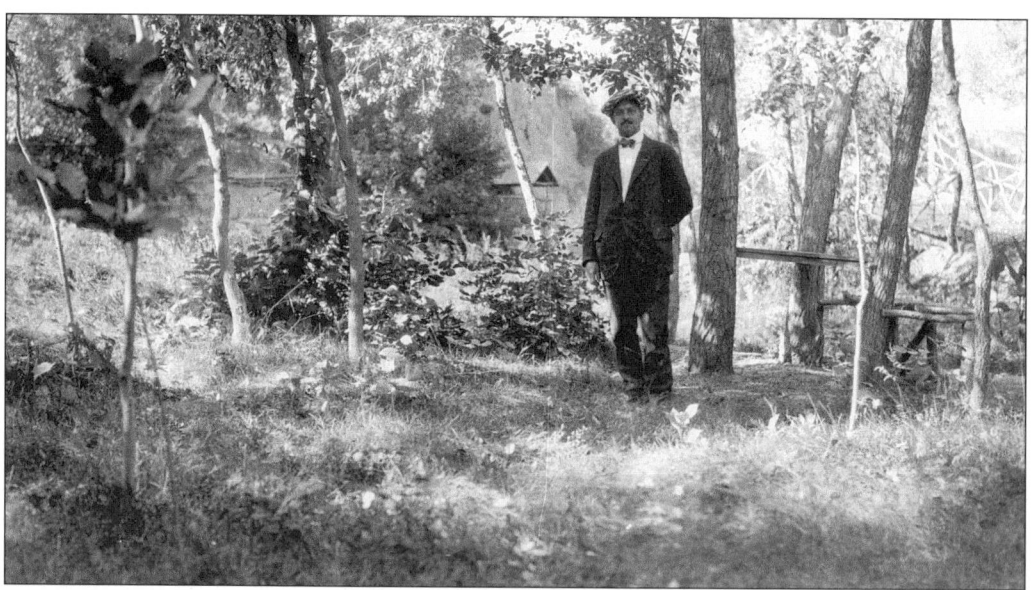

Ferdinand's son, Carl (C.J.) Verges, followed in his father's footsteps and began practicing medicine in Norfolk in 1908. C.J. was elected Norfolk's youngest mayor in 1913. In 1916, C.J. purchased the former Norfolk Brick and Tile Company land and created Verges Park. The photo shows C.J. standing in his park.

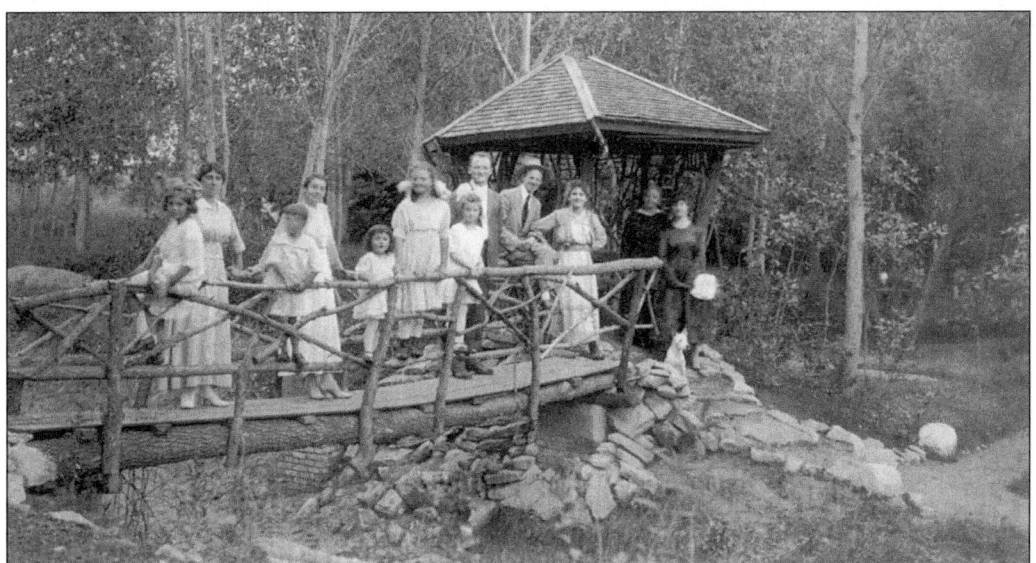

While not everyone in the photograph is identified, the group includes Dorothy, Elizabeth, and Valere Verges (at left), Dr. and Caroline Hoopman, and Elsie Marquardt. In 1923, C.J.'s son, Val, dug a cave in the side of a hill in the park. Eventually, C.J. hired miners to complete the project. They reinforced it with concrete, wired it with electricity, and added a well and pump. The cave was then used for parties, dances, and meetings.

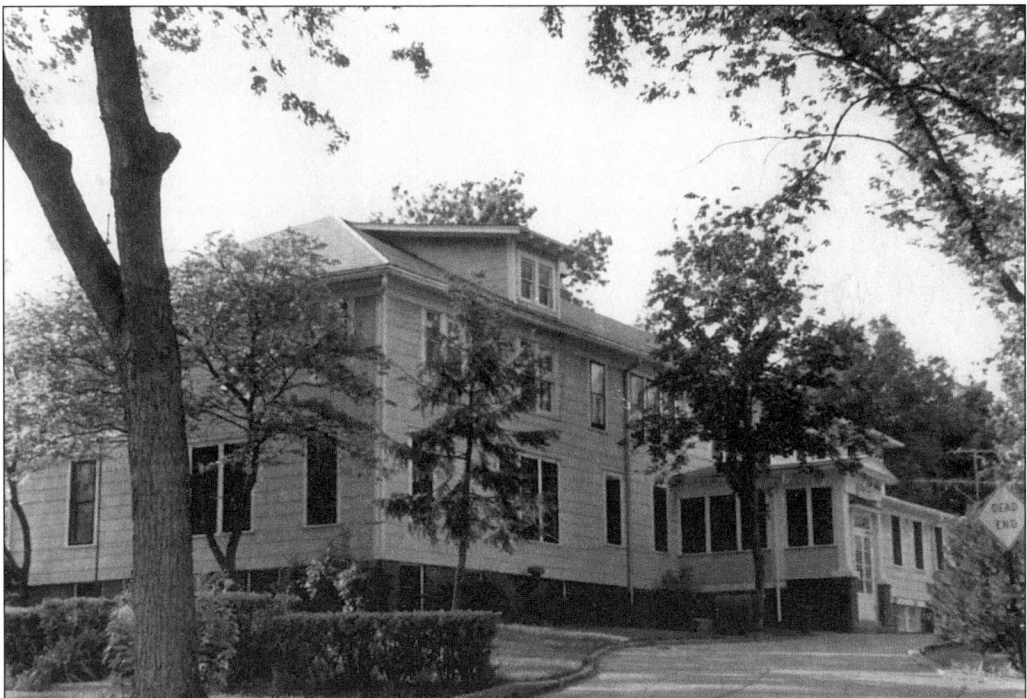

In 1918, Dr. C.J. Verges built Verges Sanitarium, a hospital for patients to stay in while they were recovering from extended illnesses. The sanitarium was adjacent to the park, and a trolley took patients back and forth. C.J. Verges died in 1967, but his son, Dr. Val Verges, practiced medicine in Norfolk until the 1980s.

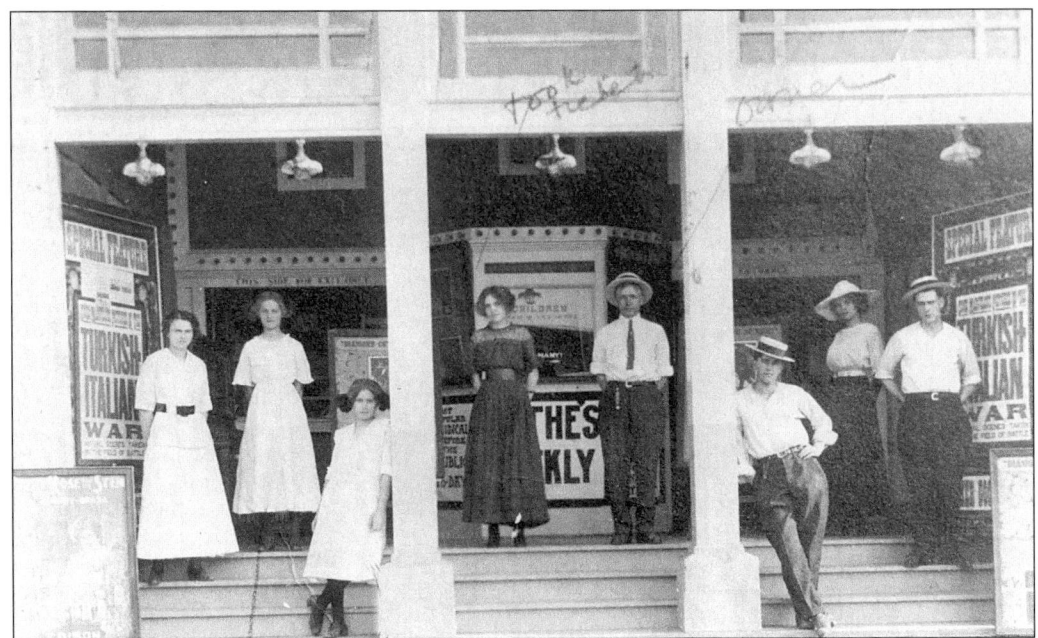

It's show time! Located at 509 Norfolk Avenue, the Crystal Theatre was owned by Robert Ballantyne, who is standing in the middle with his hands behind his back. Pictured, from left to right, are unidentified, Ruth Colwell, Grace Colwell, Ethel Colwell Ballantyne, Robert Ballantyne, Ralph Beebe, Stella McNeeley, and Norton Howe. Robert Ballantyne operated the theater from 1910 to 1911.

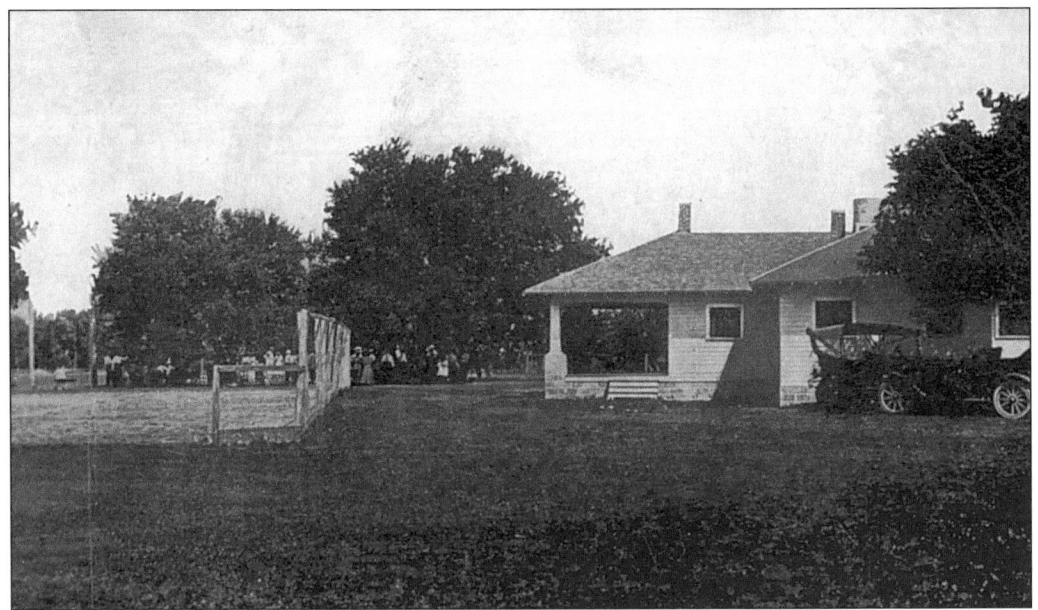

The Norfolk Country Club has been a popular spot for Norfolk citizens to relax and unwind since its opening on August 3, 1909. On opening day, large carriages and touring cars brought two hundred people to the club. It was organized by Dr. P.H. Salter, G.D. Butterfield, Ed Burnham, Storrs Mathewson, Sol G. Mayer, and S.M. Braden, who also served as the first president.

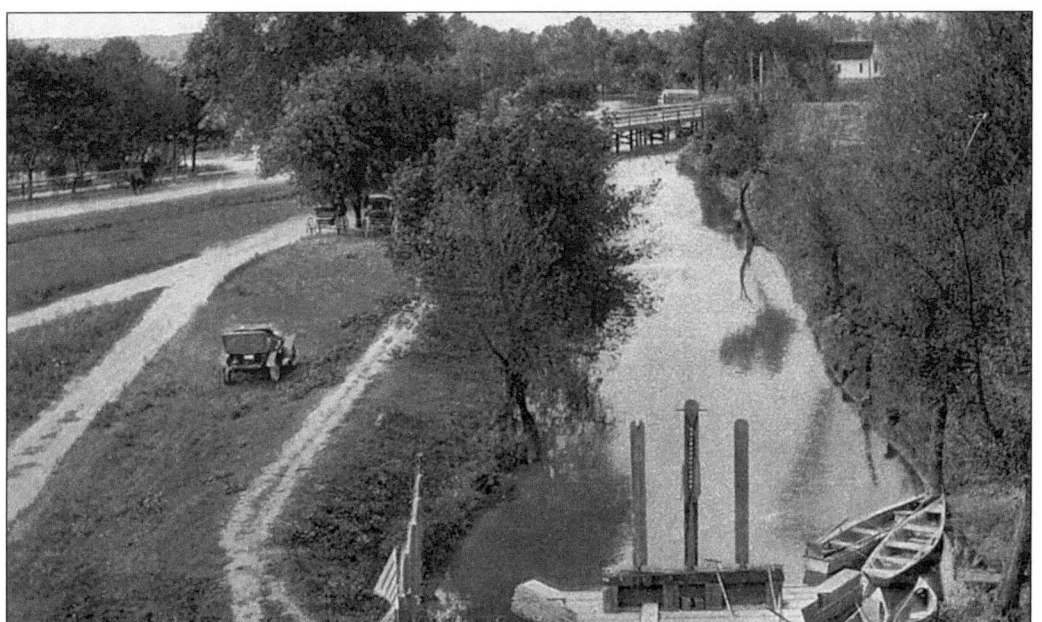

Norfolk's mill, park, and Chautauqua grounds, c. 1913, were located east of 1st Street and north of Norfolk Avenue. The City of Norfolk and Works Progress Administration (WPA) workers built Johnson Park here in 1937.

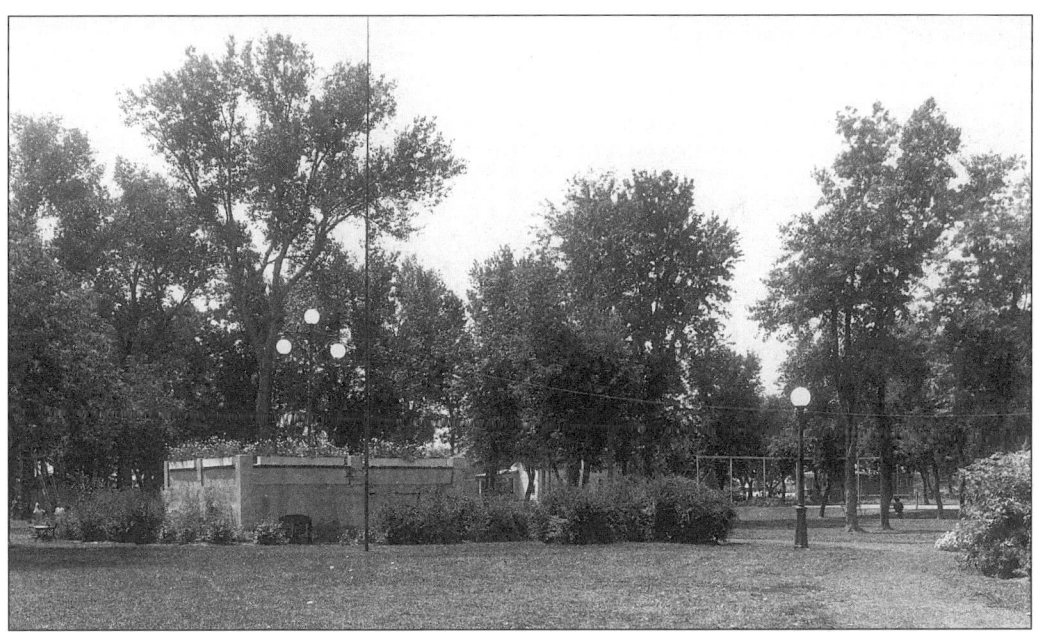

Central Park, so named because of its central location in Norfolk, was originally named People's Park, and before that Homestead Grove. In 1906, William Warneke set out to name the park "People's Park" because of its convenient location and the fact that there were no rivers or major roads that would be a danger to families with children. It featured a bandstand where concerts were held in the summer.

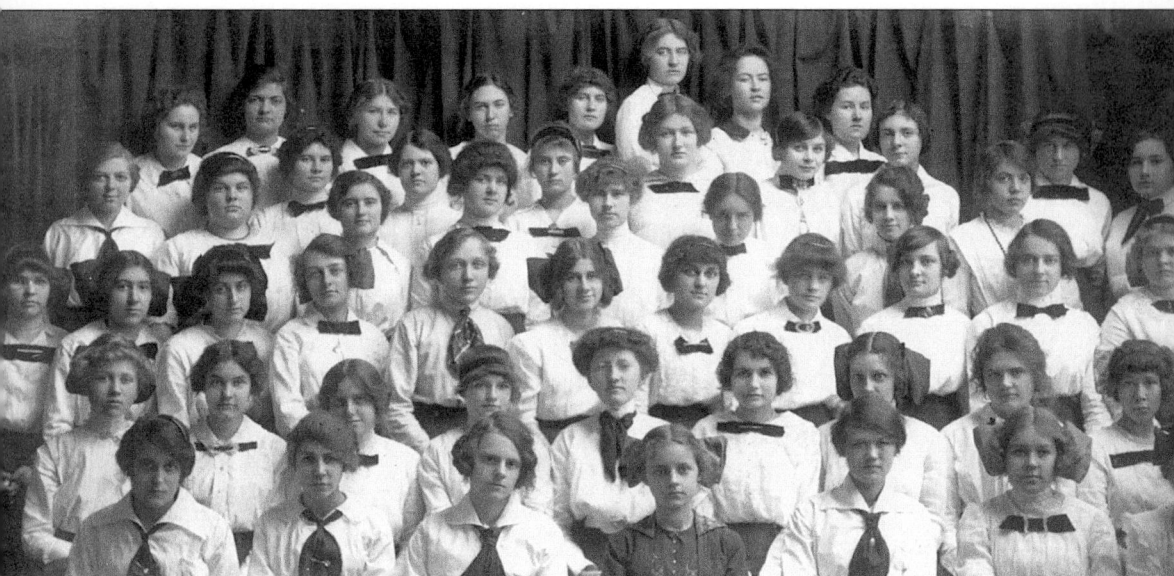

The 1914 Norfolk Senior High School Girls Glee Club is pictured here. Pictured in the first row. from left to right, are Glenn Blakeman, Bernice Ballantyne, Elsie Brueggeman, Winona Davis, Helen Borowiak, Merna Zulauf, and Clara Miller. In the second row, from left to right, are Dorothy Christoph, Mary Curran, Ruth Davenport, Frankie Slawter, Miss A.R. Thomas, Nadine France, Ruth Crosier, Lucille Durland, and Beryl Tubbs. In the third row are Mildred Dunn, Hattie Hepperley, Cora Stockton, Vivien Zulauf, Gladys Pasewalk, Victoria Maryland, Geil Wallerstedt, Myrtice Doughty, Nina Clement, Lavone Zurbrigen, and Frances Malm. In the fourth row are Leota Rish, Bernice Barrett, Irene Carrabine, Fannie Casselman, Marie Crook, Leilah Scott, Hazel Dawson, Alice Ward, Blanche Sterner, Easter Currier, Grace McCaslin, Florence Nightengale, Anna Lemley, Bernice Hibben, Beatrice Gow, and Gertrude Lenz. Finally, in the fifth row are Edith Kellogg, Lillian Clement, Elsie Zachert, Esther Taft, Dortha Kenney, Alpha Porter, Mildred Rees, and Jessie Hepperley.

Three
WINDS OF CHANGE
1917–1949

"A backward glance
A forward view
What happens next
Depends on you."

—Florence Crawford, Norfolk resident in the 1940s and '50s.

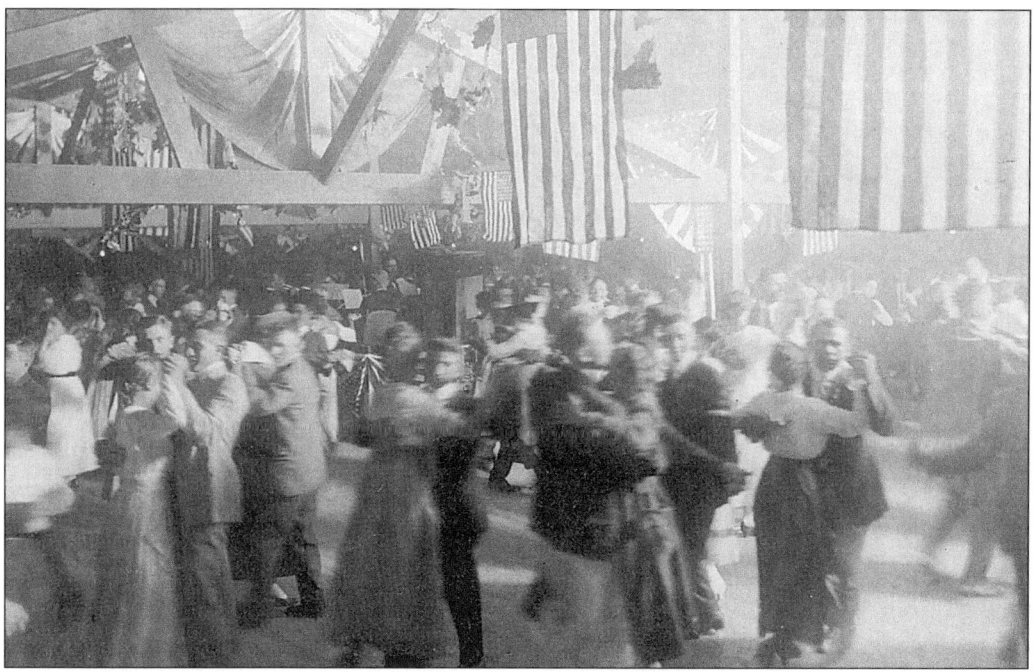

Soldiers from Northeast Nebraska and their wives and sweethearts have one last turn around the dance floor before reporting for duty during World War I. The location was King's Ballroom, which was built in 1917 by Harry King. The ballroom was host to some of the most famous bands around, including Lawrence Welk, Jimmy Dorsey, Duke Ellington, and Harry James.

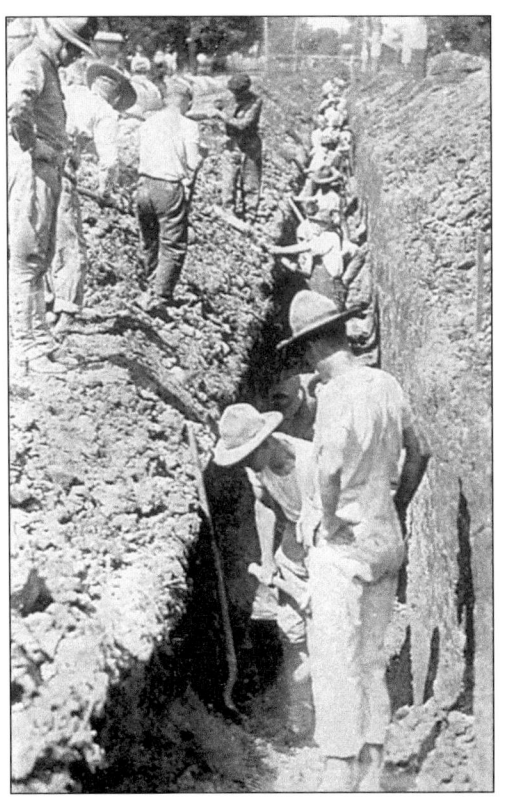

World War I brought dramatic change to the citizens of Norfolk. Young men left to fight a war, and women were left to tend to their families and their lives the best they could. Here members of Company I, made up of men from Madison County, get experience at digging trenches while making a water outlet in Norfolk. World War I was fought in the mud and rat-infested trenches of Europe.

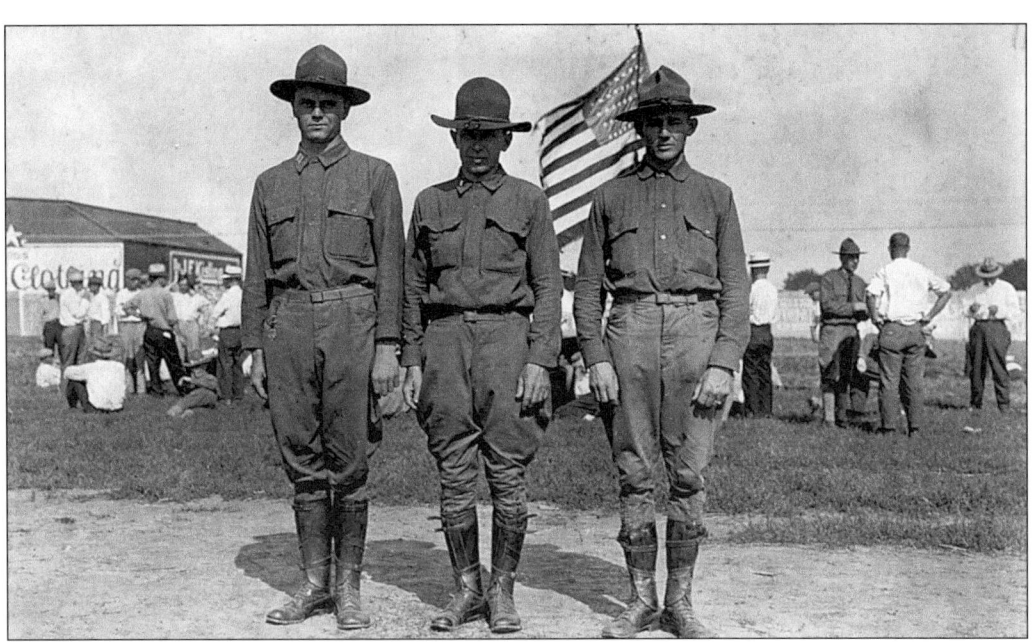

Frank Warner, on the left, was the first commander of Norfolk's American Legion Post 16. Warner was a major with the Nebraska National Guard who served in Washington, D.C. The man in the center is not identified. The man on the right is Lieutenant L.B. Hoffman, who was the Legion Commander in 1925. Hoffman served overseas in the infantry during World War I.

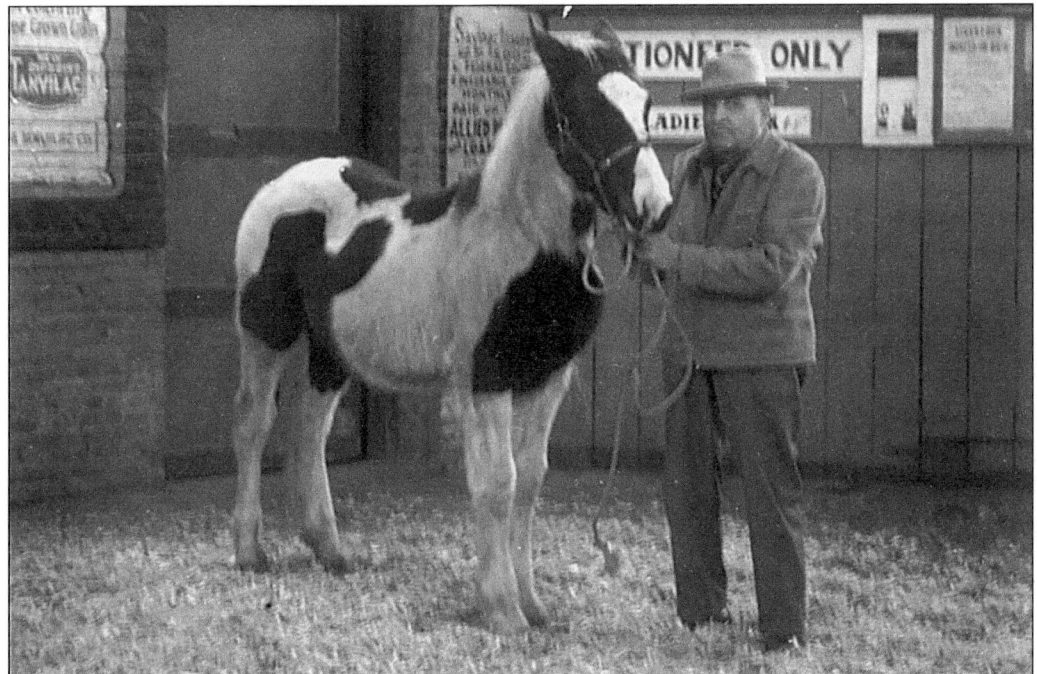

By 1919, World War I was over, men were coming home, and farmers in the area needed a place to buy and sell their livestock. This need was satisfied by the Norfolk Livestock Sales Company, which began operation in 1919. T.O. Ringer, shown in this 1936 photo, was the manager of the company during its early years.

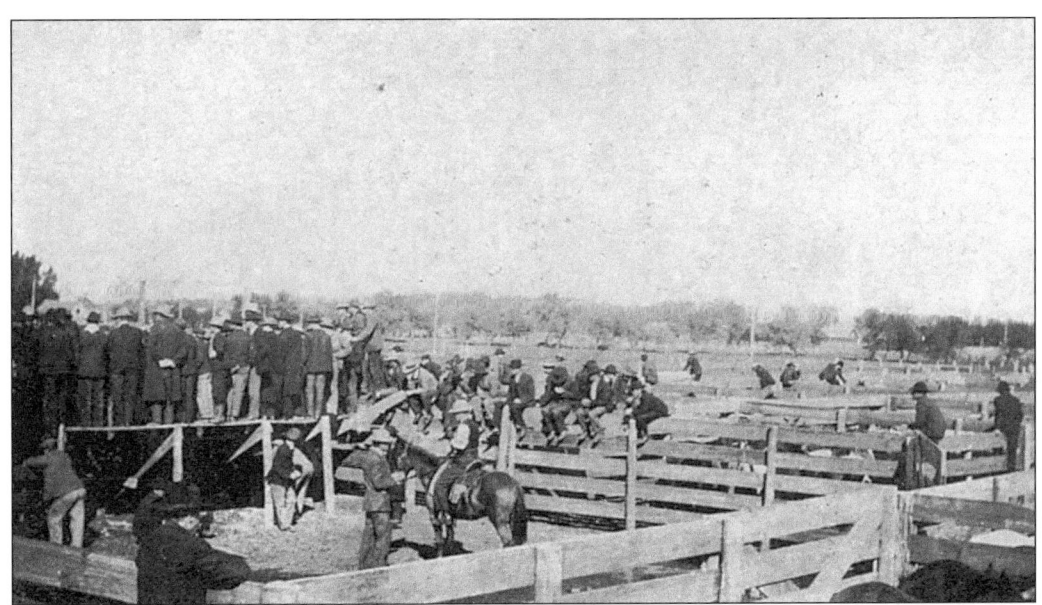

In Norfolk, Nebraska the stock exchange really was a "bull market." Here farmers and ranchers have traveled to Norfolk for what appears to be a horse auction.

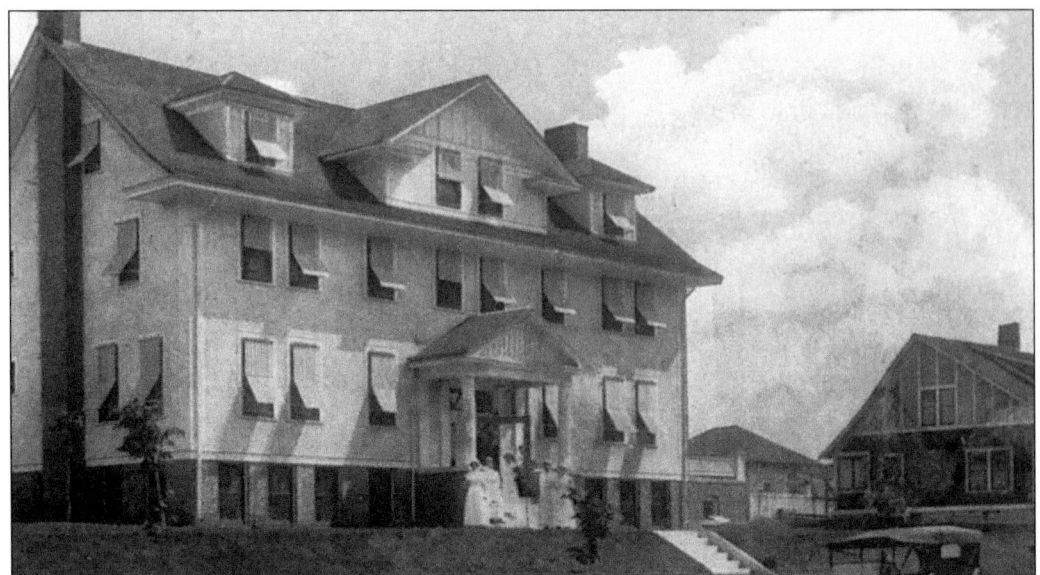

In 1912, Dr. P.H. Salter opened Norfolk General Hospital in a small house. In 1915, the hospital moved to this building located between 15th and 16th Streets on Norfolk Avenue. Salter operated the hospital for a number of years, before it was closed and converted to an apartment house. In 1935, the house was sold to the Catholic Church; it was reopened as a hospital staffed by Missionary Benedictine Sisters.

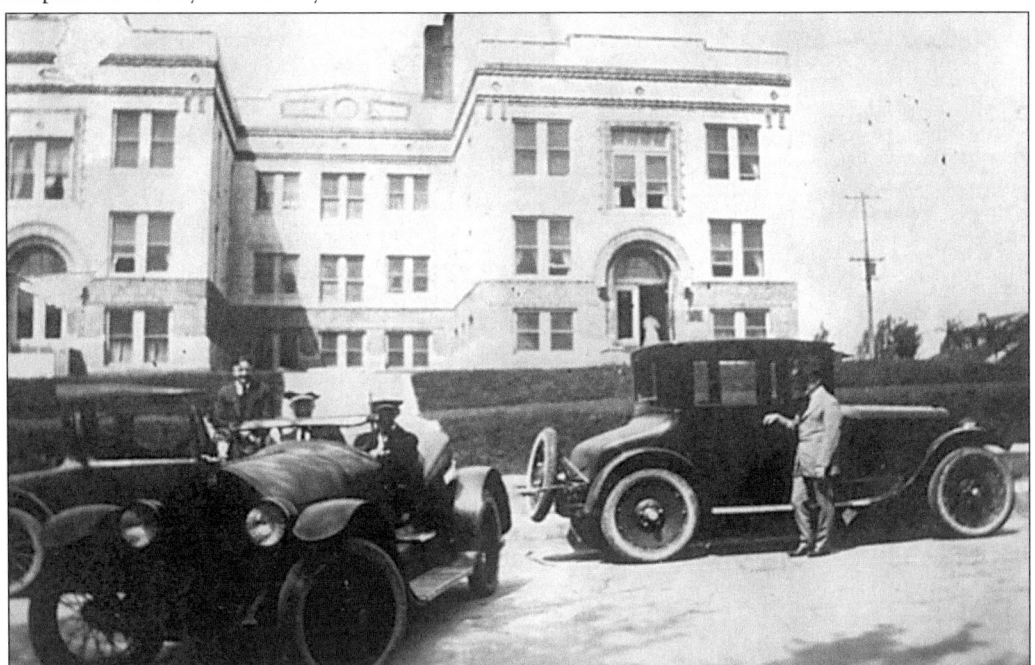

Norfolk was home to three private hospitals, but no public one. In 1922, The Lutheran Hospital Association purchased this facility at 315 North 12th Street, built by Dr. S.A. Campbell, who had fallen ill. The purchase price was $122,000. From left to right are Dr. Campbell, Dr. Fredolph A. Pollack, unidentified, and Dr. Nelson. This facility was used until 1966, when a new Lutheran Community Hospital was built.

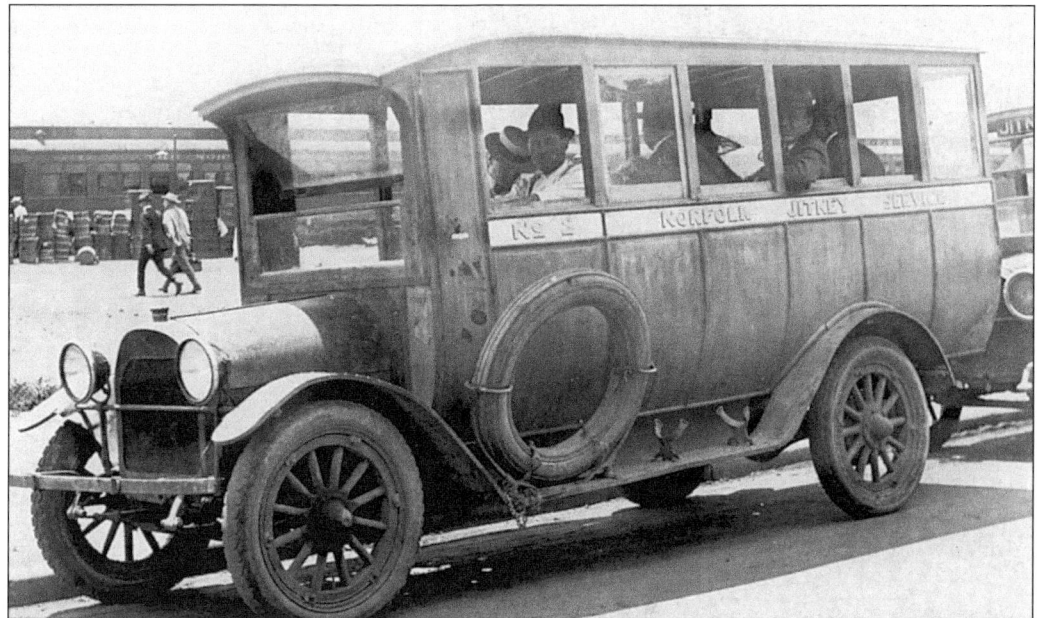

Norfolk Jitney Service ran from Norfolk Junction to downtown Norfolk during the 1910s and 1920s. Norfolk Junction, so named because it was the site of Norfolk's first railroad depot, was a small town, with its own hotels and shops. Because it was located south of Norfolk's downtown area, a jitney service was needed to transport people back and forth. Today, a jitney is better known as a taxi.

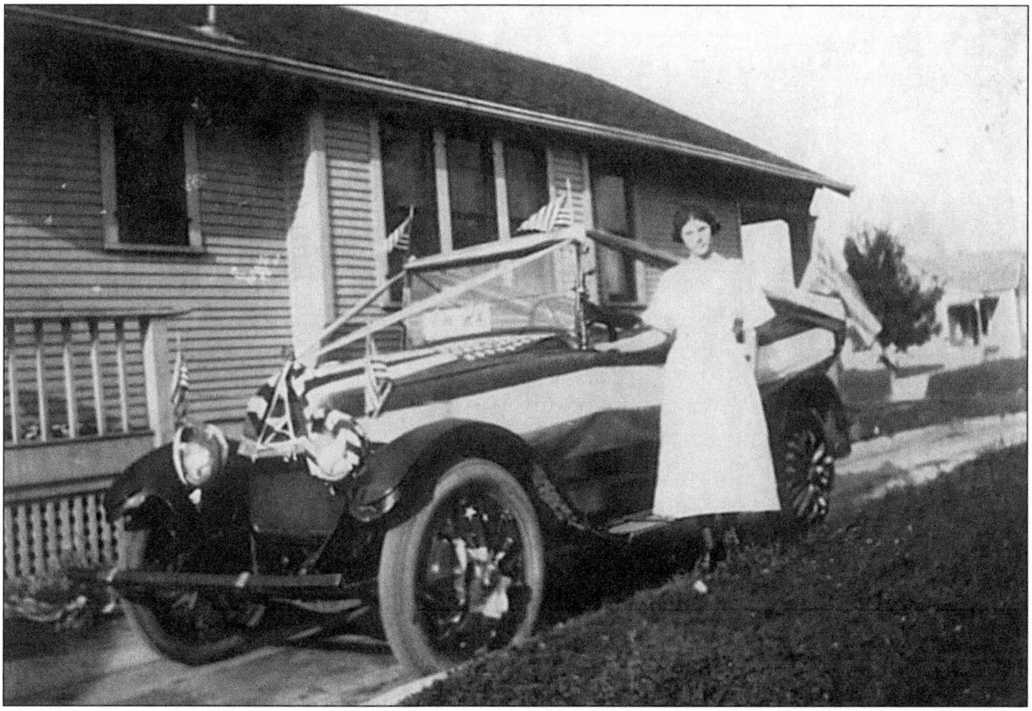

Emma Wurtz and her brother Ed Wurtz ran the jitney service. Here Emma poses beside one of their cars decorated for the 4th of July parade around 1918.

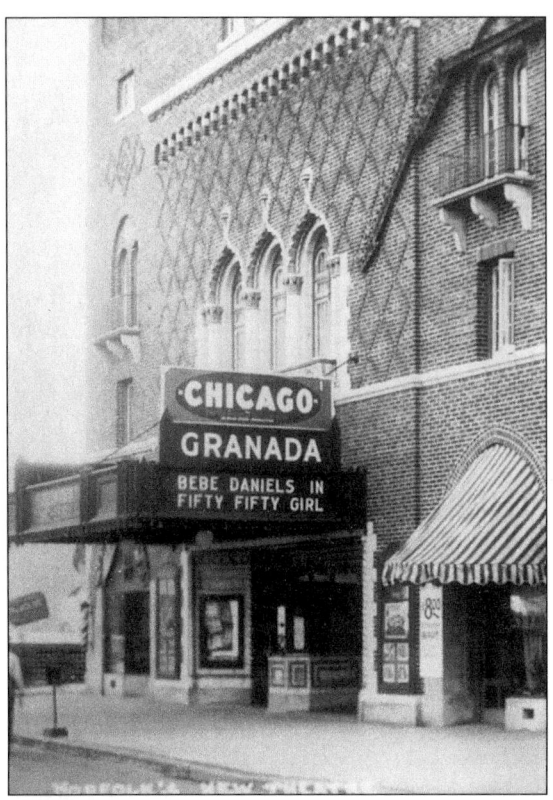

Jack Koenigstein built the Granada Theater, which opened in 1927 at 110 South 5th Street. The theater, said to have an "eclectic" design, could seat 1,100 people. Shortly after it opened, the movie *Norfolk and Its People*, which Universal Pictures produced, played at the theater. This movie was given to the Chamber of Commerce and was destroyed in the flood of 1944.

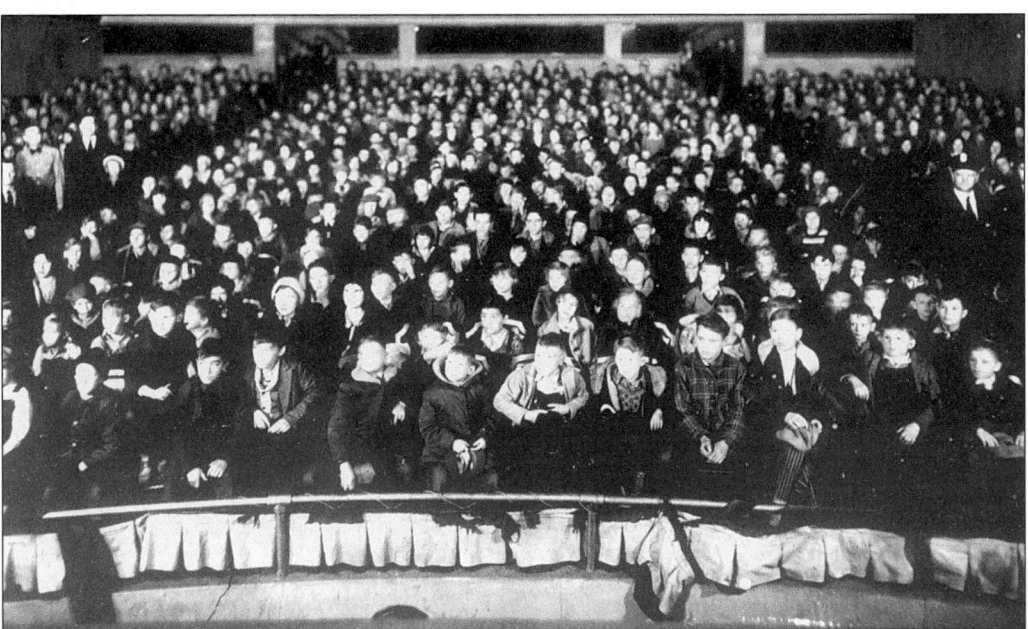

Children attend the annual Halloween Kiddie Matinee at the Granada. When children signed a form saying they would refrain from destructive acts during the holiday, they received free admission. In 1939, 948 children attended. The theater closed in 1979 due to rising maintenance costs and was opened only for special events until it was torn down in 1989.

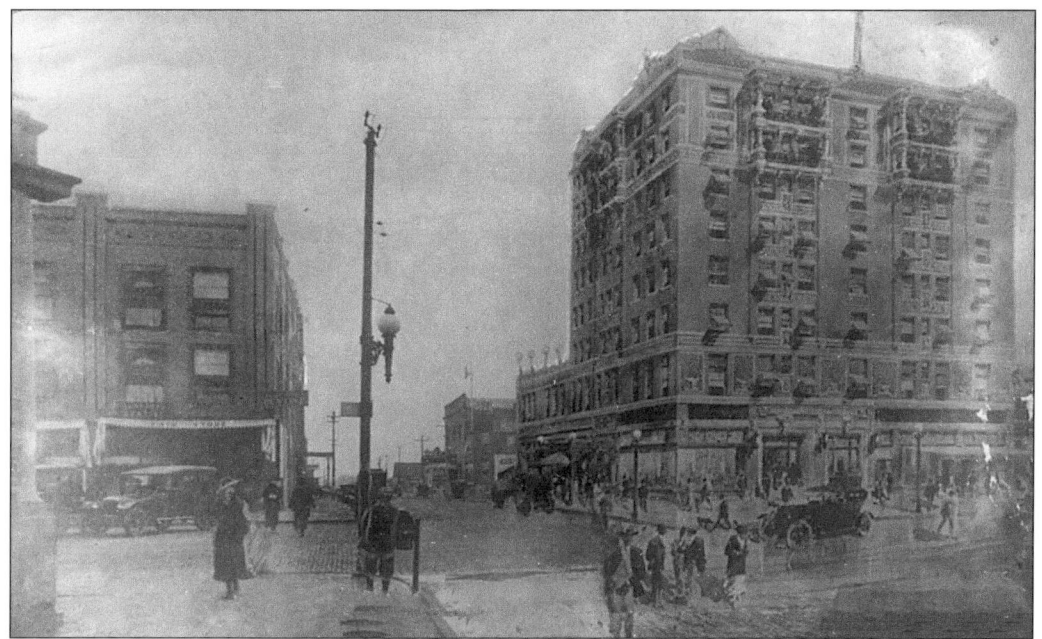

Norfolk continued to progress and change during the 1920s, and this drawing proves its citizens had great hopes for Norfolk's future. Shown here is an artist's idea of what Norfolk's newest hotel would look like. The drawing shows an eight-floor structure with balconies on the two upper floors and a very busy intersection.

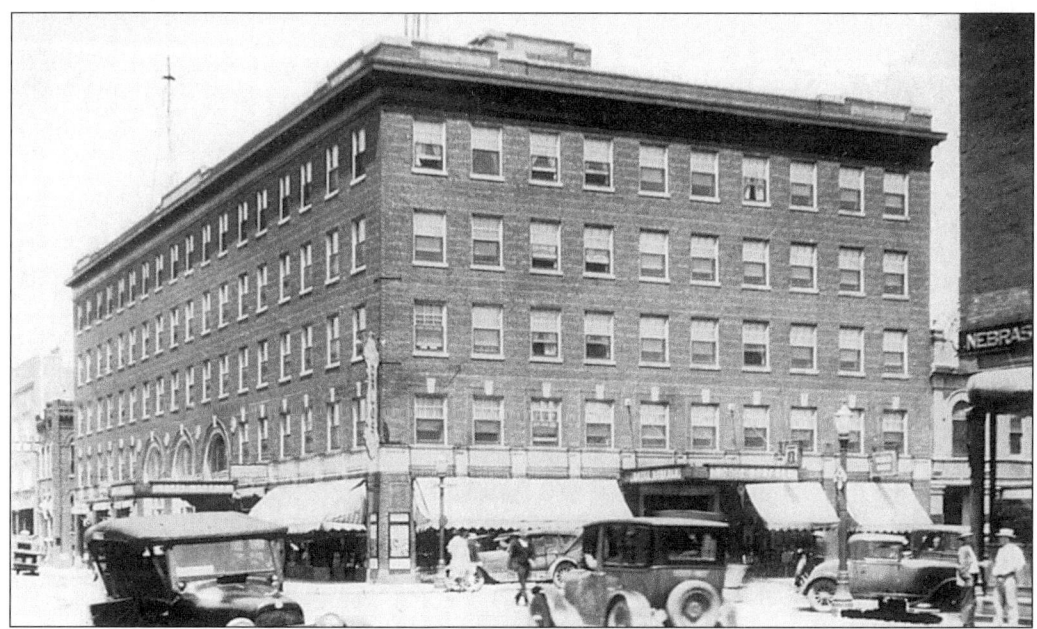

This photograph shows the Hotel Norfolk as it really looked after it was built in 1928. While it may not be as dramatic as originally planned, the hotel served Norfolk well for many years. Through the years it has had a variety of names, including the Waldorf Hotel, Hotel Madison, and, now, The Kensington. It is still in use today with businesses on the first floor and apartments above. This building has been placed on the National Register of Historic Places.0

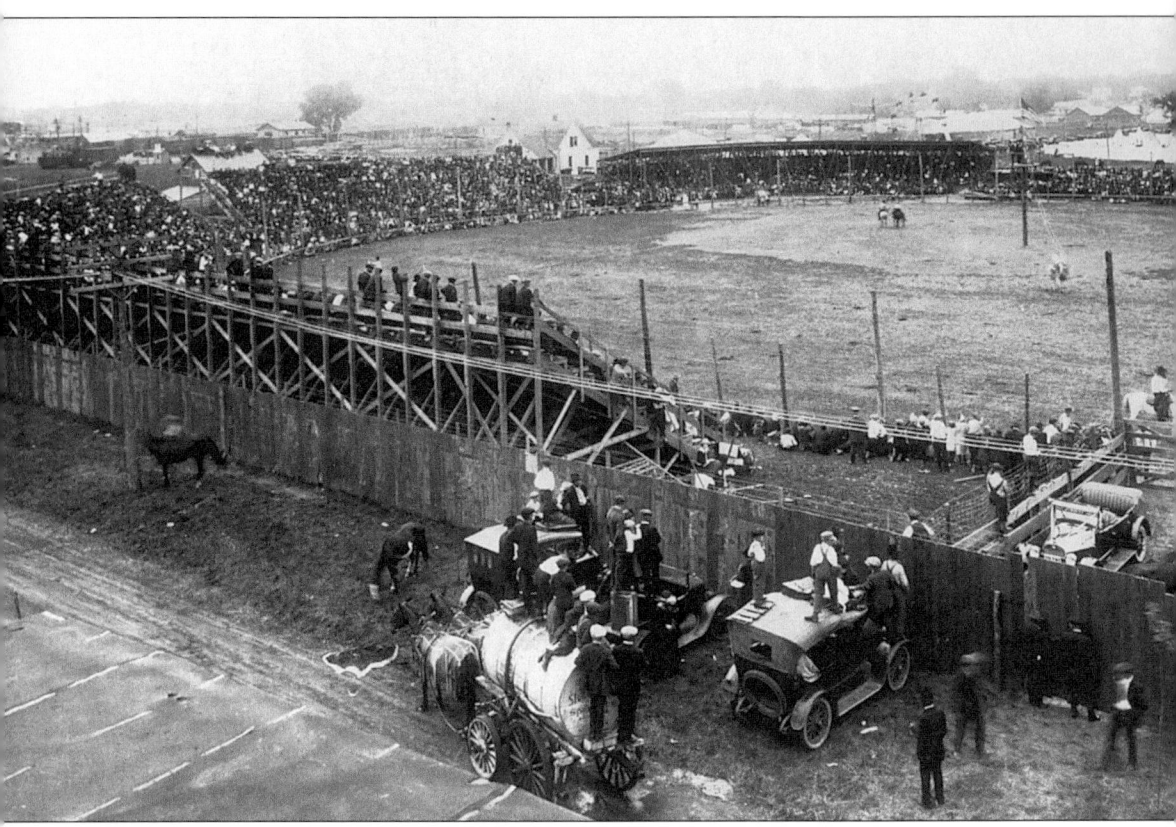

Citizens of Norfolk have always enjoyed quality entertainment. Outdoor activities, such as football games, rodeos, and festivals, were also important. This photograph was taken during the city's Harvest Festival, September 26–28, 1923. The site is Municipal Athletic Park, on North 4th Street and Prospect Avenue, which was built the year before. The scene is looking

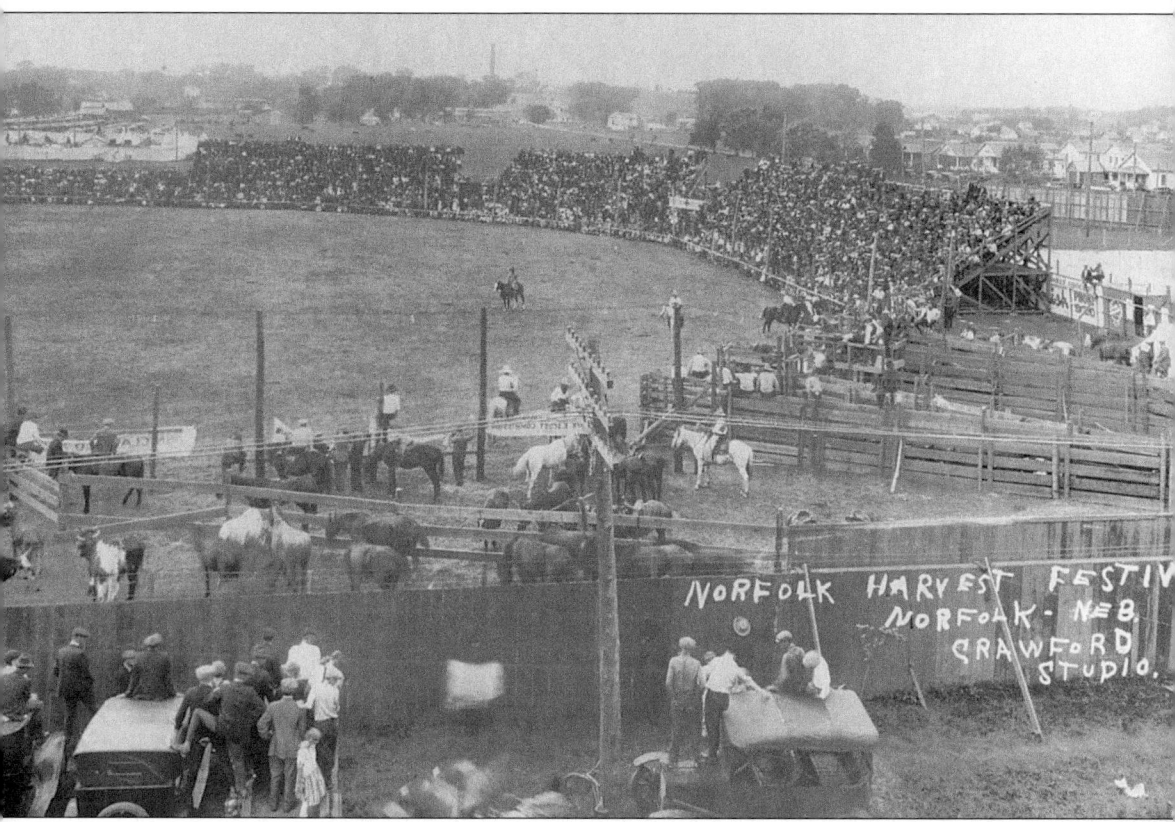

northwest from 3rd Street. In the background are tents and tipis, a carnival with rides, and many non-paying on-lookers. The park was also used for baseball and ice-skating, and was located across the street from the Norfolk Driving Park.

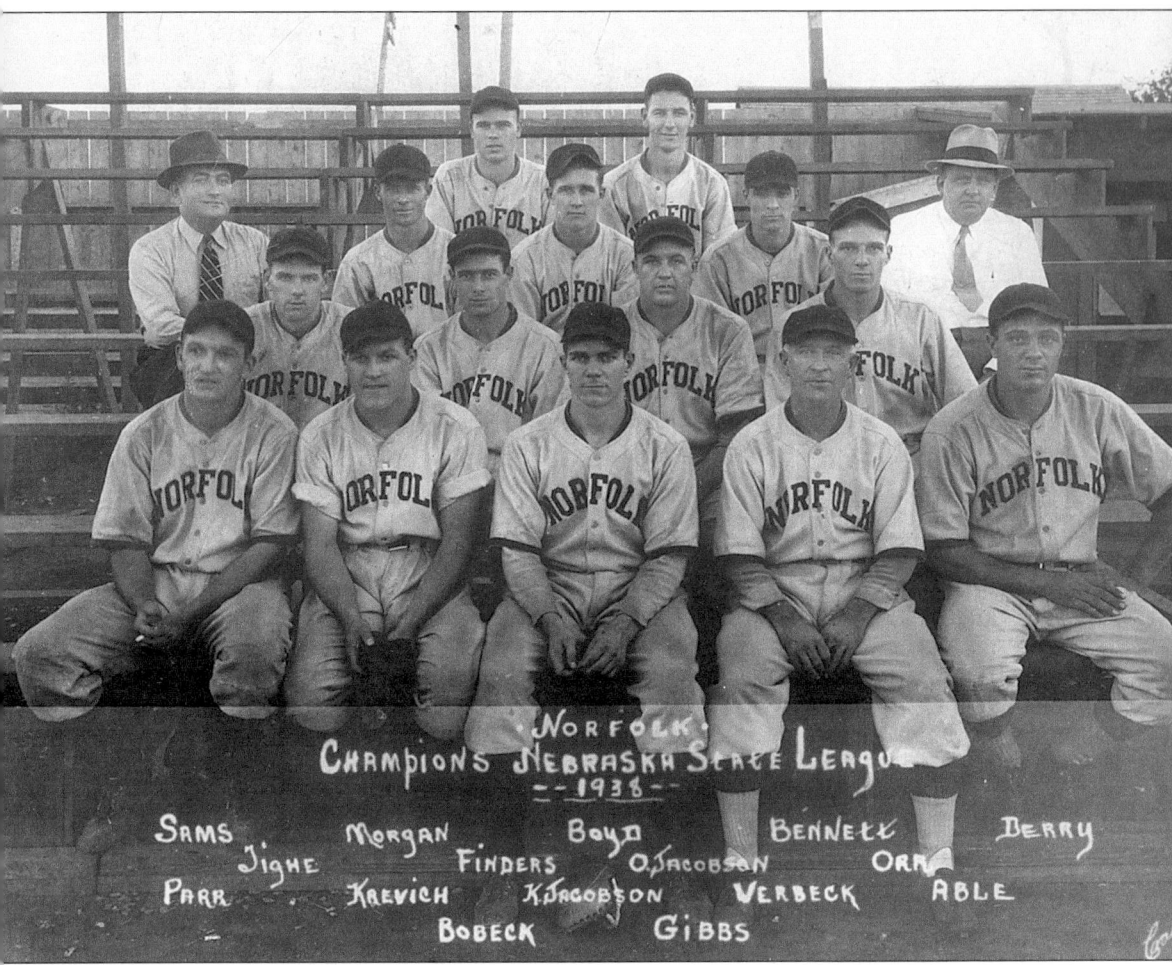

By the early 1900s, baseball was becoming America's favorite sport, and Norfolk was not about to be left out of the fun. In 1914, Norfolk entered the Western Baseball League by purchasing a franchise in Fremont, and the club became the Norfolk Drummers. There was little time for baseball during World War I, so activity was suspended until 1922 when the Nebraska State League was re-activated. The Norfolk team became the Elkhorns, and in 1923, radio station WJAG started broadcasting their games. In the next few years, lights were installed at the Municipal Athletic Park, and in 1934, the St. Louis Cardinals signed an agreement to take two players from the Nebraska State League at the end of each season. Players were so dedicated that they played in their bare feet when the field was wet and muddy instead of canceling the game. The photo above shows the 1938 Norfolk Elks when they won the Nebraska State League championship. The players on the bottom row are, from left to right, Tony Sams, Bill Morgan, Johnny Boyd, Manager E.S. "Doc" Bennett, and ? Berry. In the second row are Ned Tighe, Wendell Finders, O. Jacobsen, and Johnny Orr. In the third row are President Ben Parr, Johnny Kreevich, Kenneth "Sonny" Jacobsen, George Verbeck, and ? Able. In the top row are Leo Bobeck and Eddie Gibbs.

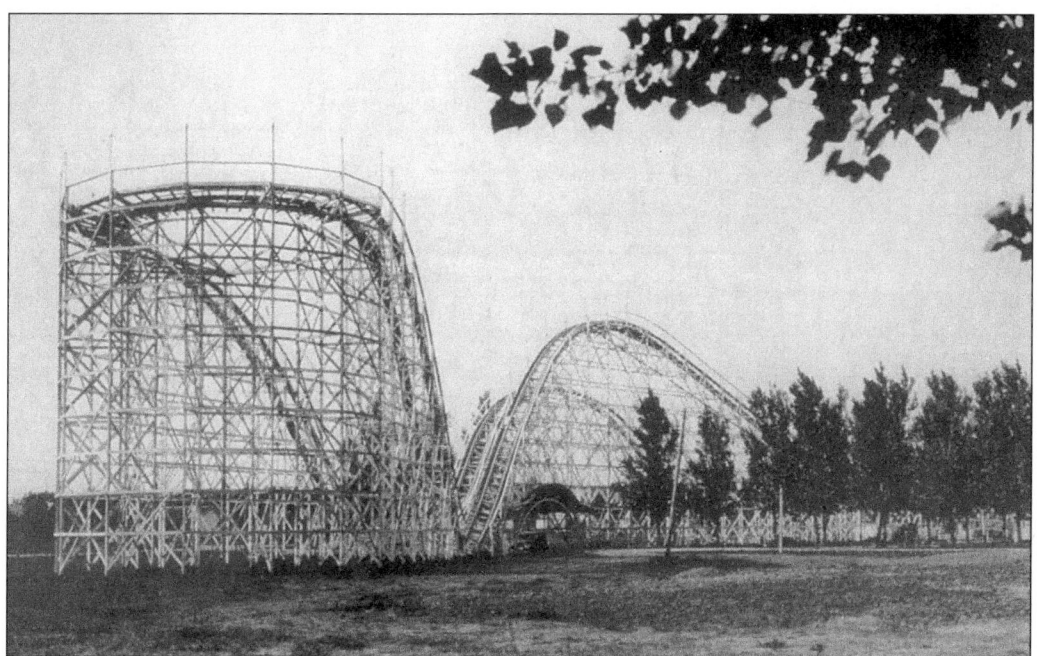

Norfolk residents had the opportunity to participate in a rare form of entertainment when Harry King, who had built King's Ballroom back in 1917, decided to build a roller coaster in the early 1920s. The roller coaster, one of the largest at that time, sat adjacent to the ballroom at 1000 Riverside Boulevard. A swimming pool and a miniature golf course were also added to the grounds in the 1920s. The roller coaster was dismantled during the Great Depression.

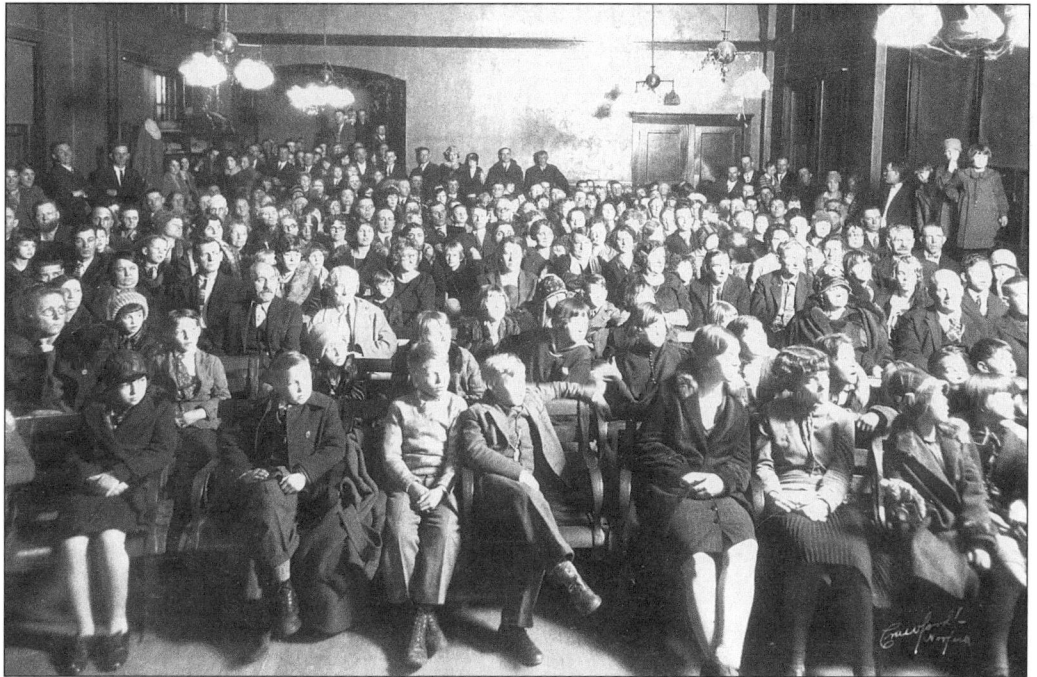

Children and adults anxiously await Santa Claus at an employees' family Christmas party at the Chicago and North Western Depot sometime during the 1920s.

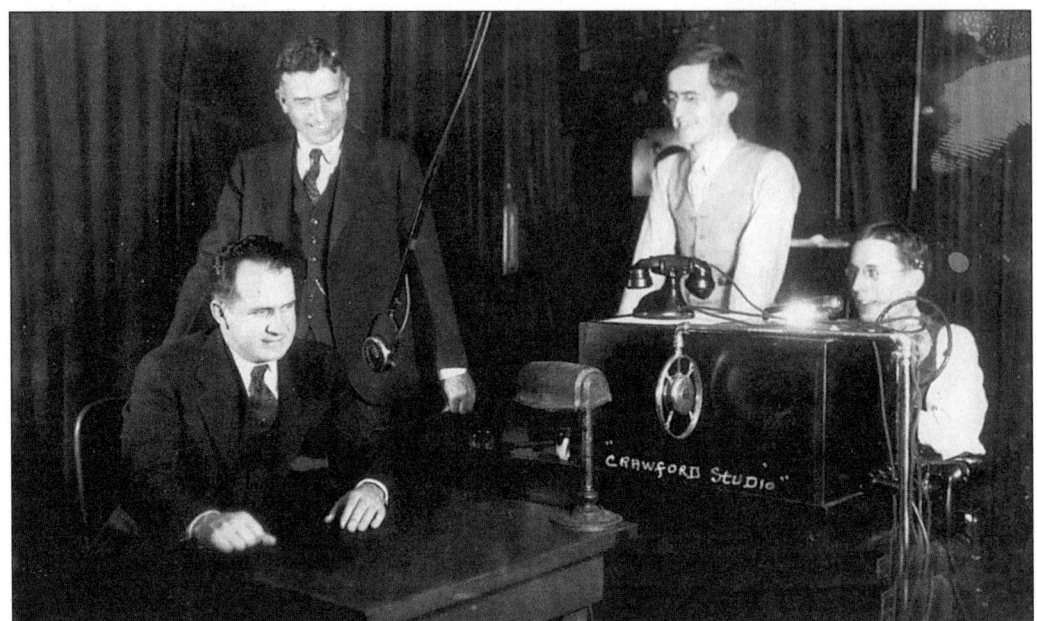

On July 26, 1922, Gene Huse, owner of Huse Publishing and the *Norfolk Daily News*, received a license to build and operate a radio station with the call letters WJAG. The station began operating that day in the *Norfolk Daily News* building at 116 North 4th Street. In this early 1930s photo, Don Bridge (left), Art Thomas, Don Huddle, and Russel Jensen broadcast from the mezzanine of the Hotel Norfolk.

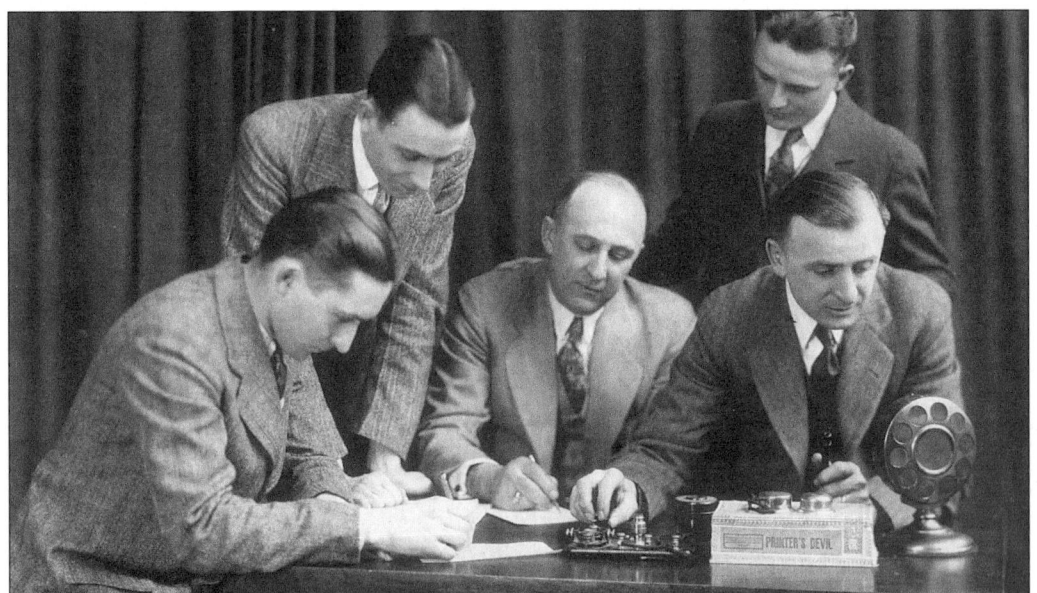

Karl Stefan, at the microphone, conducts "The School of the Air" from WJAG, teaching Morse code to listeners. Stefan was the chief announcer and noon newscaster on WJAG from 1922 to 1934. He studied telegraphy as a young man, before coming to Norfolk to become the city editor for the *Norfolk Daily News*. He initiated many new radio programs, and during the 1920s, recreated the World Series from telegraph reports. In 1934, Stefan ran for Congress where he served until his death in 1951.

First as a "fearless rider and crack shot" in Buffalo Bill's Wild West Show, Diamond Dick later had the Diamond Dick Wild West Show. Dick became famous for riding 5,500 miles from Nebraska to New York on one horse. In 1906, Dick retired as a showman and entered medical school. In 1910 Dr. Richard Tanner began practicing medicine in Norfolk. His identity as "Diamond Dick" was revealed to Norfolkans in the 1925 American Legion Rodeo.

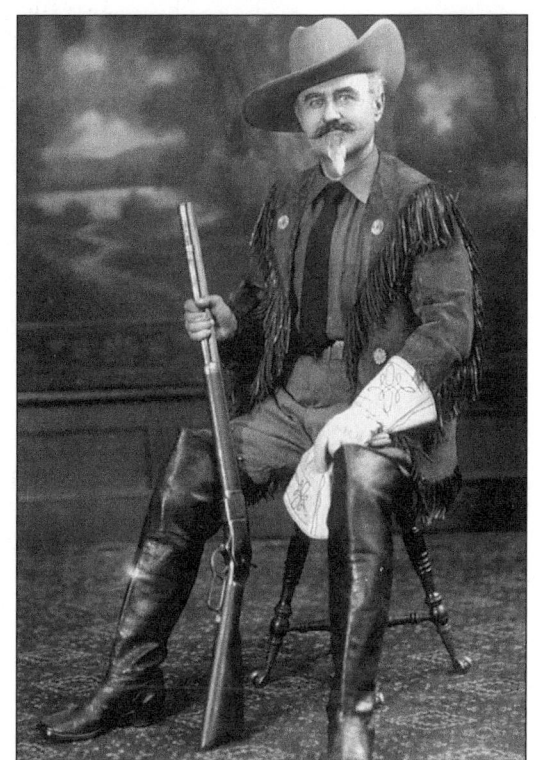

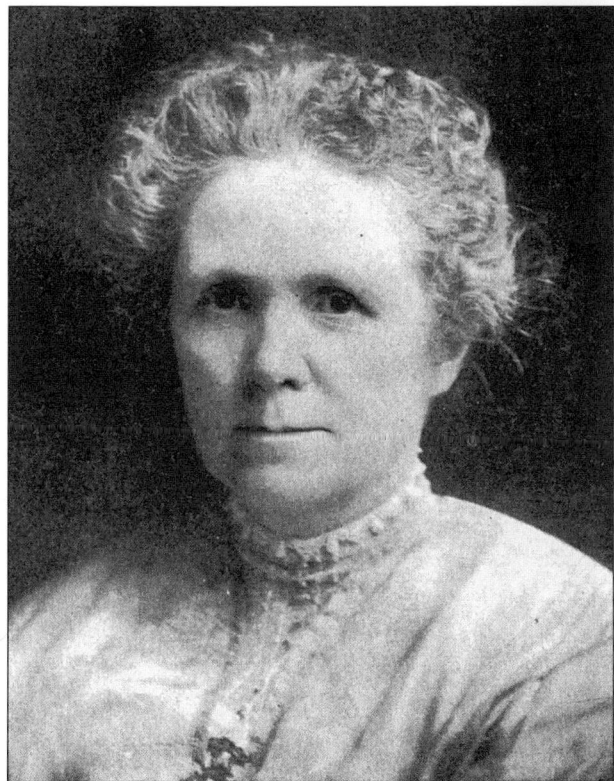

A history of Norfolk would be incomplete without mentioning Cora Beels, who wrote Norfolk's first history. She came to Norfolk in 1874 with her parents, and in 1889 married George Beels. She taught music for many years and is also credited with organizing the first Woman's Club in 1896, the Nancy Gary Chapter of the Daughters of the American Revolution of Norfolk in 1914, and the Norfolk Rebekah Branch of the Independent Order of Odd Fellows (IOOF).

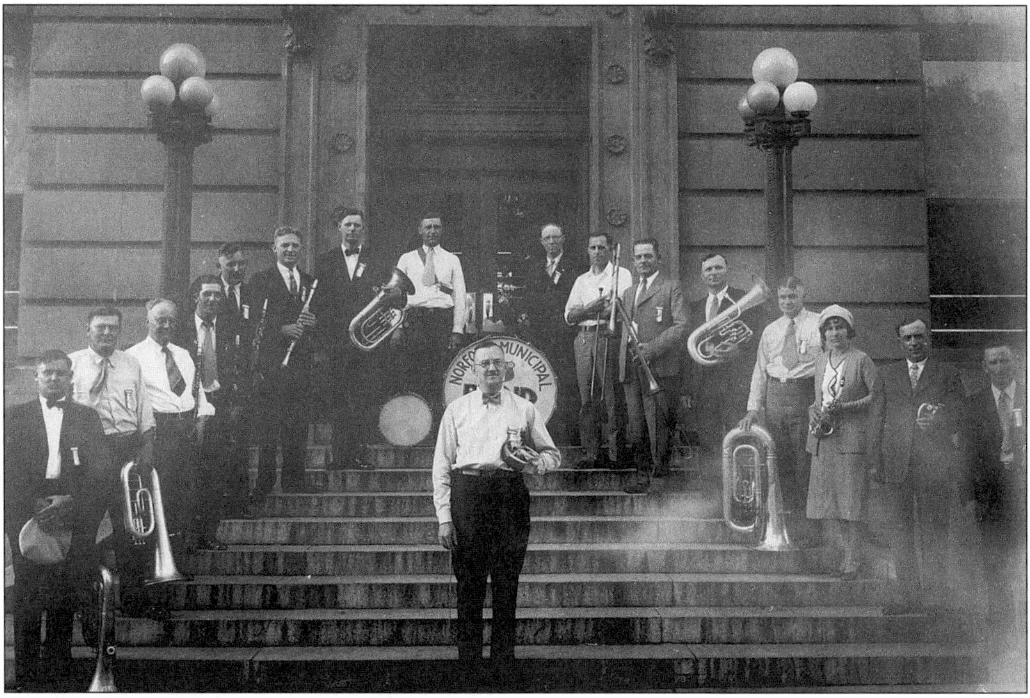

The Postmasters Convention Band poses for a photograph on the steps of the McMill Building on June 15 or 16, 1931.

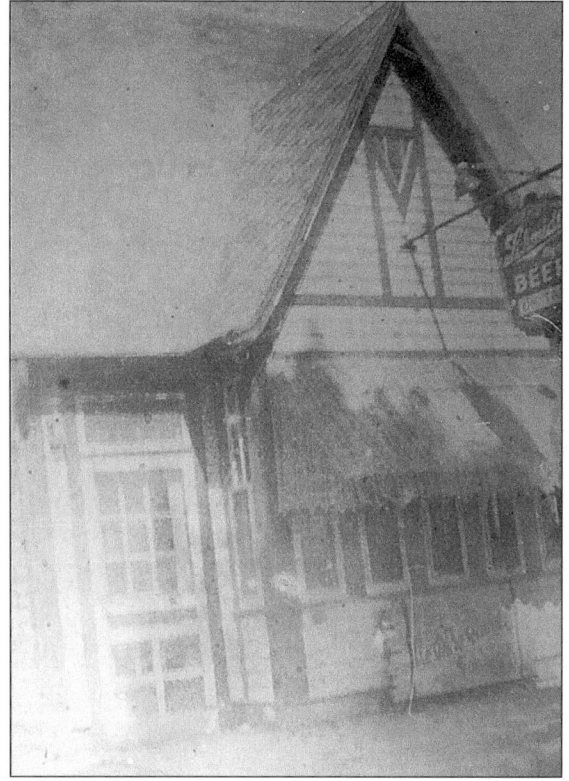

Ed Prenger opened the "Ye Olde Tavern" restaurant in 1932 on South 6th Street and Pasewalk Avenue. Prenger began serving loose meat sandwiches known as "taverns." The building was later moved to 116 East Norfolk Avenue. Years later, a new building was constructed on the same site and renamed "Prenger's."

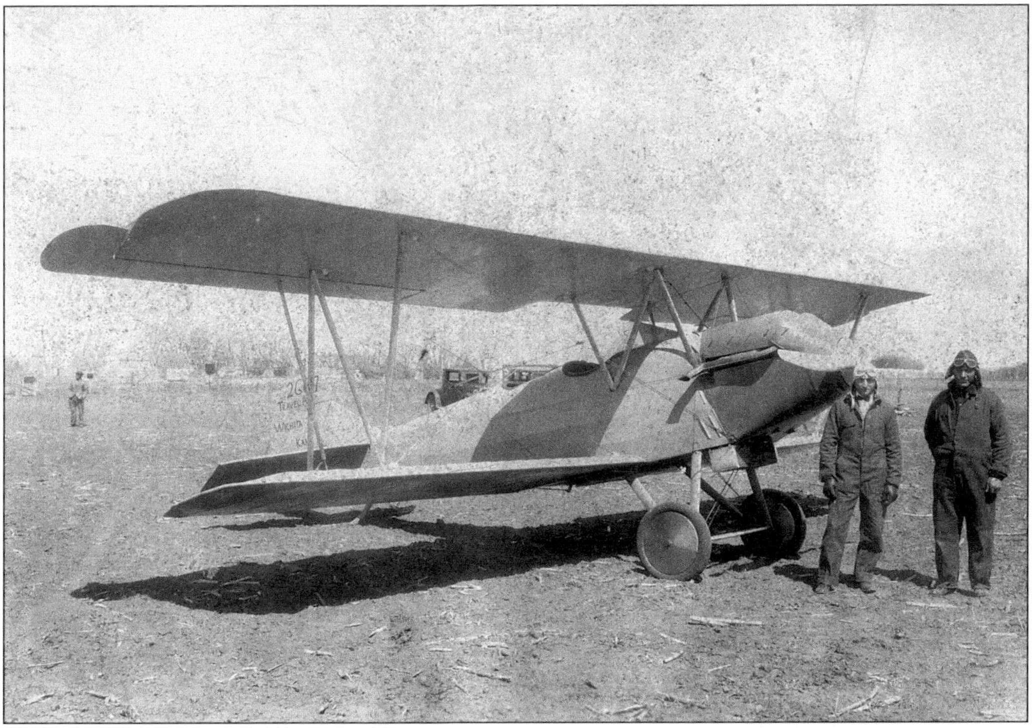

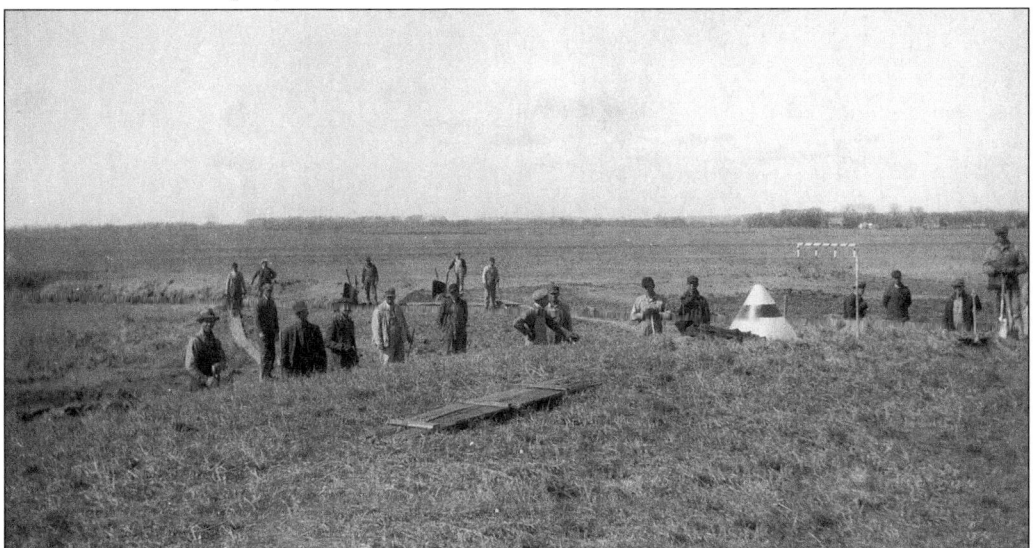

Andy Risser, left, and Henry Bruenholdte of Pilger pose beside Risser's plane. Bruenholdte was Risser's first student in Norfolk's flying school in 1928. The school had 37 students take their initial solo flights during 1928. The original airport, with two hangers, an office building, and a windsock, was southeast of Norfolk, approximately one mile southeast of the Norfolk Livestock Sales Company.

In 1934, Risser leased 160 acres of land south of Norfolk on Highway 81, where he moved his operation. Here men get the fields ready for the new airport. By the late 1930s, with the winds of war raging in Europe, the government initiated the Civilian Pilot Training Program. Students were taught to fly and then admitted to the service.

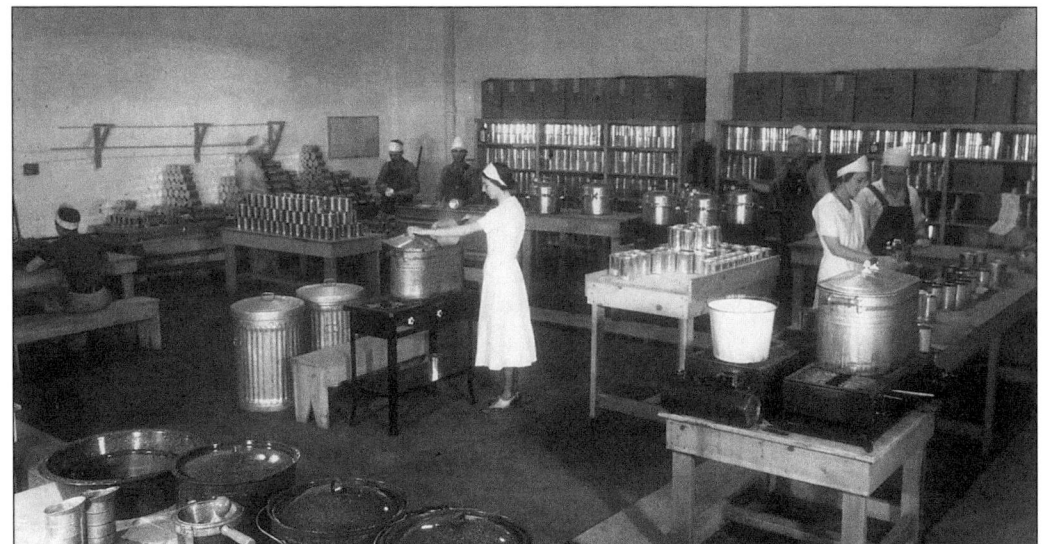

The date is September 29, 1934, and the Norfolk Canning Center operates under the Federal Emergency Relief Administration program to alleviate the effects of the Great Depression. The Depression, combined with a drought and hordes of grasshoppers that ate what few crops were left, meant that by 1937 nearly 100,000 Nebraskans were involved in some kind of government relief program.

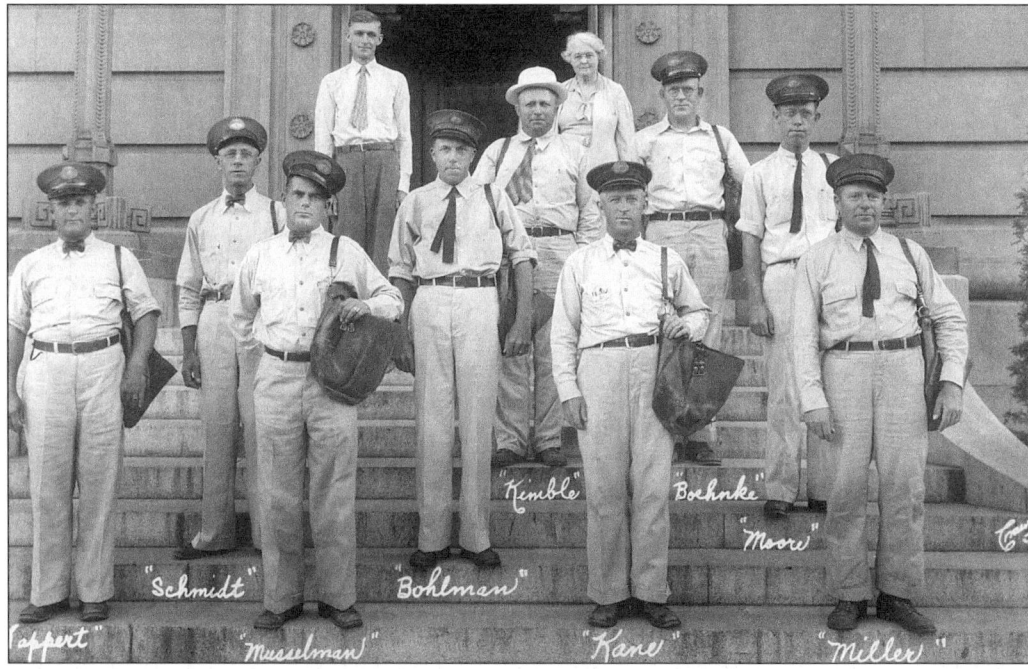

On June 15, 1936, postal carriers set out to deliver Adjusted Service Bonds, payments made to World War I veterans. The federal government was supposed to make the payments 20 years after the war, but they were delivered early because of the Great Depression. Pictured in row one, from left to right, are Tappert, Musselman, Kane, and Miller. In row two are Schmidt and Bohlman. Moore is pictured in row three. In row four are Kimble and Boehnke. Marie Weeks, postmaster, and P.M. Mueller, assistant postmaster, are in the top row.

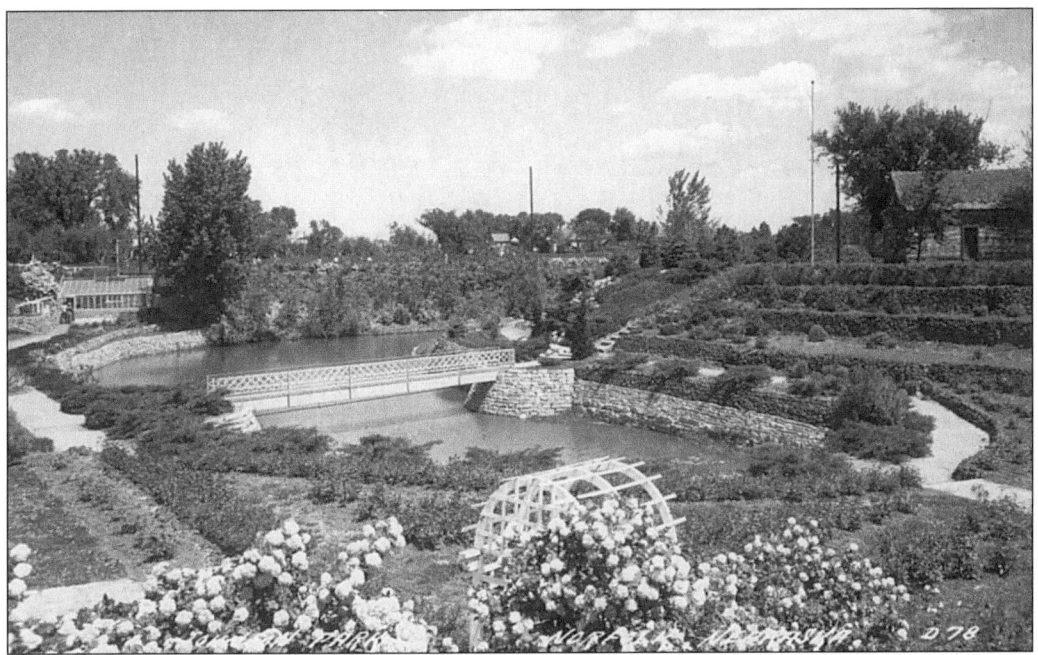

This is Johnson Park as it appeared during the summer, c. 1942. The park was the project of Nels P. Johnson, chairman of the Norfolk Park Board. The construction of the park was another Works Progress Administration project in 1937 during the Great Depression.

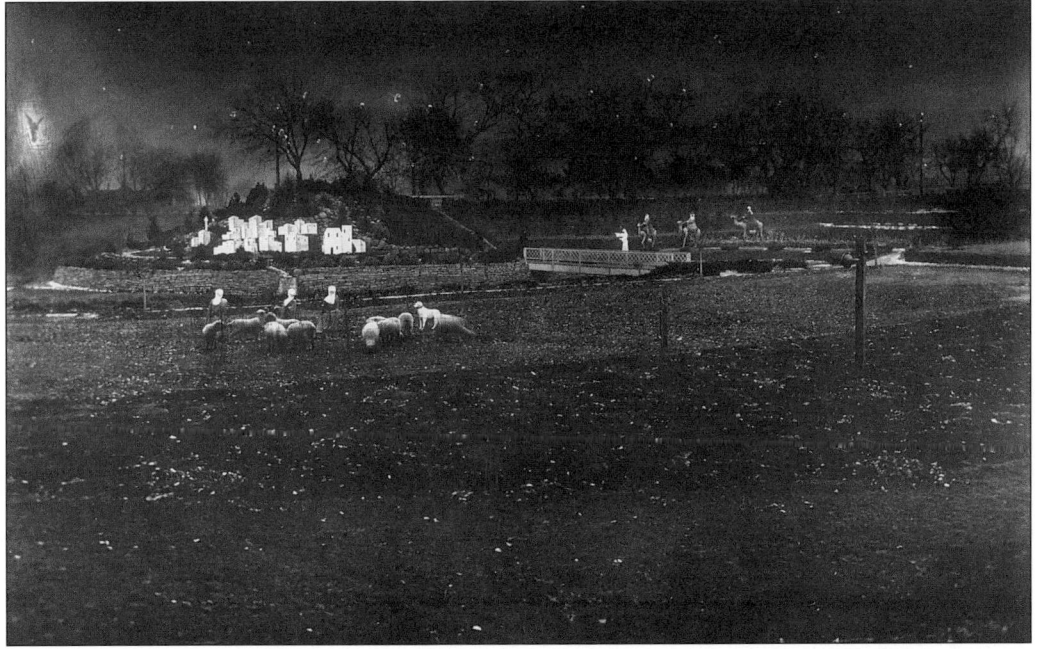

Johnson Park was a popular spot during the Christmas season. The "Babe of Bethlehem" scene started in 1937. Cars filled with curious children and adults would drive slowly by the scene, not only to capture the image, but also to listen to the Christmas carols that were broadcast from speakers surrounding the scene. The display included live sheep and life-sized figures made by A.L. Howser.

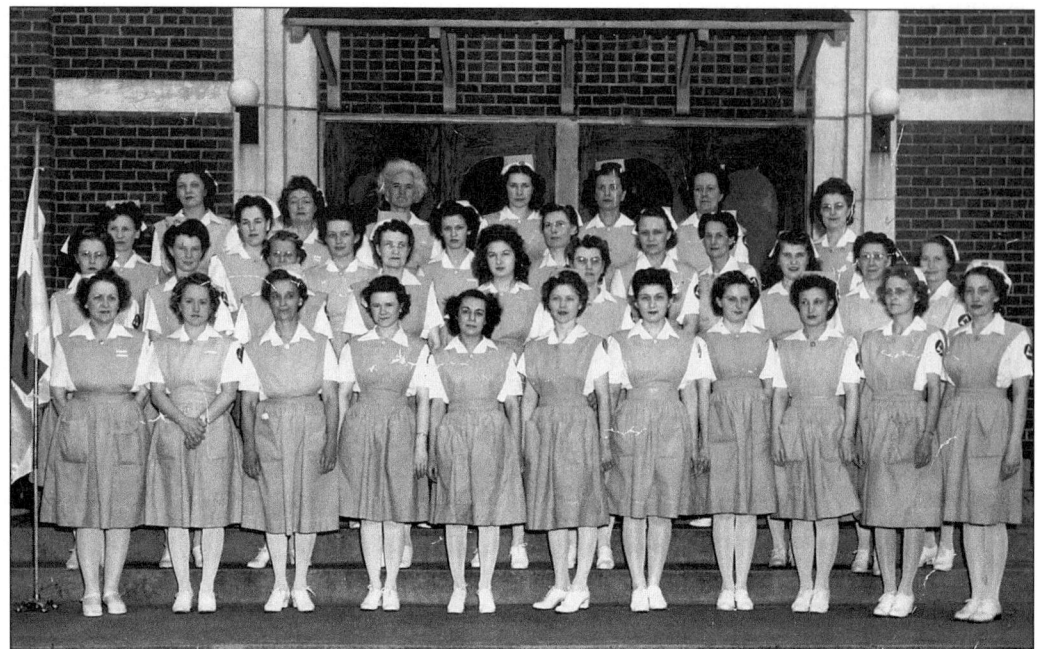

These women are Norfolk's volunteer Red Cross Aides during WWII. Some of the people shown are: Merle Benning, LaVine Blakeman, Beulah Connor, Margaret Mary Costello, Gertrude "Mid" Emrich, Marjorie Faubel, Dorothy A. Giradin, ? Hartman, Nadine Hoefs, ? Hughes, Leola Jurgens, Frances Jane Kell, Eva Perrigo, Loretta Schulte, Minnie Schultz, Frances Shapiro, ? Stone, Theola Thornton, Leota Verges, Beatrice Vrzal, Mabel Vrzal, Marian Wagner, Elaine Weihe, Bernice Wille, and Jane Woods.

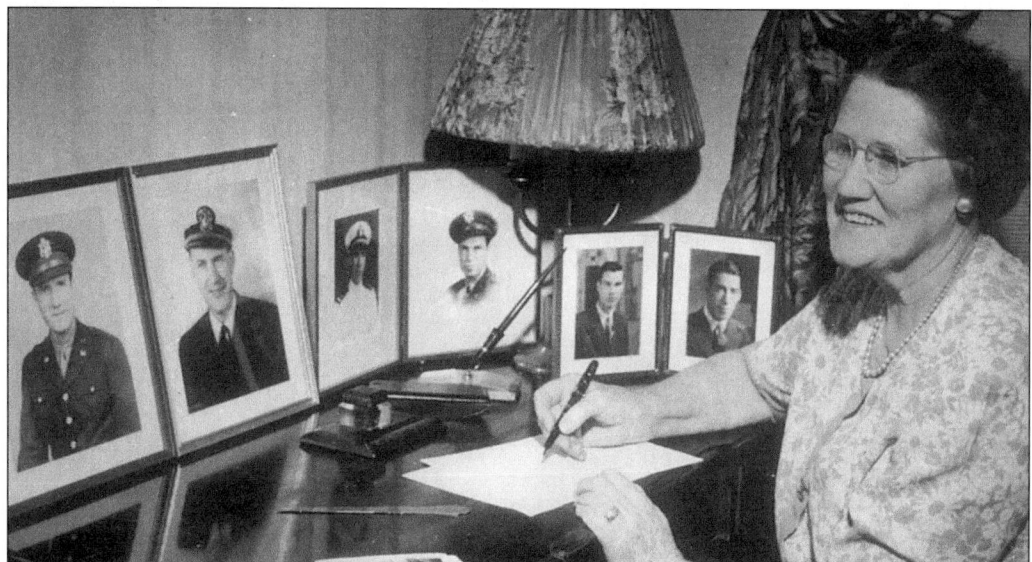

Margaret DeLay writes to her six sons who served in the Armed Forces during World War II. Their photographs are lined up on her writing desk. They are, from left to right, Harold, who served in the Army; Bernard "Mike" and Paul, Navy; Gene and Jay, Army; and John, Navy. Eugene served in Europe; Bernard, John, Jay, and Paul were in the Pacific; and Harold was stationed in Washington, D.C.

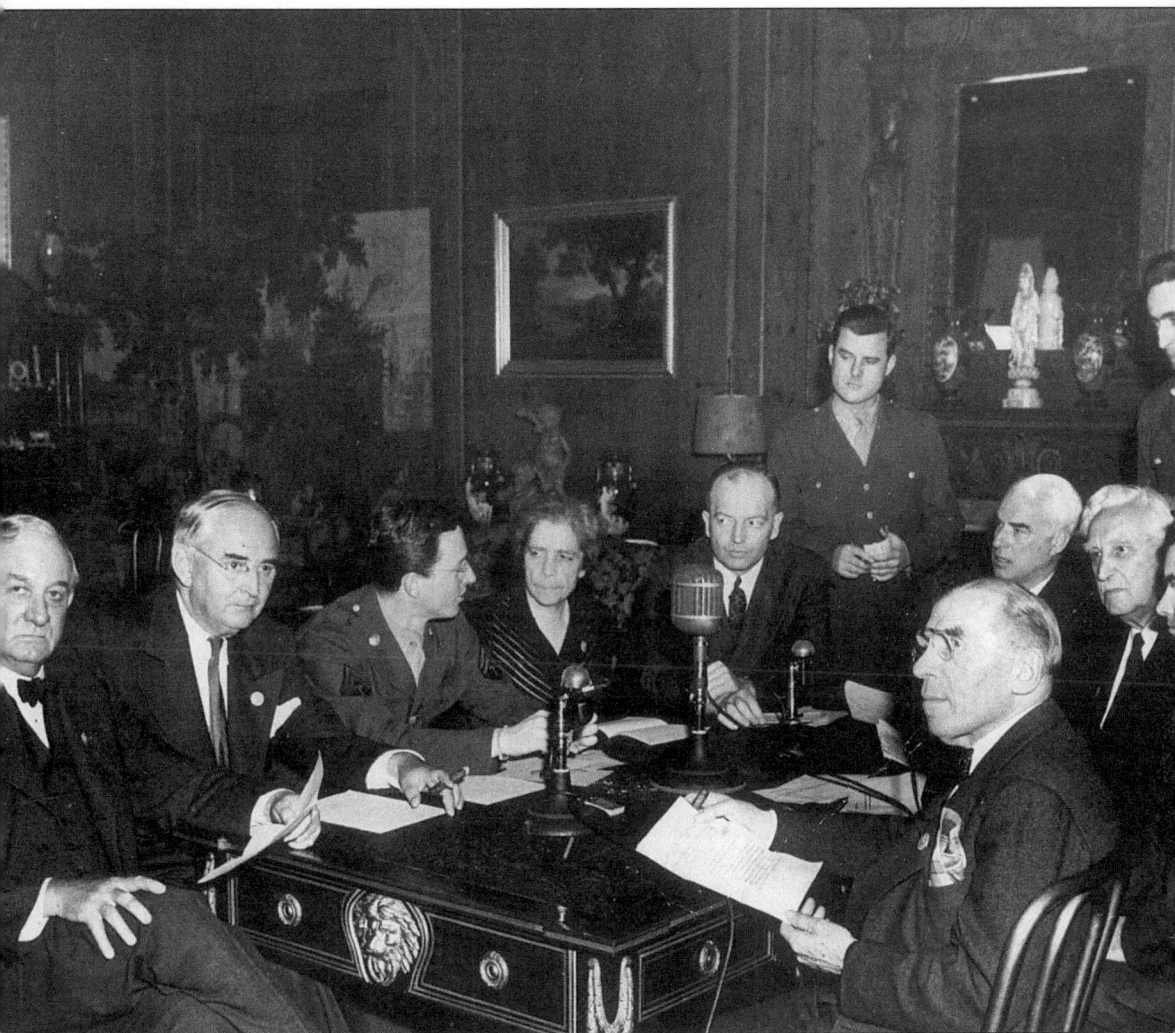

In the spring of 1945, the penthouse of the Fairmont Hotel in San Francisco, California, was the site of a meeting for the American Delegation to the Charter Conference of the United Nations. Coverage of the conference was broadcast to troops in Central and South America, the Pacific Ocean, by relay to the China/Burma/Indian theater, and the Alaska/Aleutian theater. Bob Thomas, the Commanding Officer of the Armed Forces Radio Service, later became the executive vice president of WJAG Radio in Norfolk. He participated in the conference and is standing on the left. Karl Stefan (not pictured), then a congressman from Nebraska's Third District and the minority leader of House Appropriations, was later assigned to monitor efficient use of monies spent by this delegation. Bob stated, "I'm sure there is no other such photo in existence."

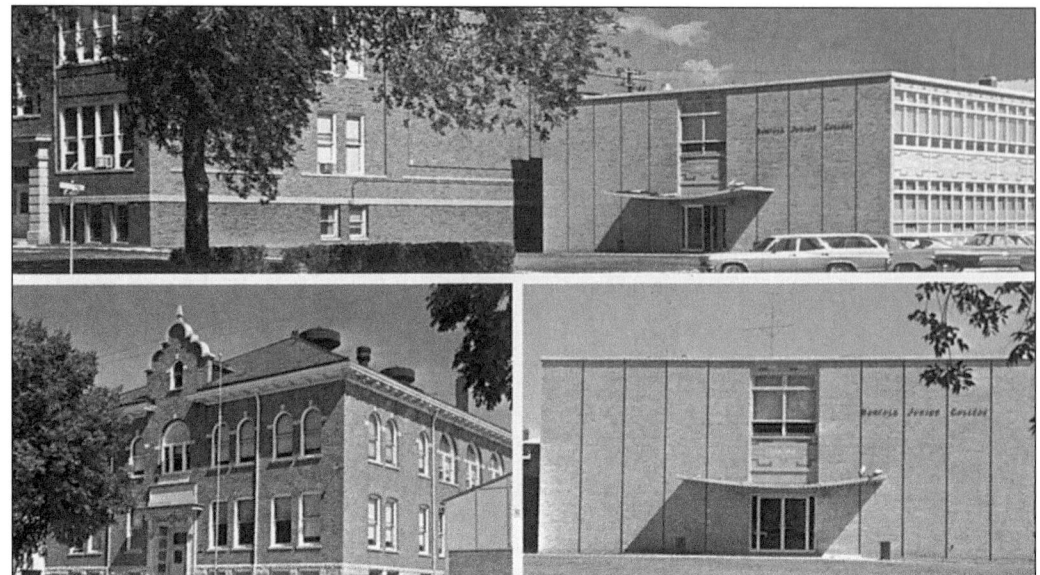

Northeast Community College has had a number of names and locations since opening in 1928. Then, it was a junior college on the third floor of the high school building at 512 Phillip Avenue. That college closed in 1932, and ten years later, Norfolk Junior College was born. It moved to 500 Phillip Avenue until the mid-1970s, when the school's new facility at 801 East Benjamin Avenue was built. This photo shows the Phillip Avenue campus.

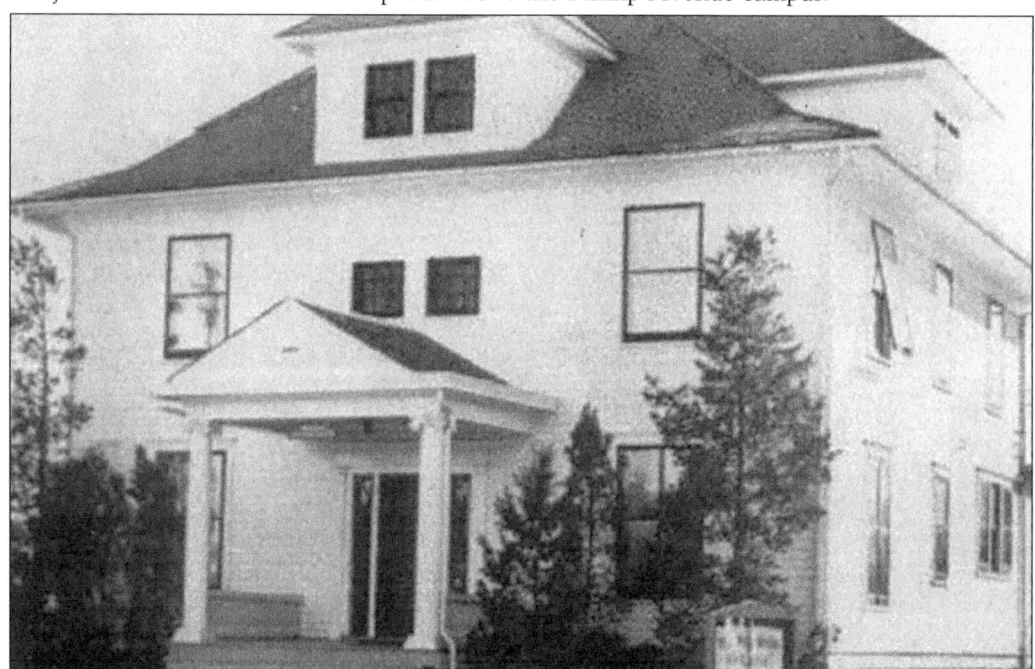

On October 16, 1944, Christian leaders met in Wymore, Nebraska, to plan for Nebraska Christian College. In August of 1945, Nebraska Christian College opened at 909 Park Avenue. In 1958, the facility pictured here was built at 901 Park Avenue. That building was used until 1969, when the college was built at 1800 Syracuse Avenue. The school's mission is to "teach and train Gospel preachers who will be true to Christ and the Bible."

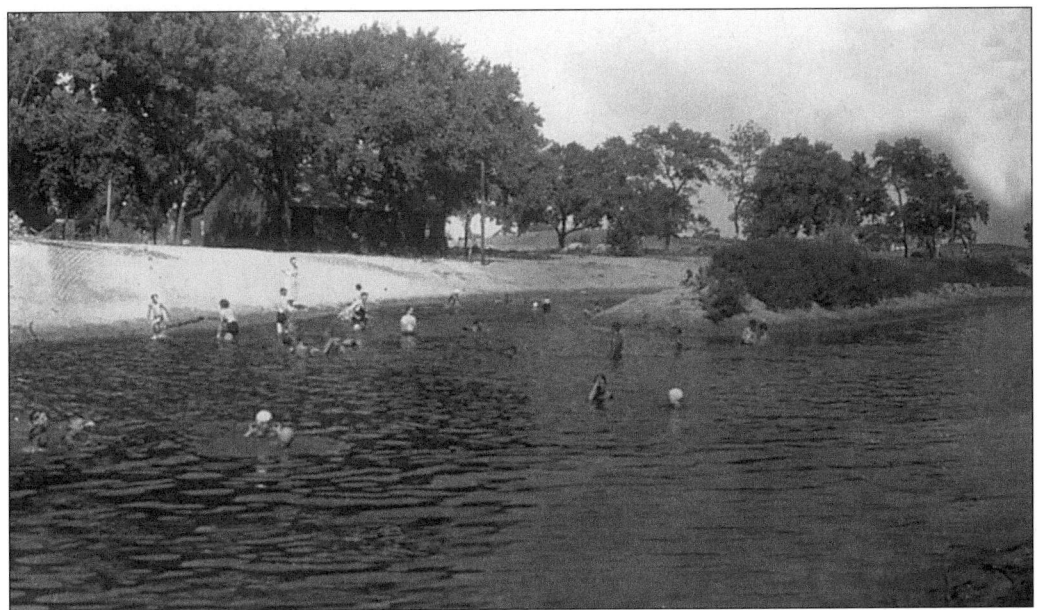

Ta-ha-zouka Park, which is next to the Elkhorn River on Highway 81 south of Norfolk, was established in 1936 and dedicated in 1937. The name Ta-ha-zouka is an American Indian word meaning "Horn of the Elk." An Indian tradition says the Elkhorn River's most common name was Ta-ha-zouka.

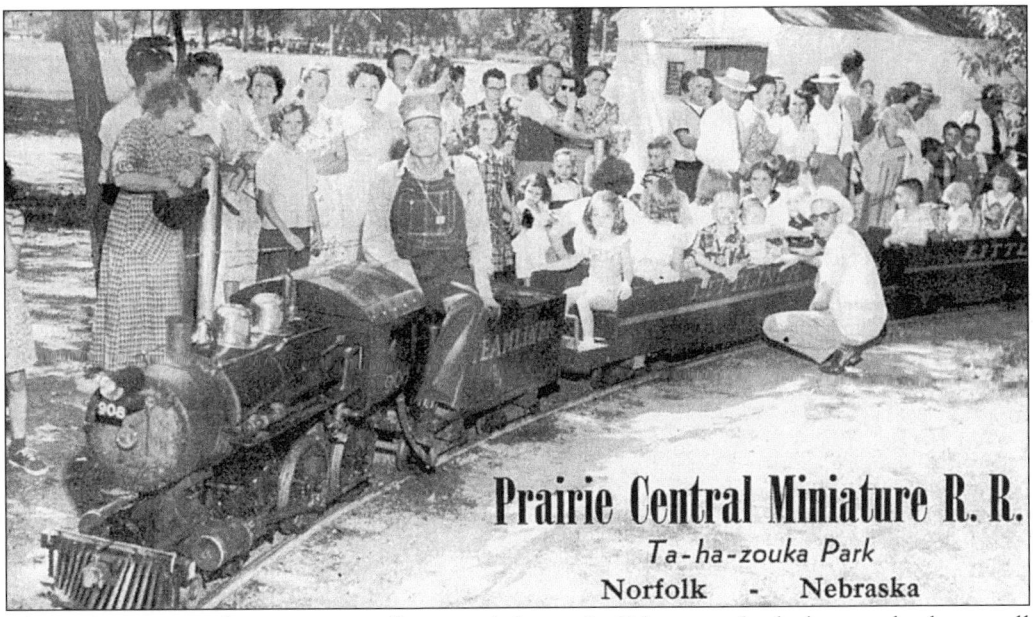

Prairie Central Miniature R. R.
Ta-ha-zouka Park
Norfolk - Nebraska

The park was once home to a small zoo with bears, buffaloes, peafowl, deer, and other small animals. A small train, shown here, also ran through the park for a number of years. Pehr Wagner started the operation known as the "Prairie Central Miniature Railroad." Now the park is a popular spot for campers and people enjoying family reunions, softball games, and picnics.

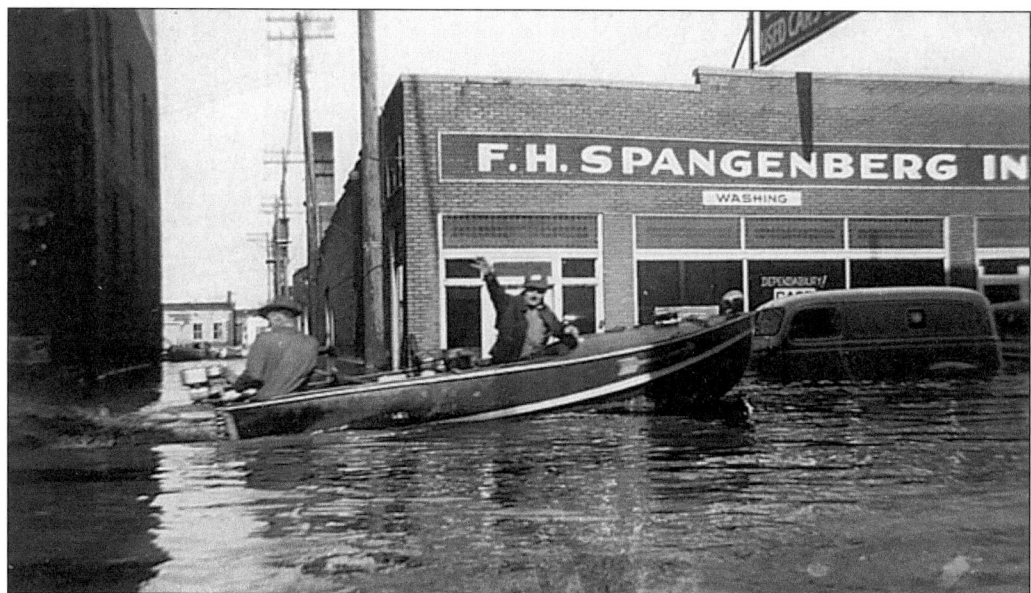

Heavy rains fell north and west of Norfolk during the morning of May 10, 1944. Another three inches fell on May 11, and in the early-morning hours of May 12, a wall of water 21 feet high broke the dike along the river's bank north of Braasch Avenue. The result was a flood the likes of which Norfolk had never seen before. This is the alley off 4th Street between Norfolk and Braasch Avenues.

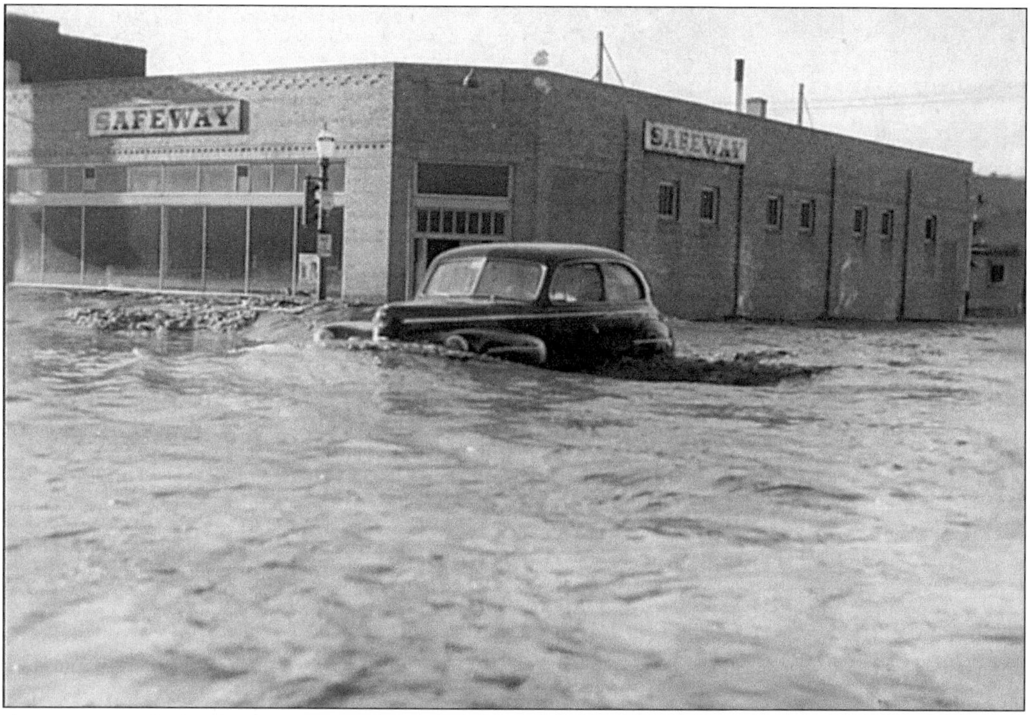

A car is stranded in high water in downtown Norfolk at the corner of Norfolk Avenue and 3rd Street during the 1944 flood, which damaged 176 city blocks, 180 businesses, and 460 private homes.

Ryal Miller Chevrolet Company, like many other businesses in Norfolk, experienced extreme damage from the flood. The business, located at 126 North 4th Street, was in the hardest-hit area. From the look of the water line on the boxes, the water reached about five feet in the store.

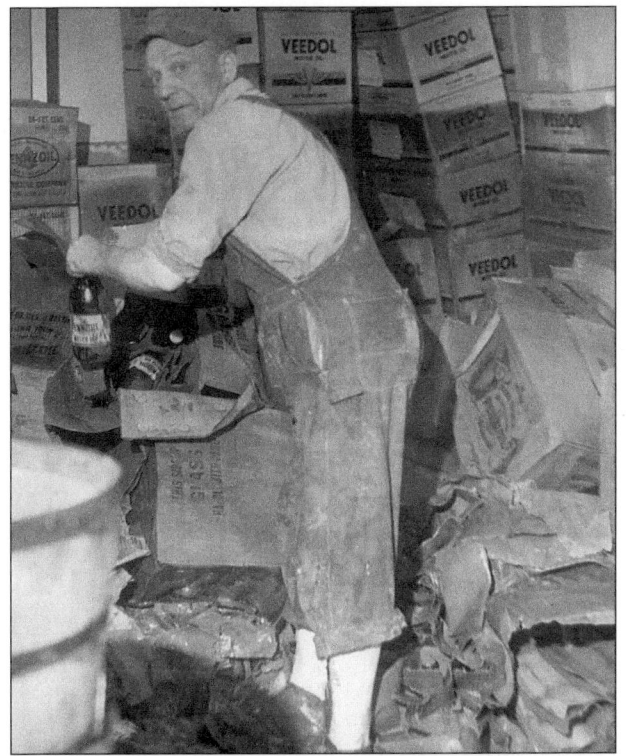

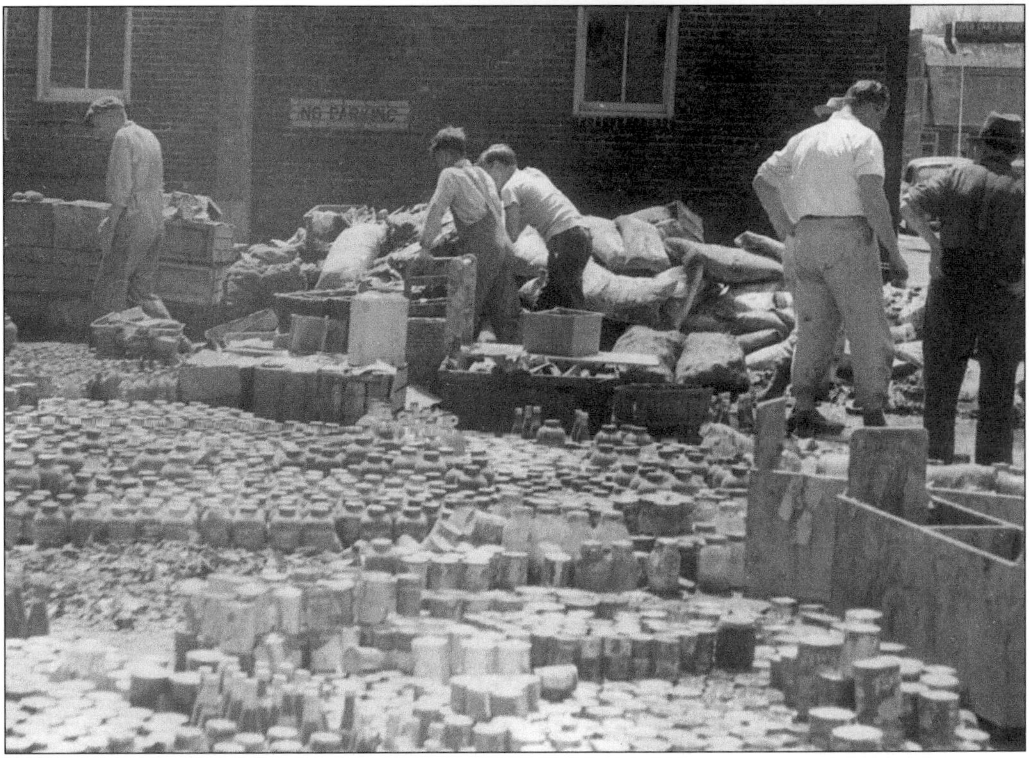

Workers sort through canned goods in the Safeway parking lot following the 1944 flood.

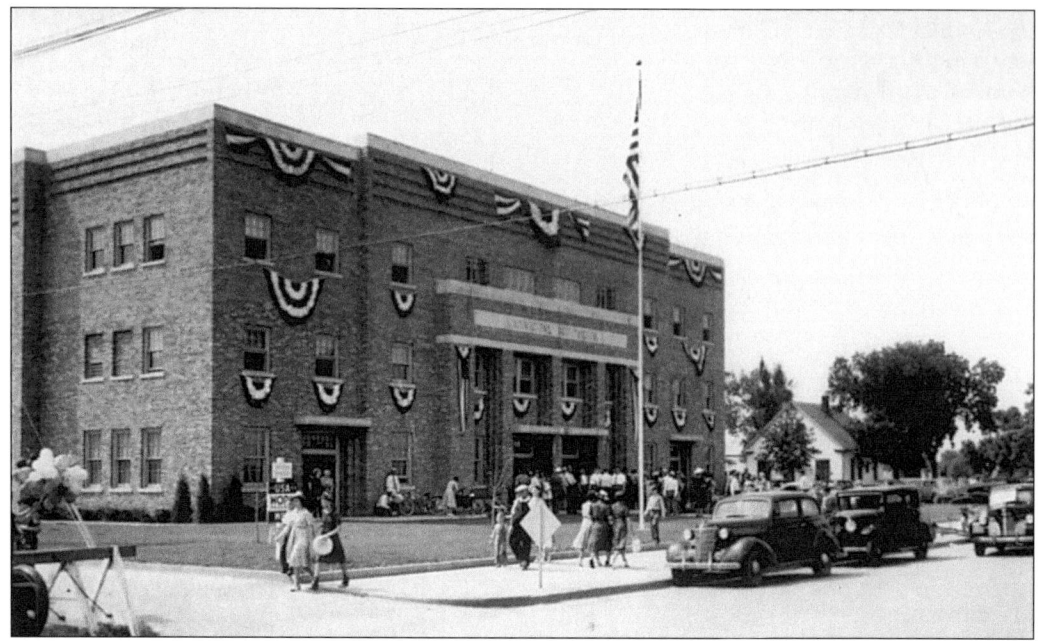

Norfolk's new city auditorium was dedicated in 1939. The Works Progress Administration (WPA) was responsible for constructing the building, called the Municipal Auditorium. The City of Norfolk uses the building for concerts, sporting events, and craft shows. Norfolk city offices are currently located in the building as well.

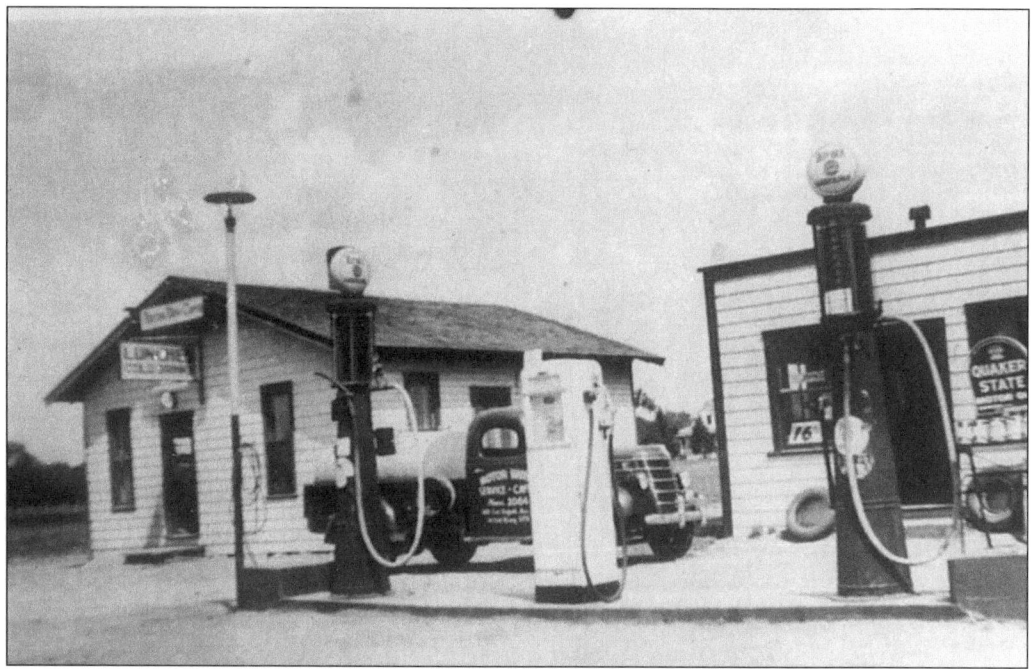

Mary's Café and Home Oil opened in 1942 on East Highway 275. Mary O'Gorman operated the 24-hour café; Jim Meyer and Dave Milligan ran the gas station. In 1955 a new building was constructed to house both businesses. The café and station are still a family business to this day with Mary and her son Pat O'Gorman as owners.

Katie Ashbrook listens to music at the Baldridge Ice
Cream Palace at 3rd Street and Madison Avenue.
The "Palace" served up lunches, Coca-Cola, and ice
cream treats to satisfy all the local teenagers.

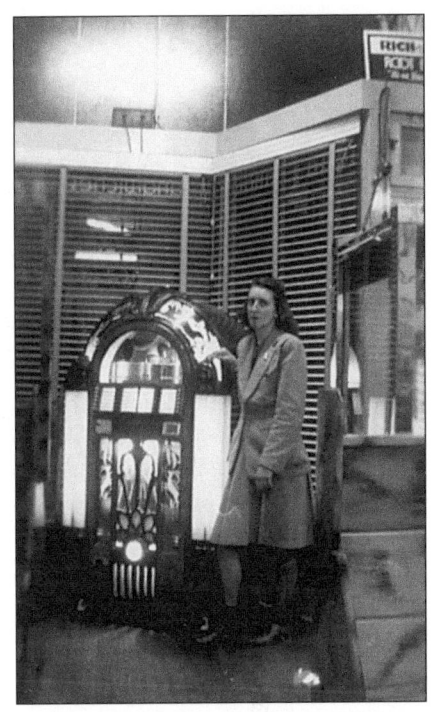

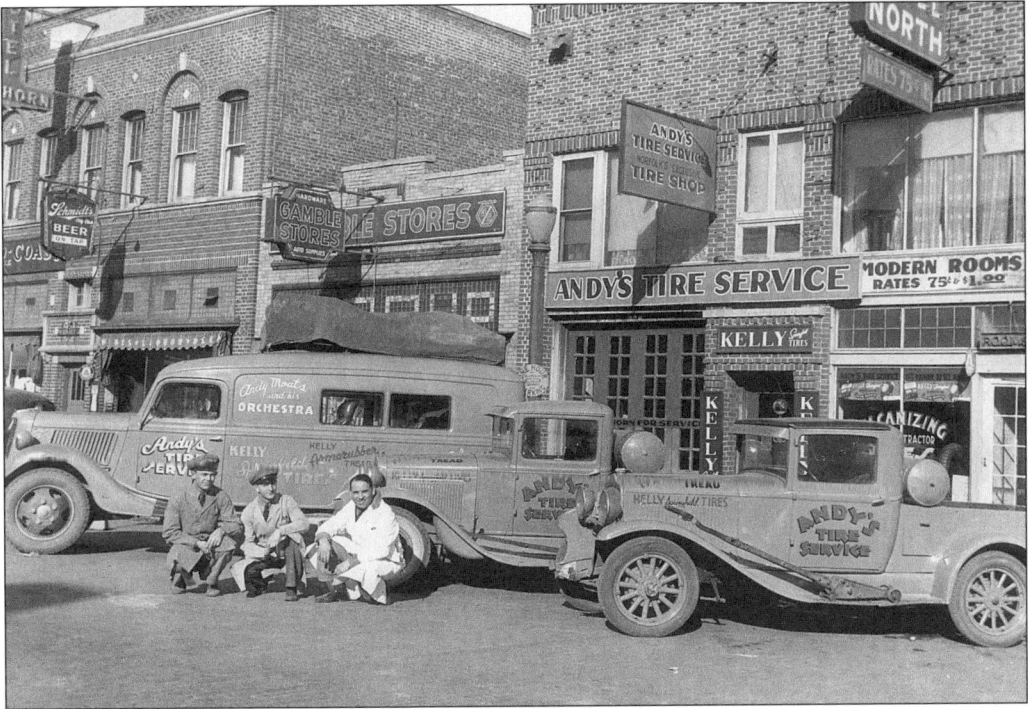

By the late 1940s, Norfolk had an active, thriving downtown area, as is reflected in the signs
that decorate part of Norfolk Avenue. Here Andy Moats (on the right), and two of his
employees, Roy Bierce (left), and O.L. Ashbrook (center) pose for a photo in front of Andy's
Tire Service. Moats also had a big band orchestra that toured the area.

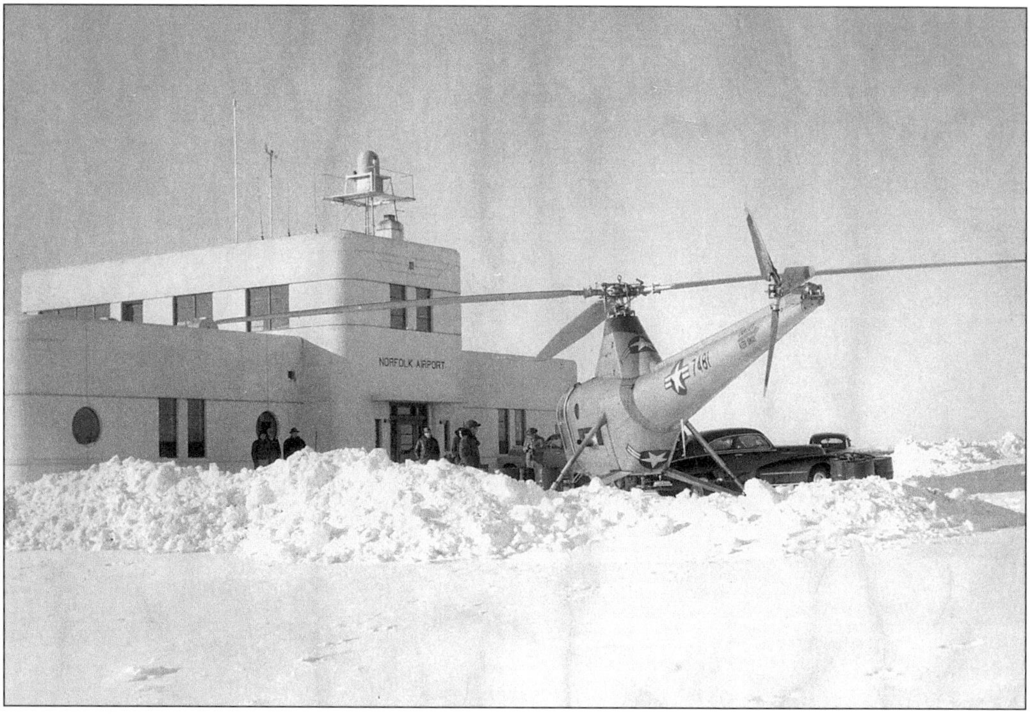

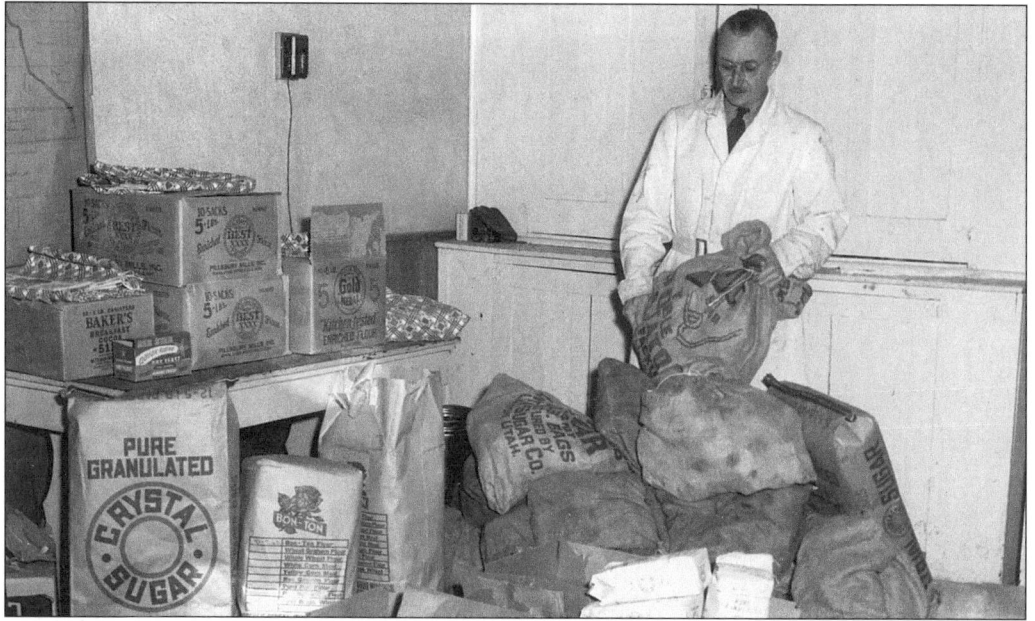

Next to the flood of 1944, the winter of 1948–49 is the most talked about disaster to occur in Norfolk. Food had to be airlifted to people and animals living in rural areas. Helicopters, such as the one shown above, were used to transport food to stranded persons. The Norfolk Municipal Airport became headquarters for "Operation Snowbound," the name of the relief effort meant to help those in need.

F.C. Hague, Red Cross food chairman, looks over food supplies the Madison County Red Cross is putting in parcels to be dropped to snowbound farmers needing help.

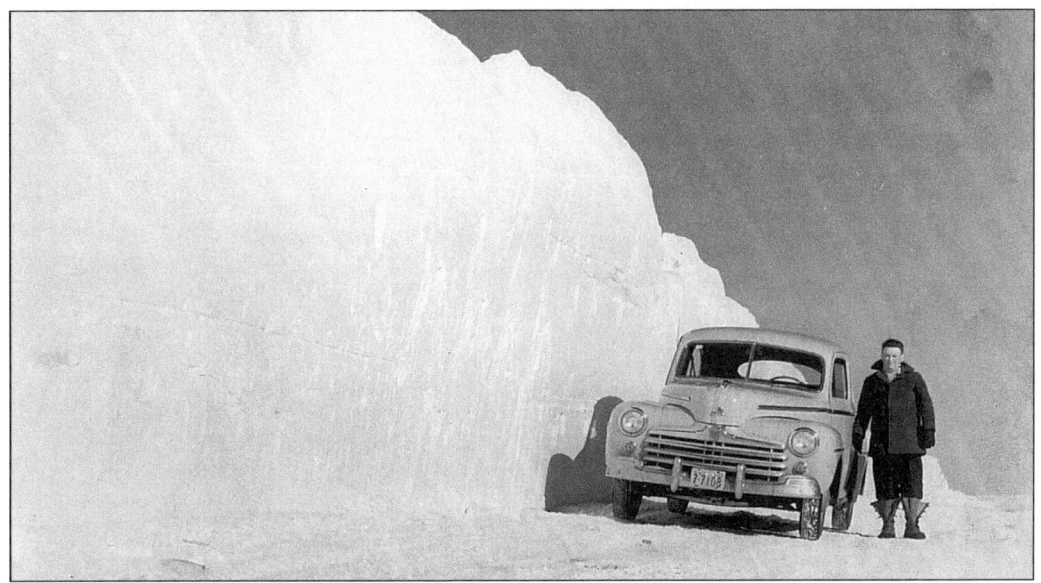

The drifts were pretty high on Highway 275 east of Norfolk. Some areas of the state received as much as 47 inches of snow over the course of the winter, and the wind often blew up to 60 miles an hour. By spring, most Northeast Nebraskans, especially those living in rural areas, were used to being stuck in snowbanks and stranded at home.

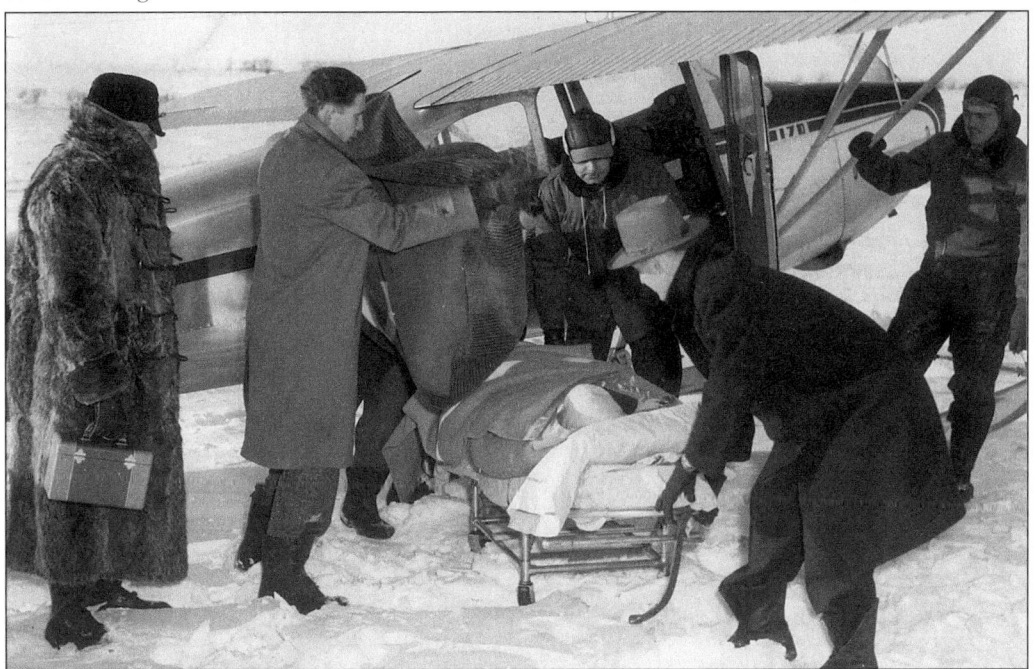

During the 1948–49 blizzard, Carol Anderson, the daughter of Mr. and Mrs. Morris Anderson of Newman Grove, was flown to Norfolk with acute appendicitis. Here Carol is being taken from the plane for transport to Lutheran Community Hospital for surgery. Those involved are Dr. F.L. Frink, Murray Wagner, Dick Warren, pilot John Youngheim, Forrest Swoboda, and Cloyd Cannon Jr. After the operation, Youngheim flew back to the snowbound Anderson home to get the girl's parents.

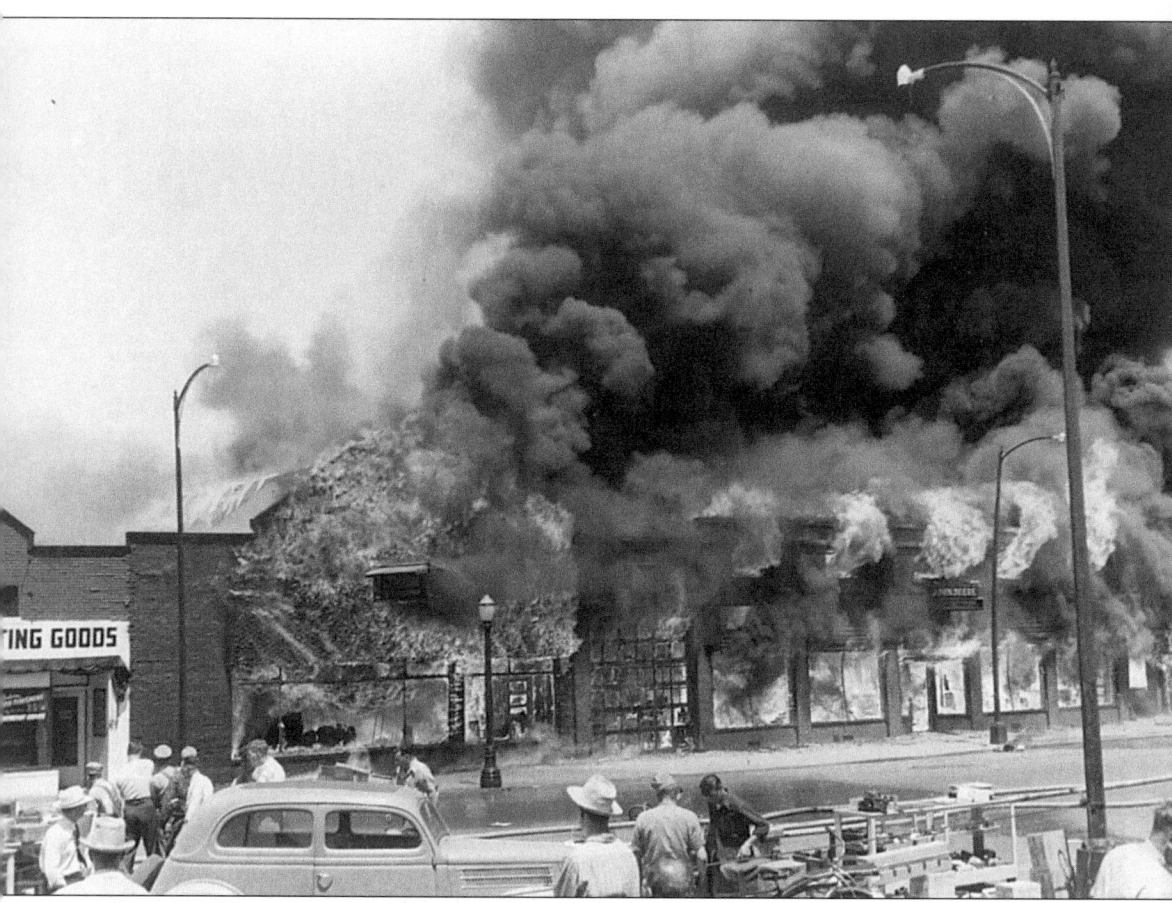

The Chicago Lumber Company burned on May 27, 1948. The fire is said to have started when a tar pot being used to repair a roof of a neighboring building overheated and caught fire. The fire destroyed the entire block.

Four

THE GOOD TIMES
1950–1969

"Life is for doing, learning, and enjoying."

—Peter and John Roger McWilliams

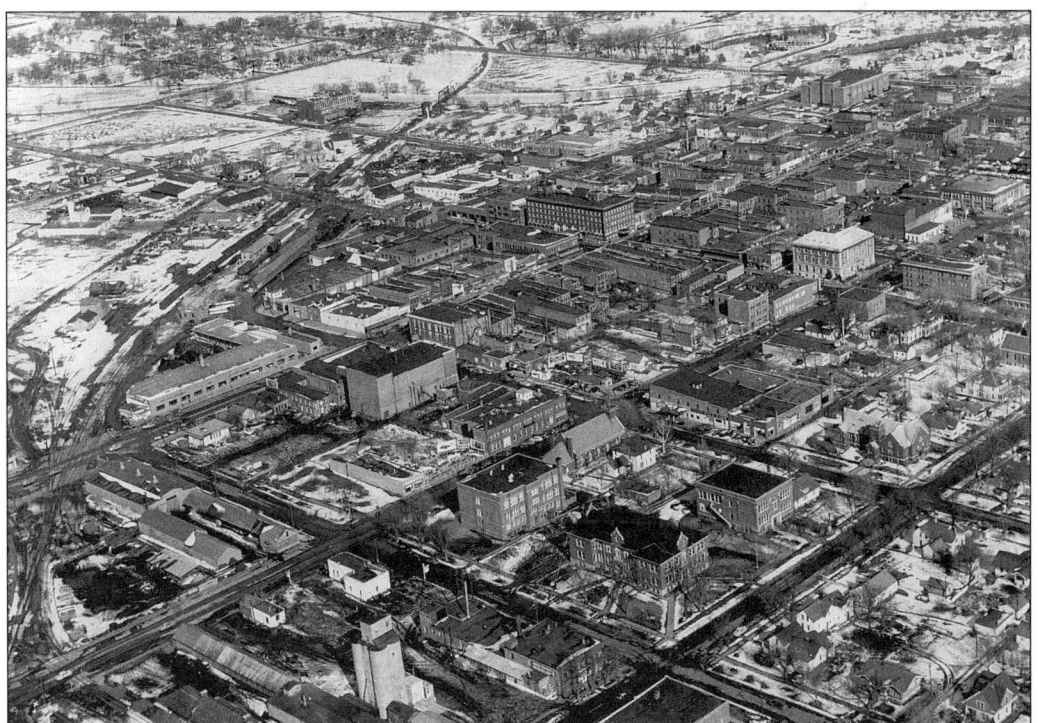

By the 1950s, Norfolk was enjoying post-war prosperity. It was home to more than 11,000 people, three railroads, two colleges, two hospitals, several hotels, sixteen churches, and modern schools. Norfolk was just beginning to stretch its wings. In the next 50 years the town more than doubled in size. Business and industry became major players in its growth and development, and the area continued to thrive.

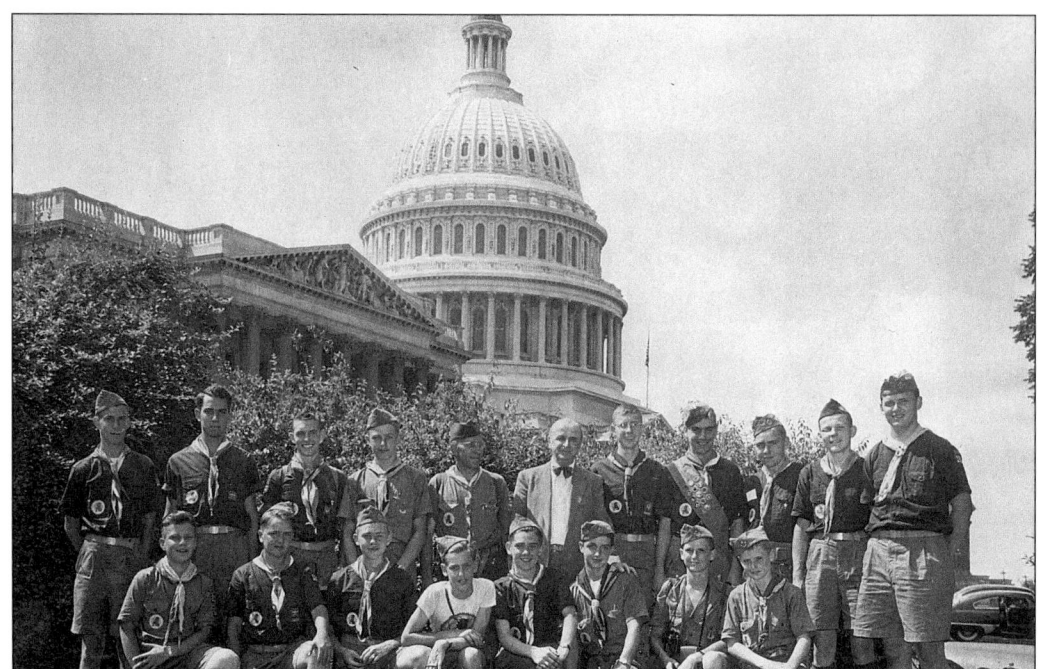

In this 1950 photo, Congressman Karl Stefan is shown in Washington, D.C., with Boy Scouts from the Covered Wagon Council Troop 6. The boys are all from Northeast Nebraska. Stefan, a former radio personality for station WJAG, was elected to Congress in 1935.

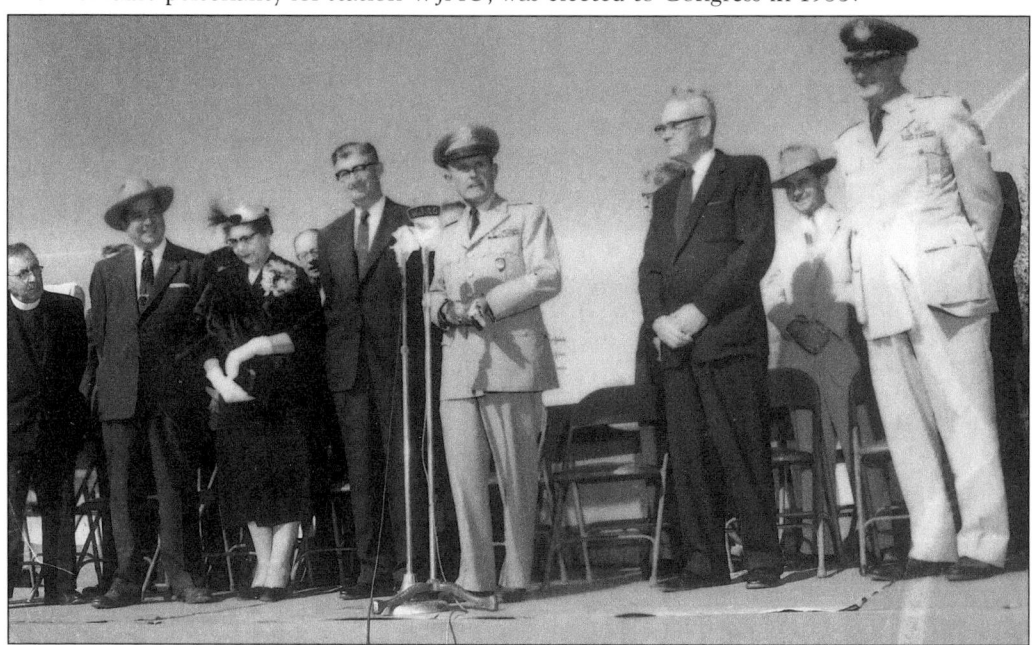

General Alfred Gruenther, originally from Platte Center, Nebraska, and NATO Commander in 1955, speaks to a crowd at Karl Stefan Memorial Airport on September 29, 1955. The airport was dedicated that day to the late congressman who died on October 2, 1951, while still in office. The woman pictured is Mrs. Ida Stefan, the widow of Karl Stefan. To Gruenther's right is Dr. Allen P. Burkhardt, Superintendent of Schools.

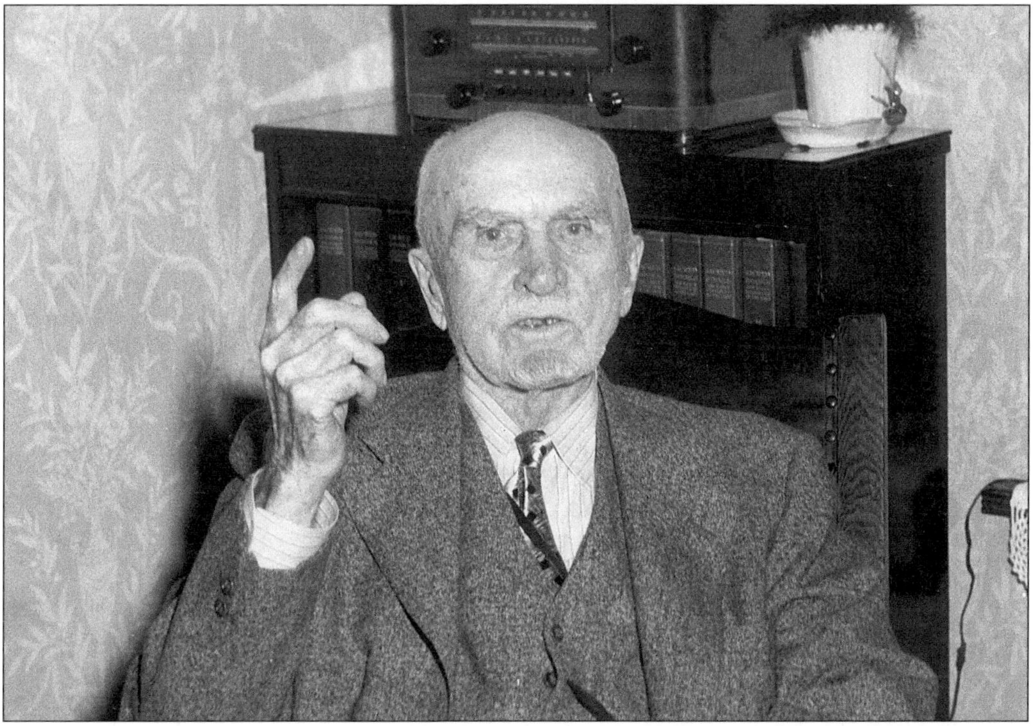

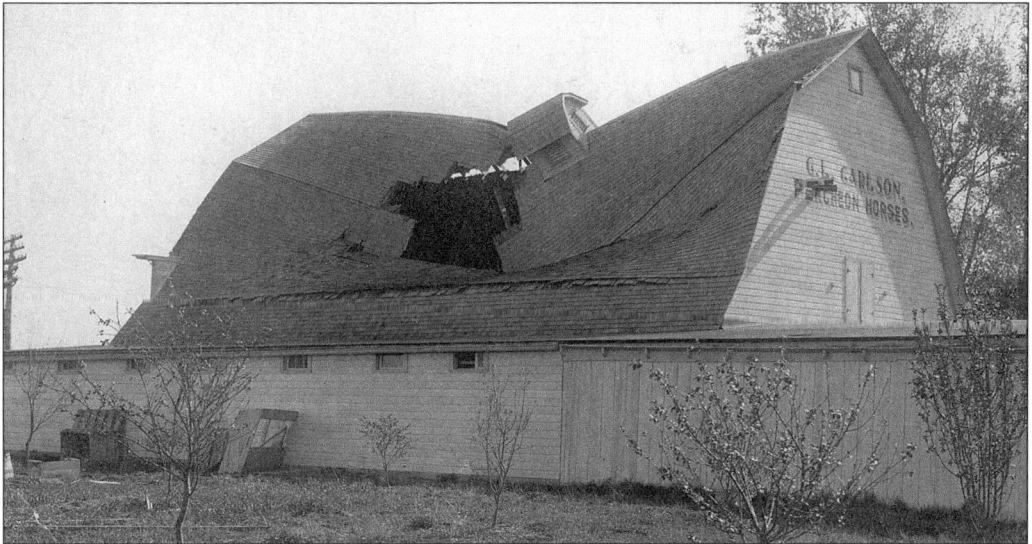

George Lloyd Carlson makes a point during his 100th birthday party on January 1, 1953. In 1880, Carlson, while visiting a doctor in Yankton, South Dakota, first devised the capsules-system of artificial insemination for animals. Carlson studied and worked around the world before settling in Holt County, Nebraska, in 1896. He moved to Norfolk in 1903 and built a barn where he could demonstrate the economic benefits of artificial breeding.

A tornado destroyed part of Carlson's barn. Carlson once bred a horse named Nicolas to 747 mares within a period of one hundred days, which resulted in 529 foals. He also wrote a book entitled *Studies in Horse Breeding* that was used as a text book in colleges in Canada, England, South Africa, and Australia. He died on April 17, 1953.

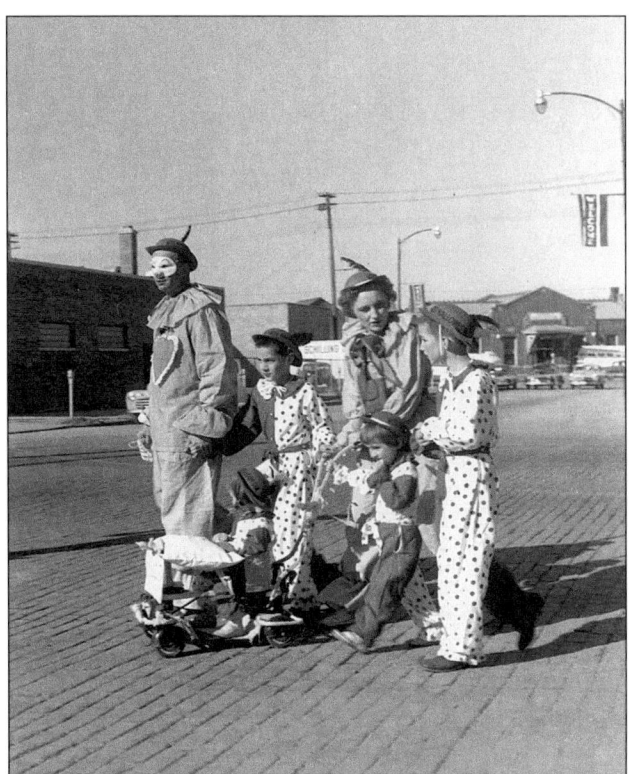

Norfolk has long hosted a city festival, including the Harvest Festival, which was popular during the early 1900s, and Hallow'esta, a late-October celebration that included activities for the entire family. The timing of the festival was a reason for people to dress in costume, as did this family who decided to do a little "clowning around." The photo was taken in 1952.

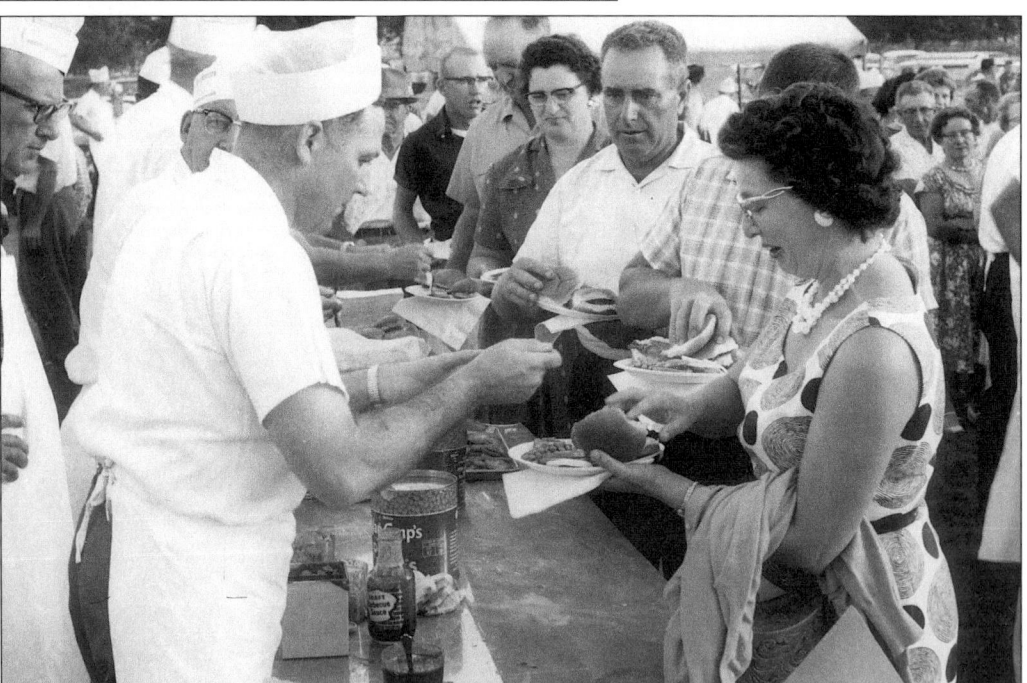

For years, the Norfolk Area Chamber of Commerce hosted an annual Farmer's Barbecue. It was Norfolk's way of saying thanks to area farmers for their support during the year. The event included lots of good food and live entertainment. In this 1965 photo, guests wait to be served.

Sharon McManus, who once lived in Norfolk, appeared in several movies, including *Anchors Away* with Gene Kelly and *This Time for Keeps* with Esther Williams. In this photo, Sharon was just nine years old. She is the daughter of Mr. and Mrs. William McManus.

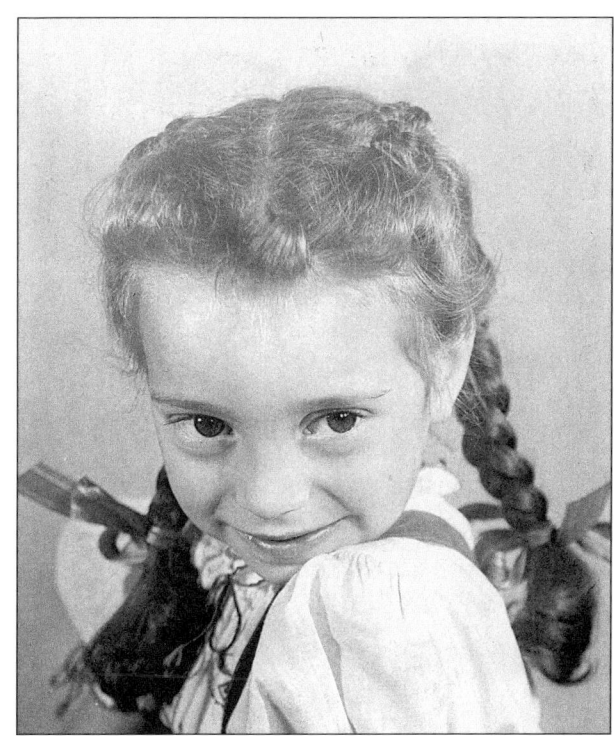

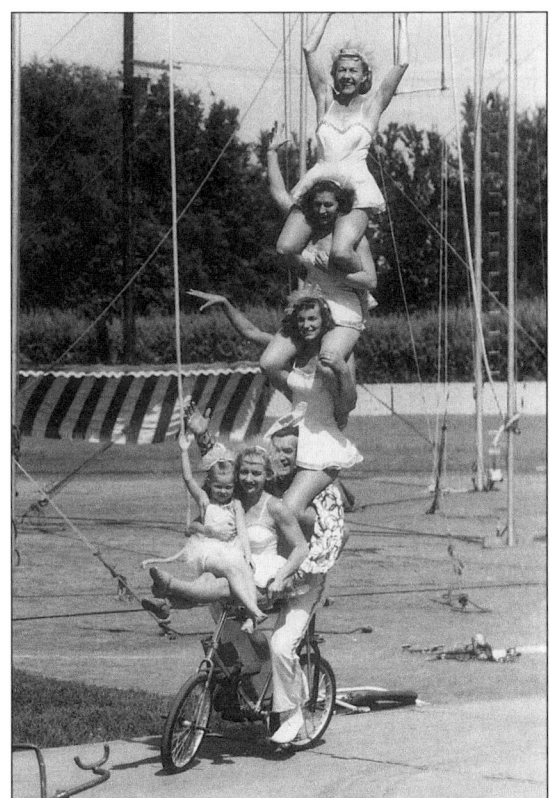

The Shrine Circus has been a family favorite for many years. Here, performers do a balancing act on a bicycle during a 1962 circus. The annual event raises money for Shriners' Hospitals for Children.

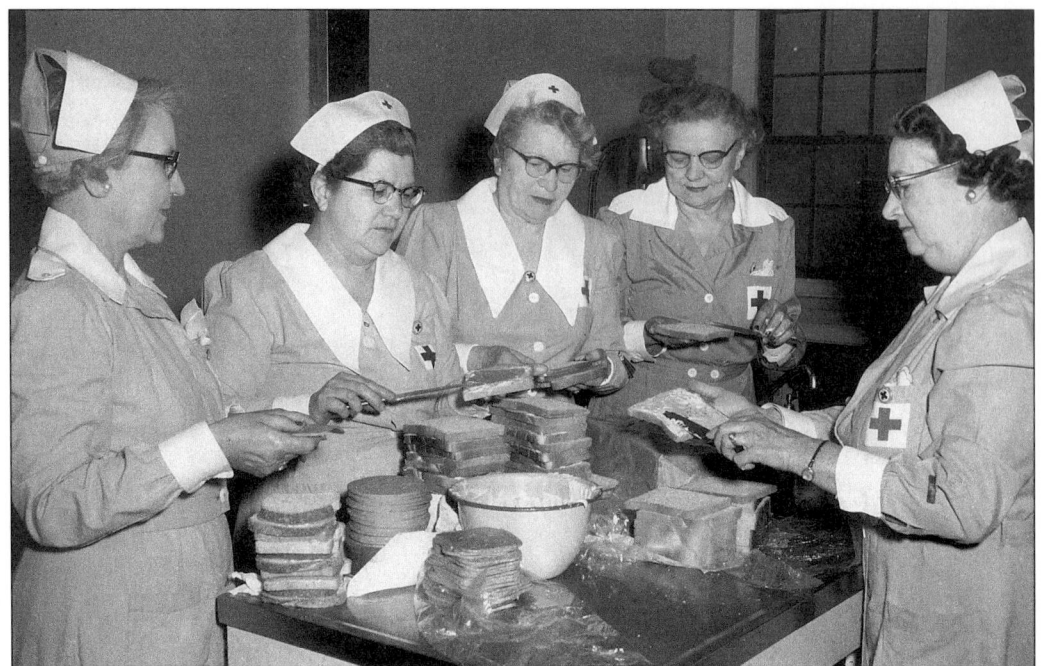

The American Red Cross relies on the support of volunteers like the "Grey Ladies." In this May 1954 photo, from left to right, Mrs. Frank Phillips. Mrs. Clyde Reed, Mrs. L.V. DeVore, Mrs. J.B. Kocum, and Mrs. Robert Craft Sr. prepare sandwiches at the City Auditorium for disaster volunteers following a tornado. The Grey Ladies program was one of several initiated by the chapter to help provide services in time of need.

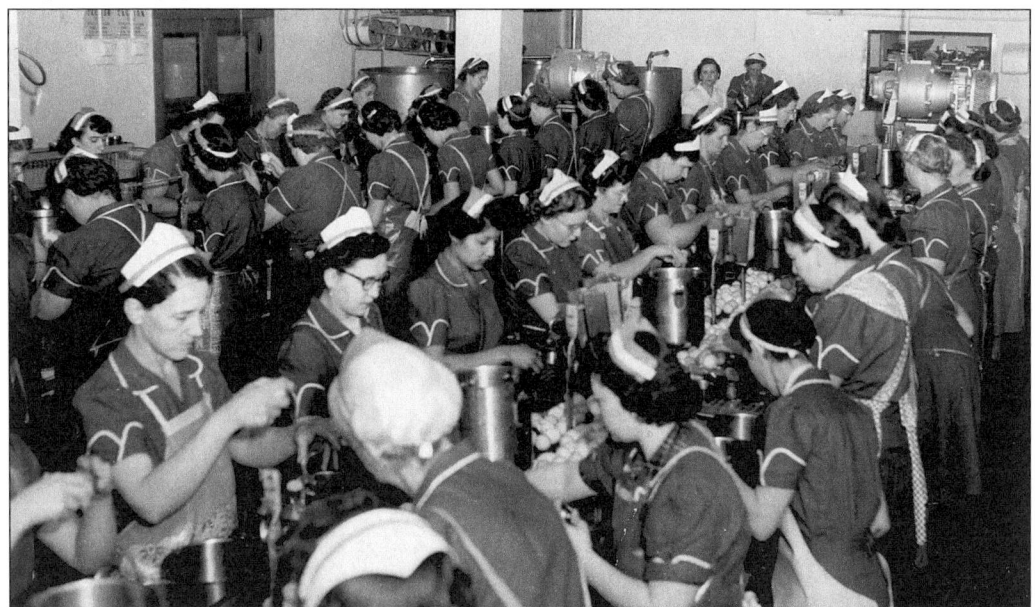

The Omaha Cold Storage Company, doing business as OCOMA Foods, was located on the southeast corner of 1st Street and Northwestern Avenue. The factory employed as many as two hundred during the early 1950s. Here, women handle some of the thousands of eggs that the plant processed each year. The plant operated from 1952–1958.

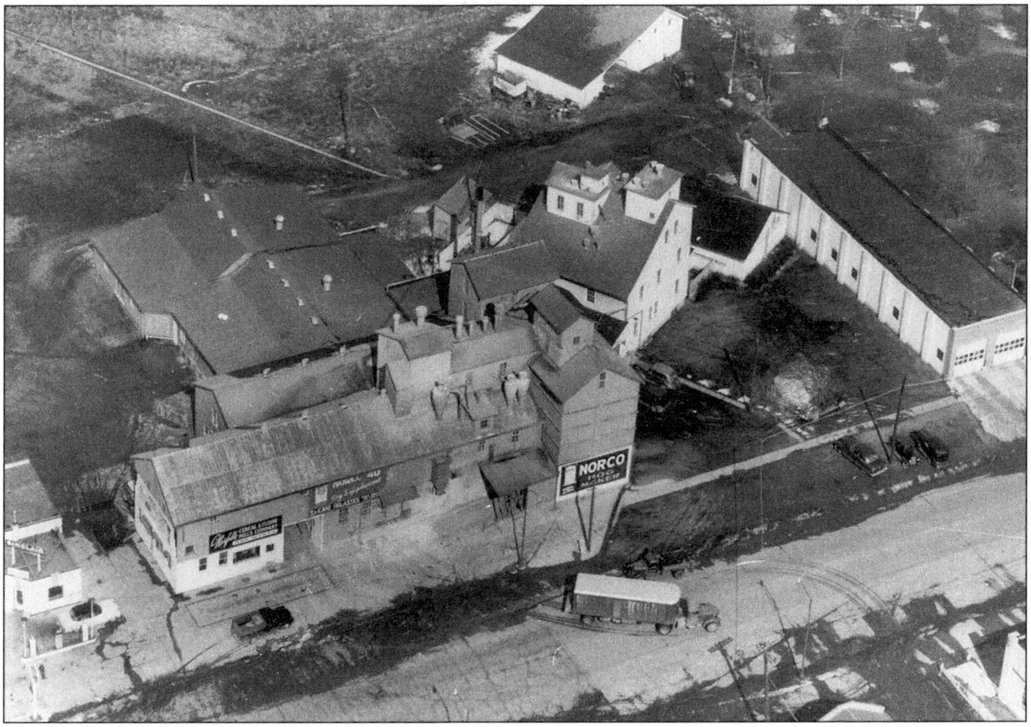

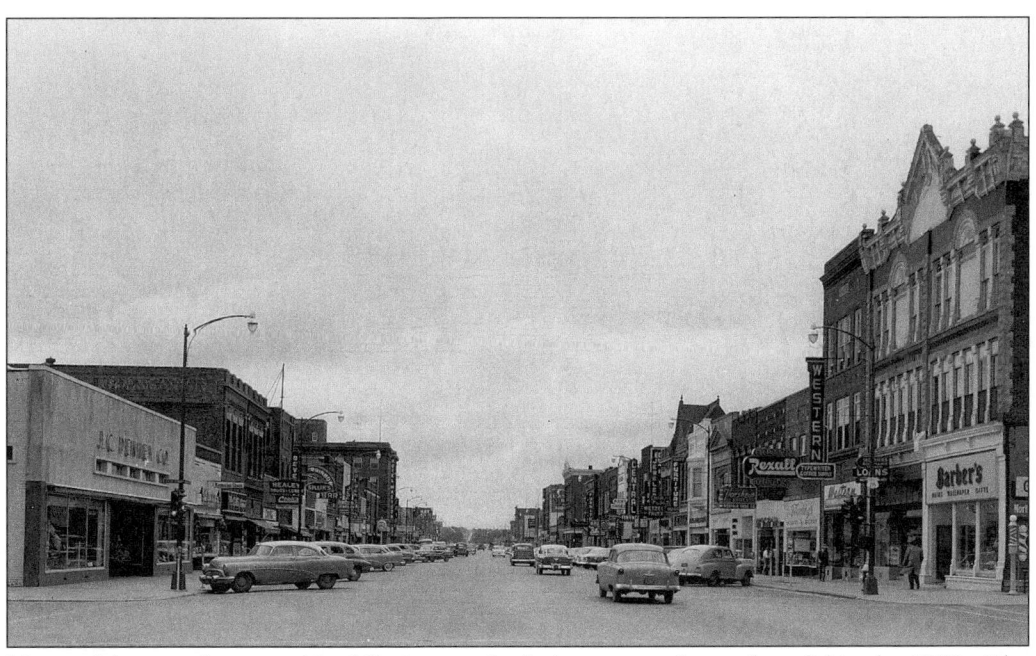

Pictured here is Norco Feed Mills as it appeared in 1955. The site was home to Norfolk's first flour mill and saw mill, built by Colonel Charles Mathewson in 1870. This expanded and modernized mill was torn down in 1976, and the site became home to a shopping center.

Many of the storefronts on Norfolk Avenue look the same today as they did in the 1950s. The street, however, has changed dramatically with the addition of center islands, trees, and flags.

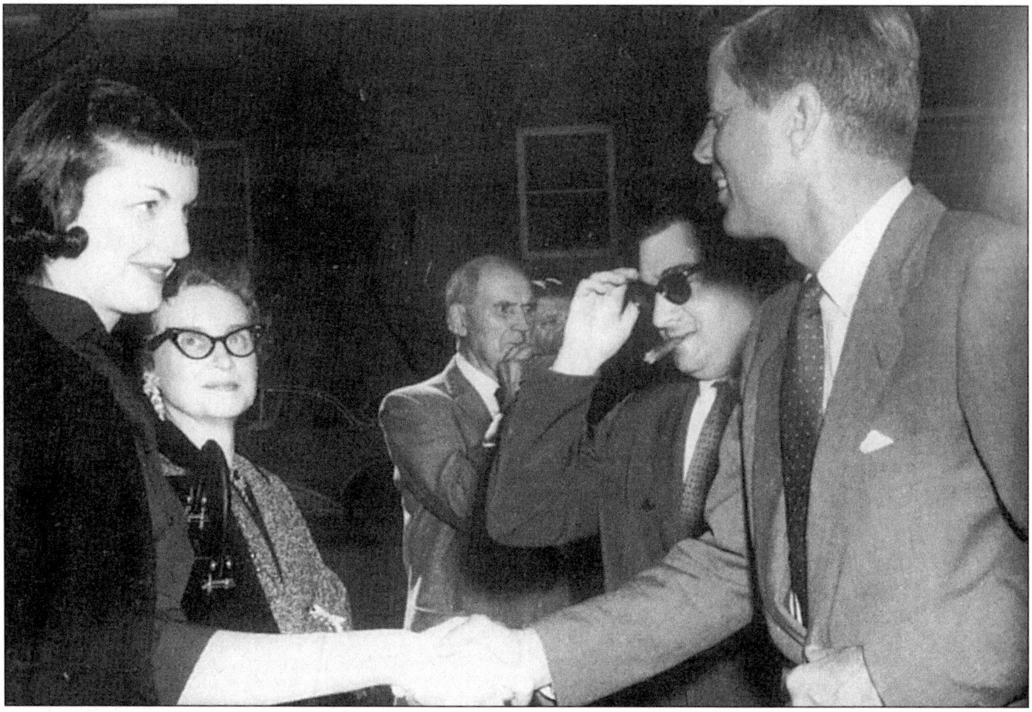

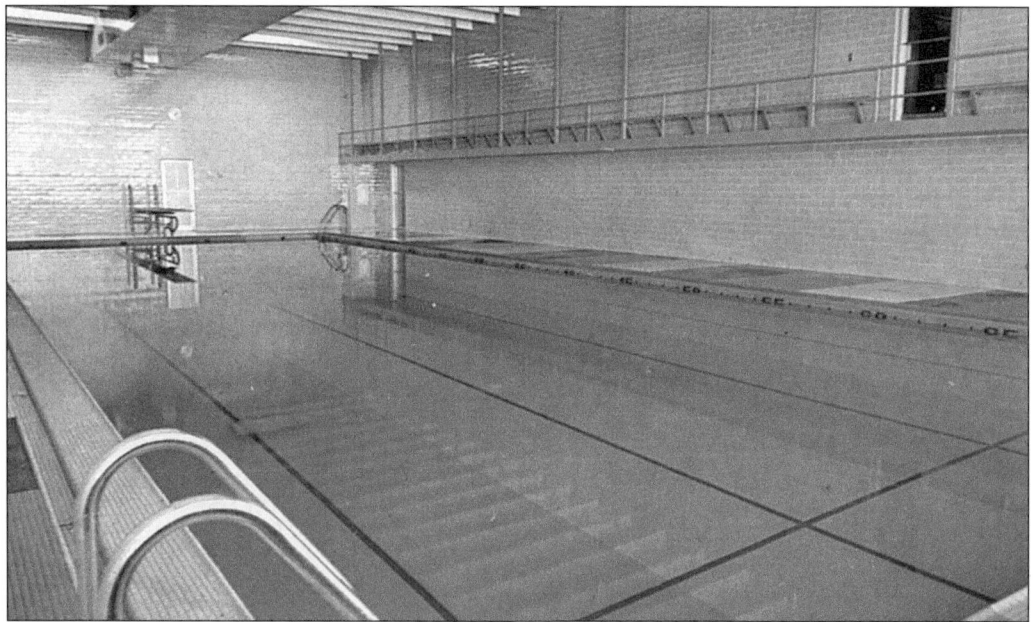

John Kennedy shakes hands with Mrs. Claude Trimble of Norfolk while Mrs. George Dittrick of Norfolk and Kennedy's press secretary, Pierre Salinger, look on. Kennedy was a senator from Massachusetts when this photo was taken on October 5, 1959, at Hotel Madison in Norfolk. He was here during his campaign for president.

The John G. Moore Pool opened at the Norfolk YMCA on May 11, 1959. The pool, which cost $127,000, was 28 feet wide and 75 feet long. It was named after John G. "Chief" Moore, who was general secretary at the YMCA for 42 years from 1920 to 1962.

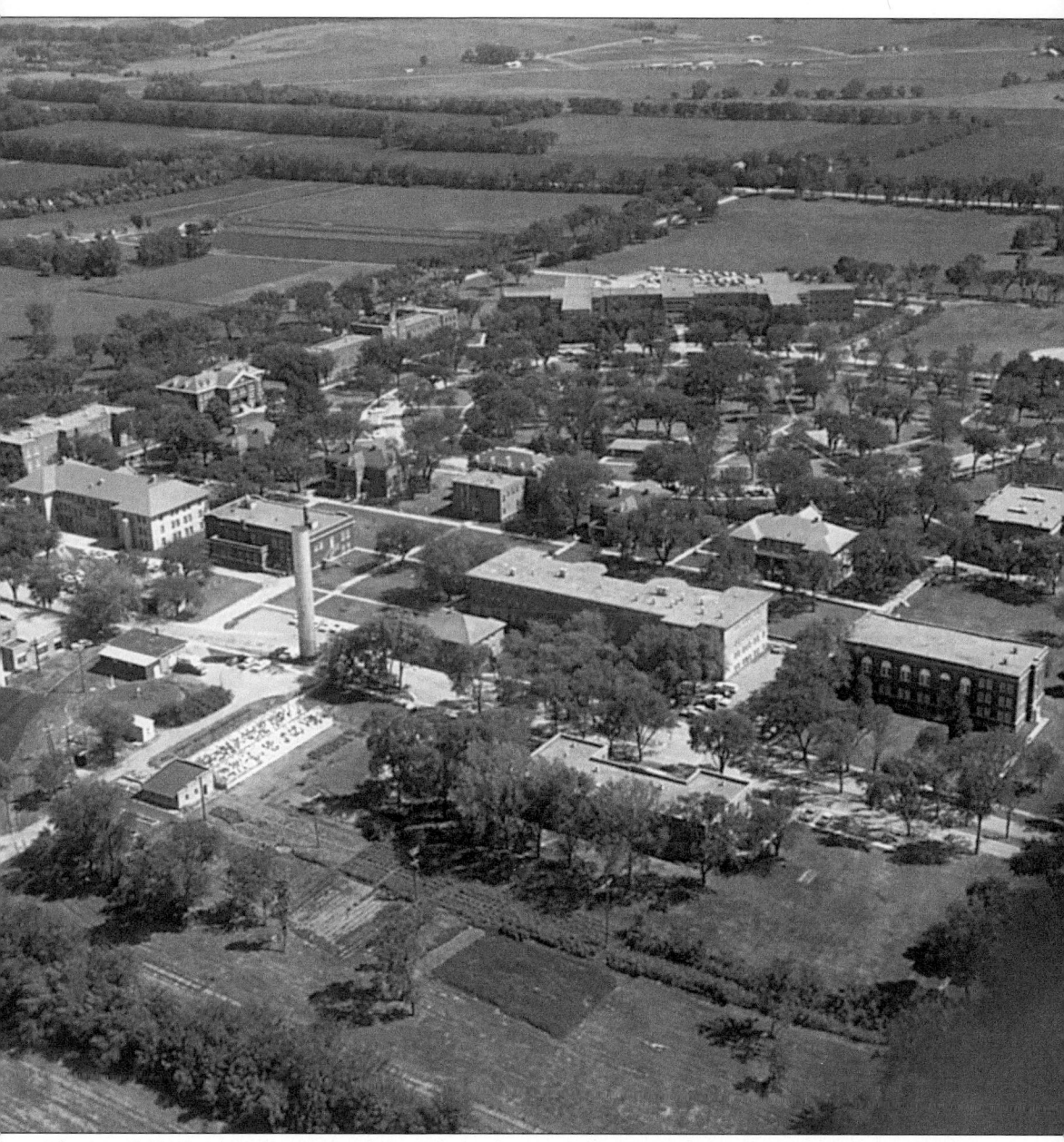

The Norfolk State Hospital, once known as the Norfolk Hospital for the Insane, experienced years of rapid growth and eventual decline as treatment for mentally ill persons progressed. However, the facility, now known as the Norfolk Regional Center, still plays a vital role in Norfolk's economy and is one of Norfolk's most noted landmarks. This photograph was taken in the 1960s. The hospital is located at 1700 North Victory Road.

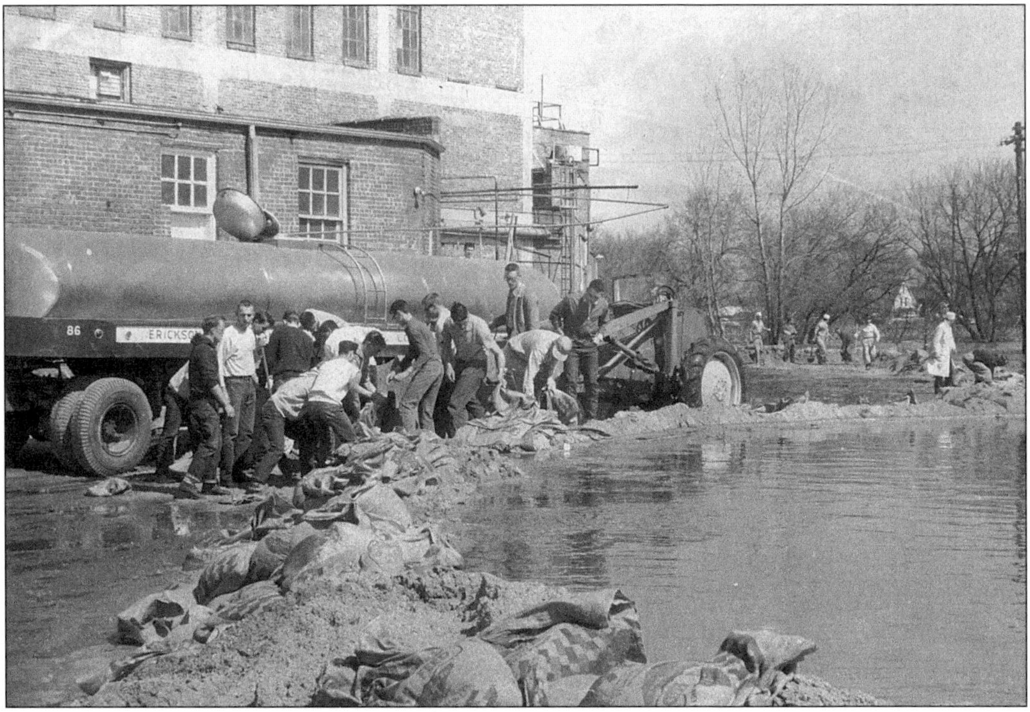

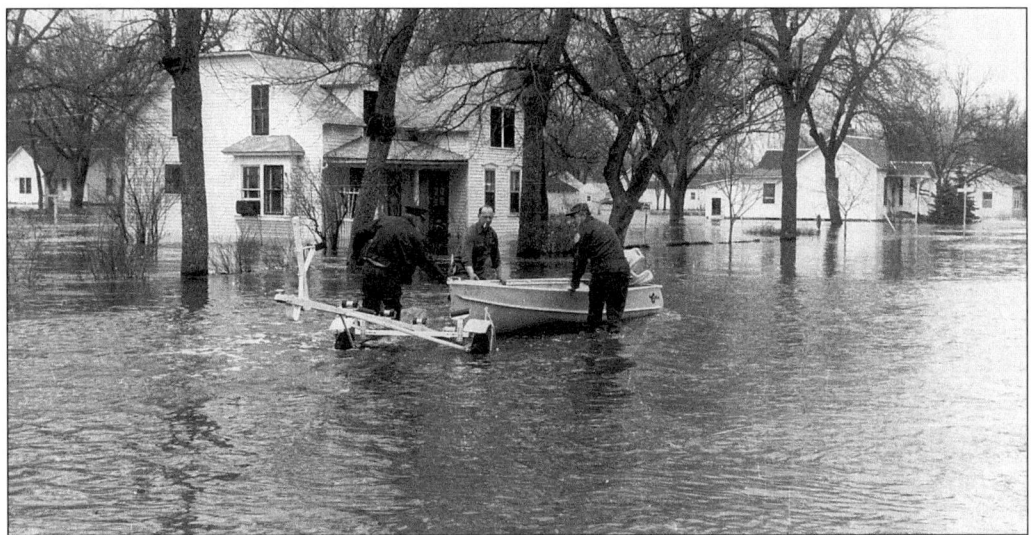

Norfolk has a long history of floods. In fact, it has been said that American Indians warned settlers not to stay in the area because it flooded too often, but they didn't listen. Norfolkans went on to endure major floods in 1870, 1880, 1881, 1888, 1897, 1903, 1912, 1917, 1944, and even 1962, which is when this photo was taken. Here workers prepare sandbags to keep flood waters at bay near Henningsen Foods on North 3rd Street.

Sometimes the only way to get around when the water gets too deep is by boat. Here members of the Norfolk Fire Department pull a boat off a trailer in the residential neighborhood of 1st Street and Elm Avenue. The March 1962 flood was caused by rapid snow melt accompanied by heavy rains that broke the dike on the river. The flood caused more than $700,000 in damages to one hundred blocks.

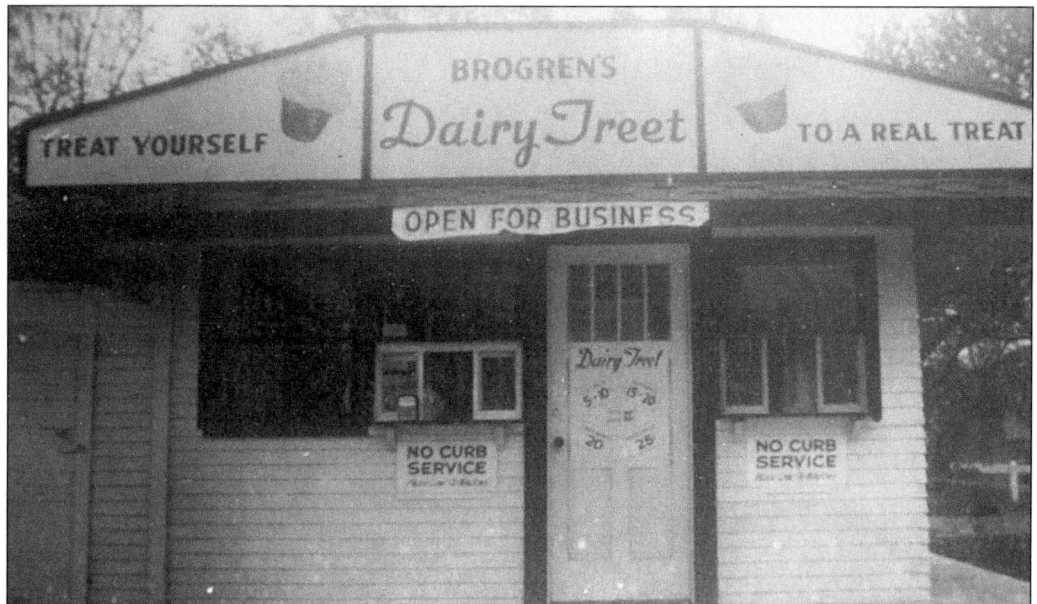

Tastee Treet has been around since before the days of bobby socks and poodle skirts. Here is the original Tastee Treet, when it was still Brogren's Dairy Treet in the 1940s. The owners, Terry and Diane Brogren, continue the Brogren family tradition started more than 50 years ago by Louis Brogren, Terry's father. He bought the Tastee Treet franchise in 1950. It continues to be best known for its Tastee Beef sandwiches and root beer floats.

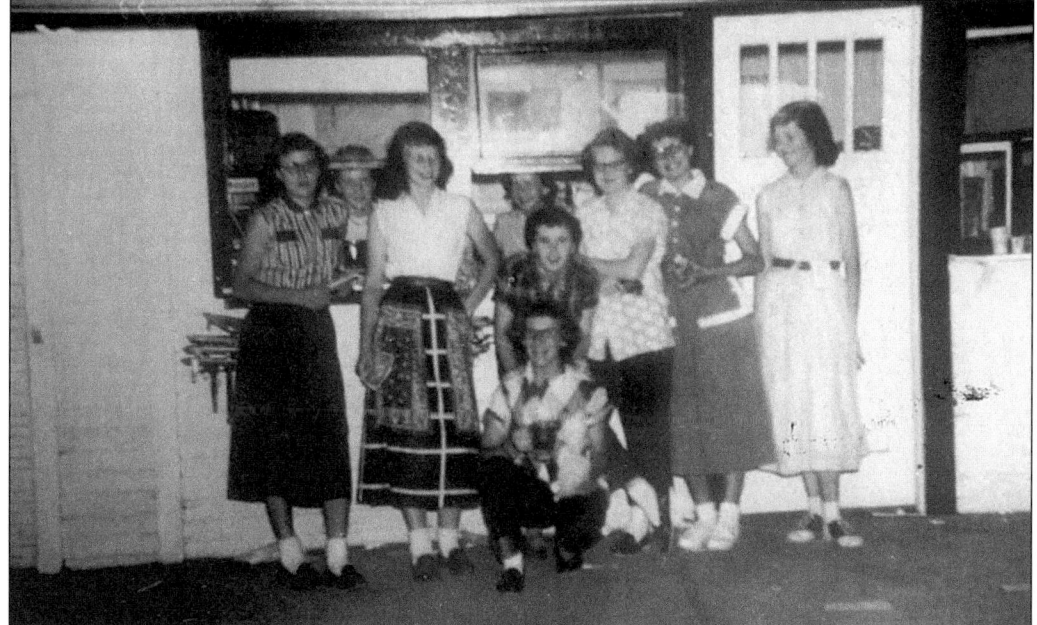

Tastee Treet was one of the first restaurants in Norfolk to use carhops to serve customers. A few of the carhops stopped long enough to have their photo taken. They are, from left to right, Janet Arns, Lila Shipley (in window), Margaret Hinken, Dee Demmel (in the center window), Jeanette Best (in front of Dee), Delilah Kaspar (kneeling), Elaine Zobel, Janet Retzlaff, and Mary Jo Hupp.

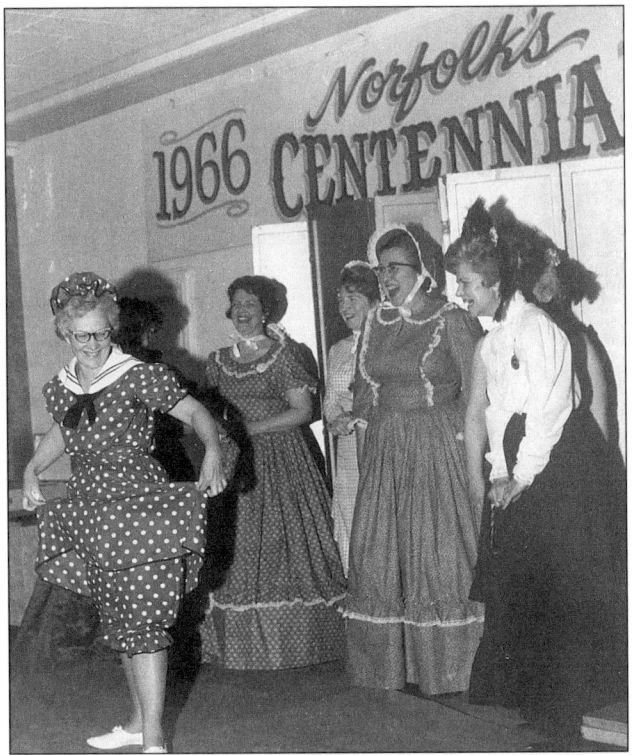

Norfolk celebrated its centennial in 1966 with a week full of activities for everyone. Norfolkans were encouraged to wear clothing from the 1860s. Here, women model their outfits for each other during the kick-off at Hotel Madison Ballroom. They are, from left to right, Marie Egley, Frances DeLay, Delores Francis, Carmel Smith, and Ruth Fleming.

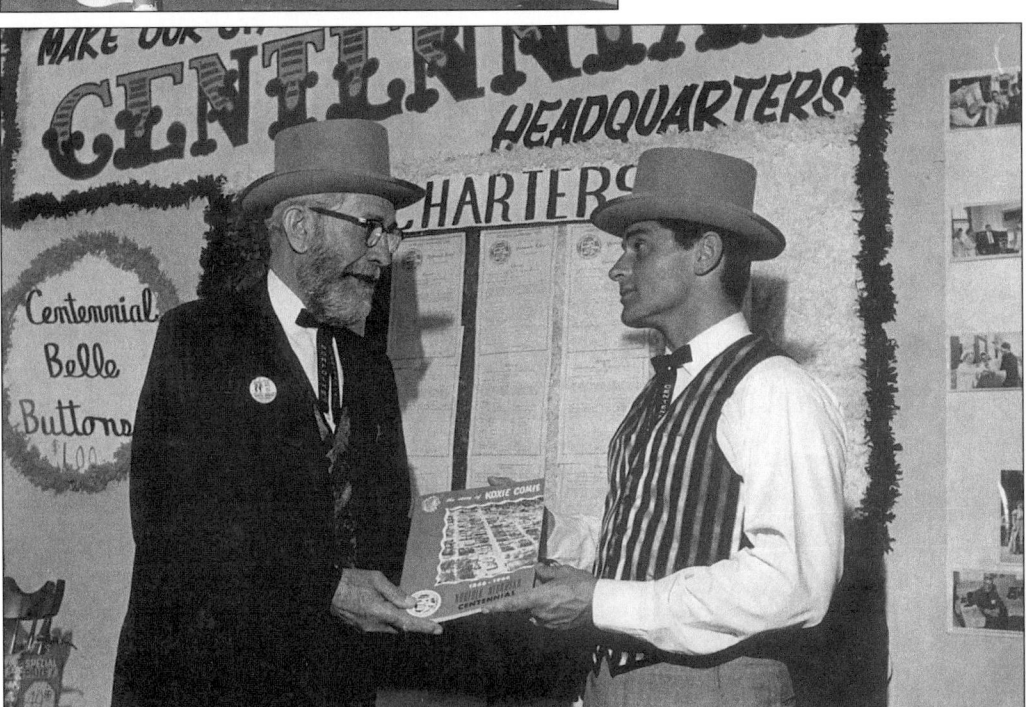

Bob Harrison presents a copy of Norfolk's centennial book, *The Story of Koxie Comie*, to Don Stewart, a Norfolk native who had since moved to California and was working as a television actor. The presentation was made at Norfolk's Centennial headquarters.

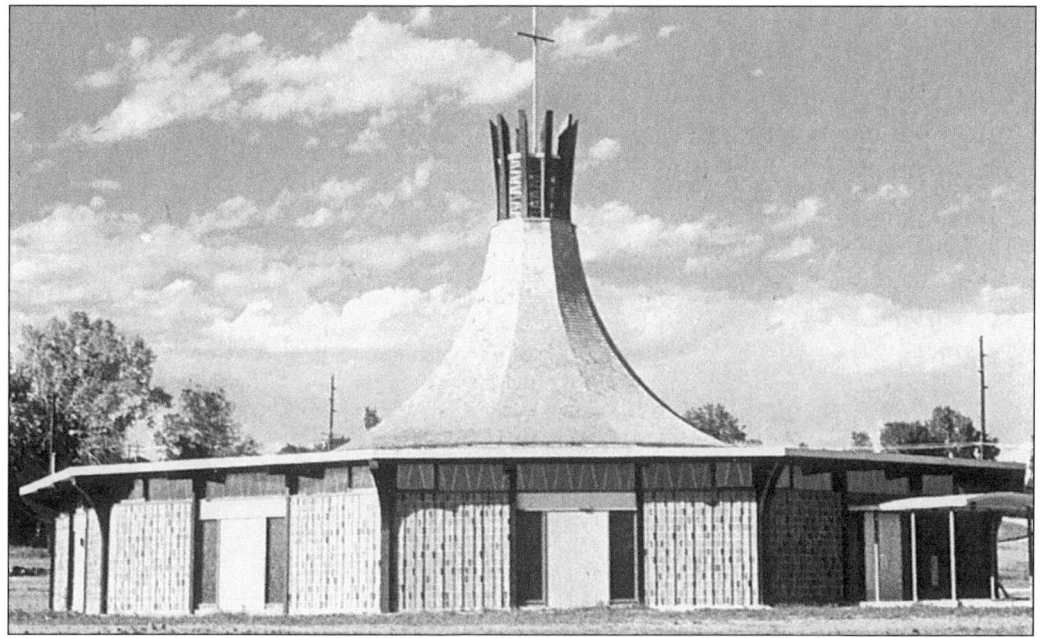

Our Savior Lutheran Church, built in 1964, was one of the first churches in Norfolk to break away from traditional church design. Since this photo was taken in 1966, two additions have been added to accommodate the church's growing congregation. Norfolkans place a great emphasis on religion; Norfolk is home to over 40 churches and 7 parochial schools.

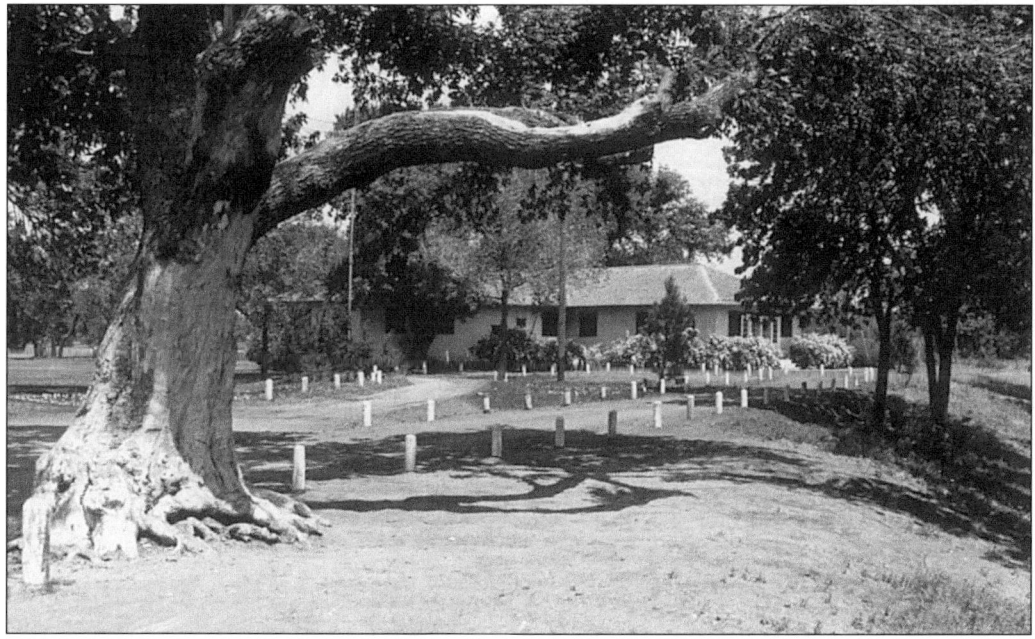

The Norfolk Country Club has changed significantly since this photo was taken, c. 1950. At that time it only had a 12-hole golf course. The course was expanded to 18 holes in 1965–66 at which time a new clubhouse was built.

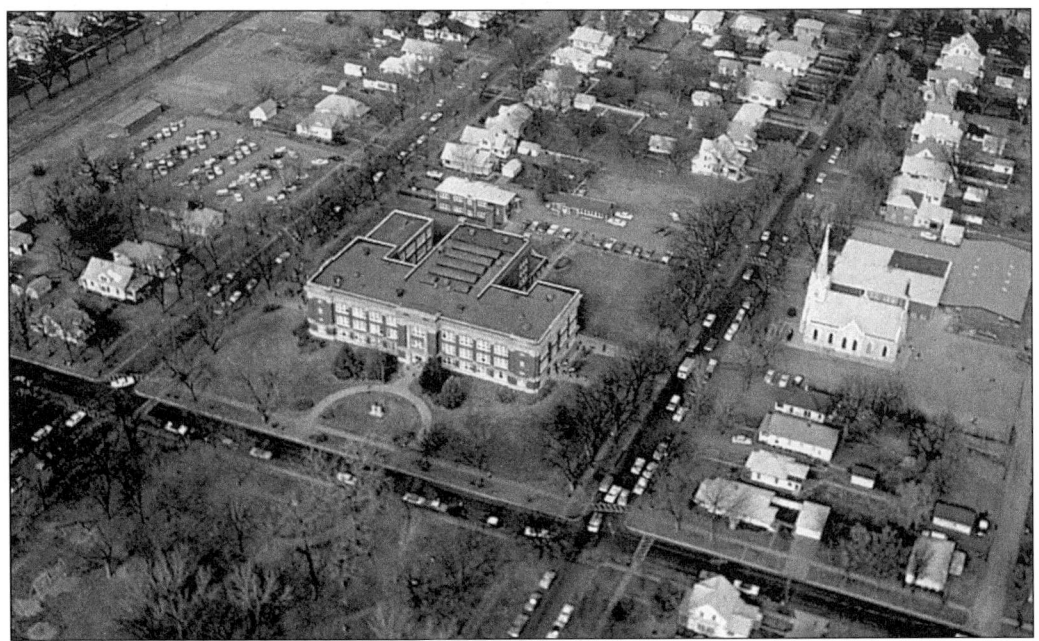

This aerial view of Norfolk High School was taken in 1966. This building has been alive with activity ever since it was built in 1922. The high school moved to a new building in 1968, and this one is now used as the Junior High School.

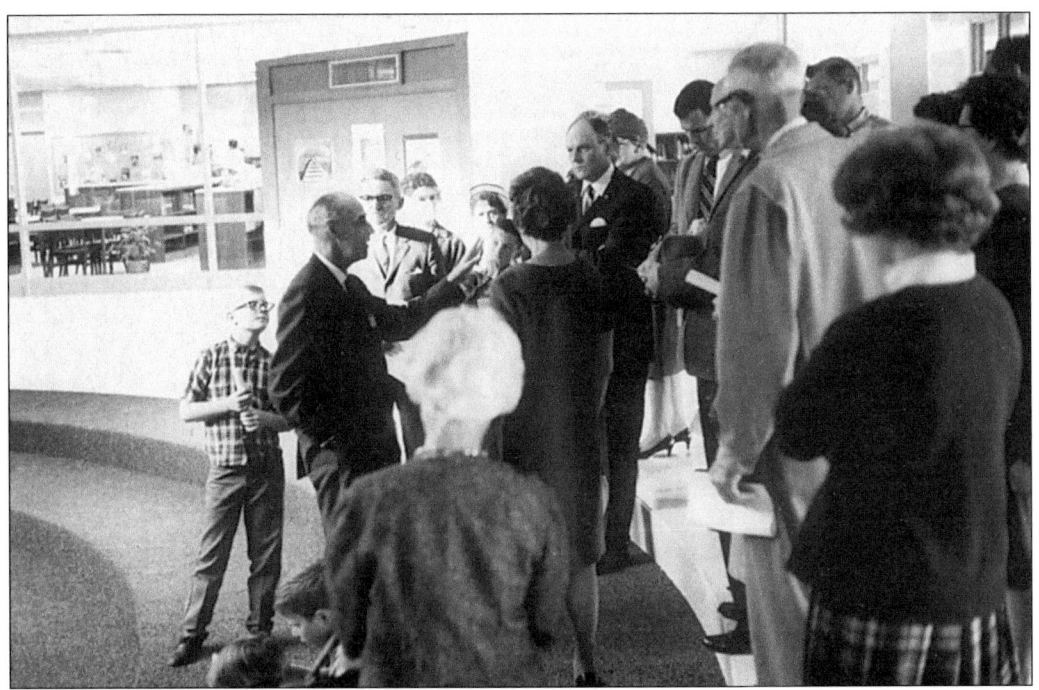

Don Maclay, who was Superintendent of Schools from 1960 to 1968, gives a tour through the new high school during open house on October 22, 1967. Mr. Maclay later became Administrator of Northeast Vocational Technical Community College.

In 1966, at Norfolk's Centennial, members of the Women's Relief Corps stand by the statue of Abraham Lincoln that is in Prospect Hill Cemetery. The organization had the statue erected in 1939 as a tribute to those men and women who served in the Civil War. The club was Norfolk's oldest patriotic organization at the time.

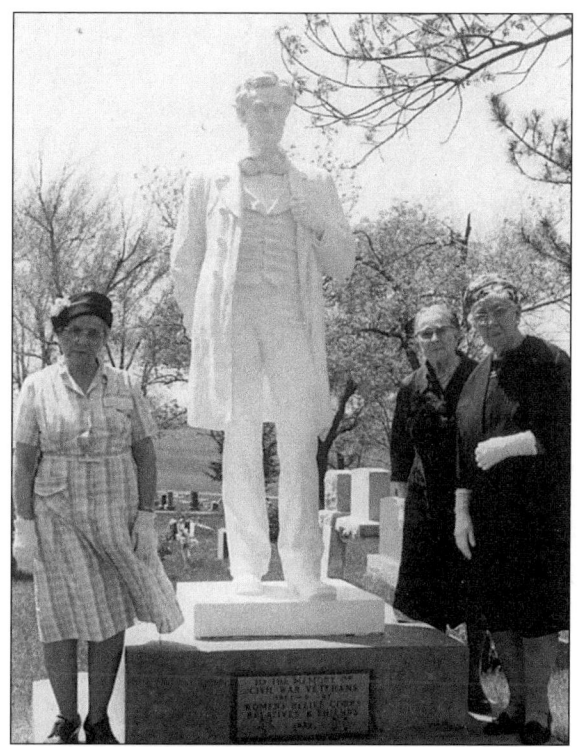

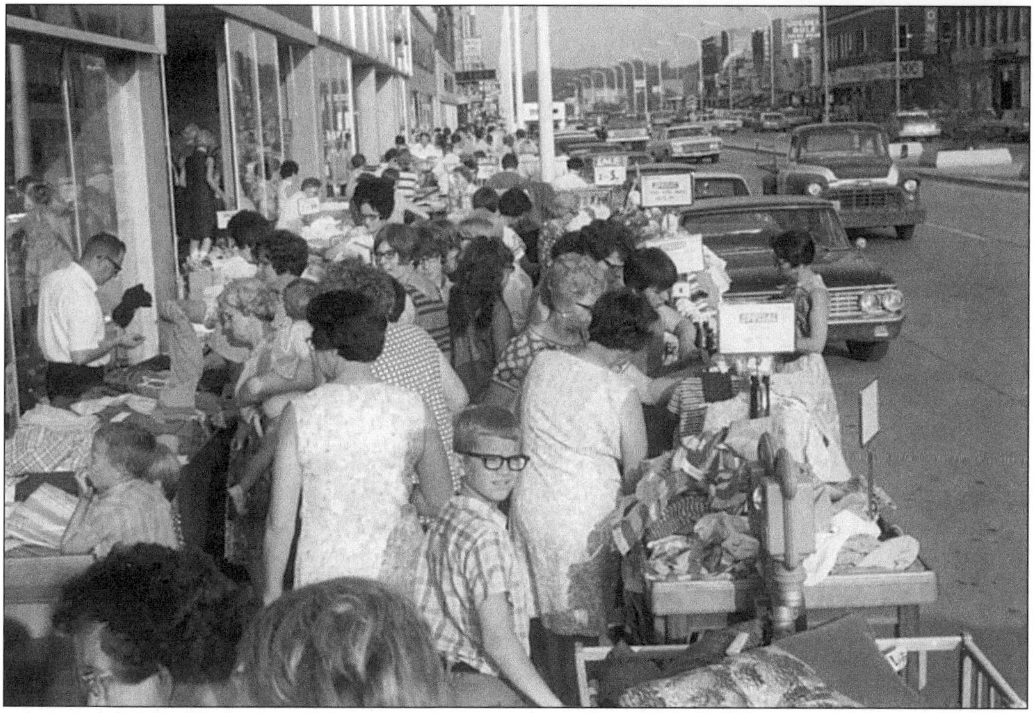

"Dog Days" has been a popular summer event for years. It's an opportunity for downtown merchants to sell their stock of summer merchandise and a chance for shoppers to find some real bargains, as is shown in this July 24, 1968 view of Norfolk Avenue.

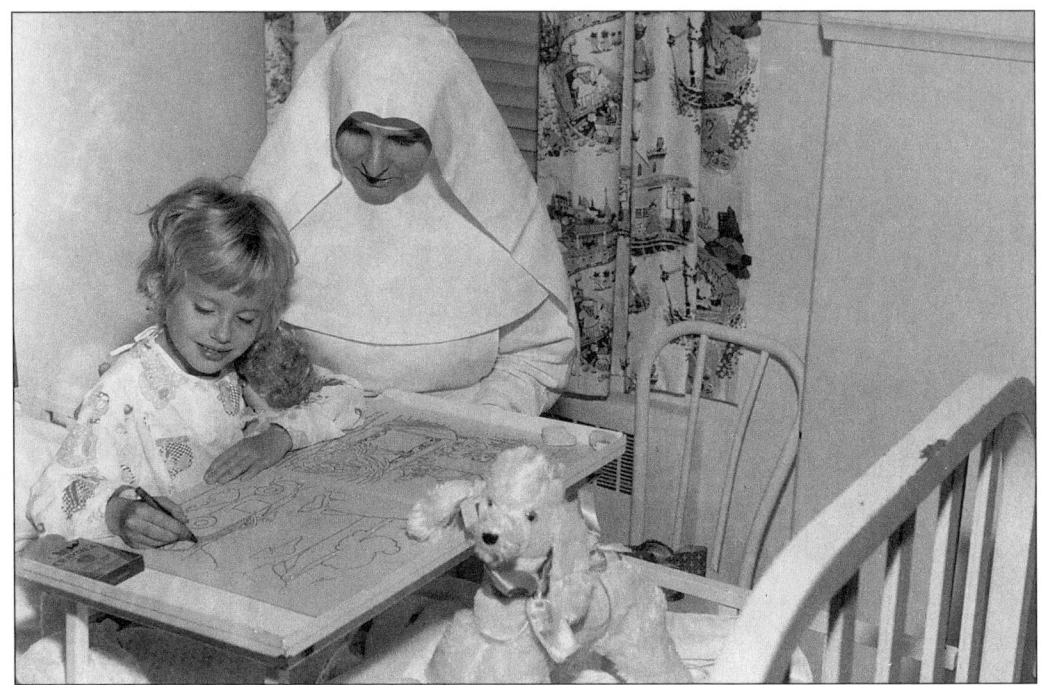

The Missionary Benedictine Sisters have lived, worked, and prayed in Norfolk since 1935 when seven Sisters opened Our Lady of Lourdes Hospital. Here, Sister Richildis Schramm visits with a young child who is a patient in the hospital. Our Lady of Lourdes merged with Lutheran Community Hospital in 1996, becoming Faith Regional Health Services. The Sisters continue to serve the hospital in a variety of ways.

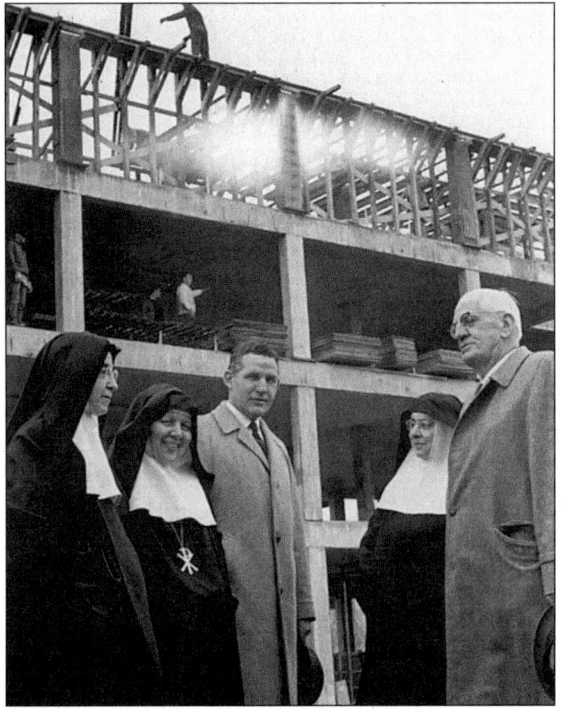

Here, Benedictine Sisters discuss the construction of the new Immaculata Convent with builders. The Convent, located at 300 North 18th Street, was dedicated in 1965. In addition to the hospital, the Sisters also ran Saint Joseph's Nursing Home and a private boarding school for girls named Assumption Academy.

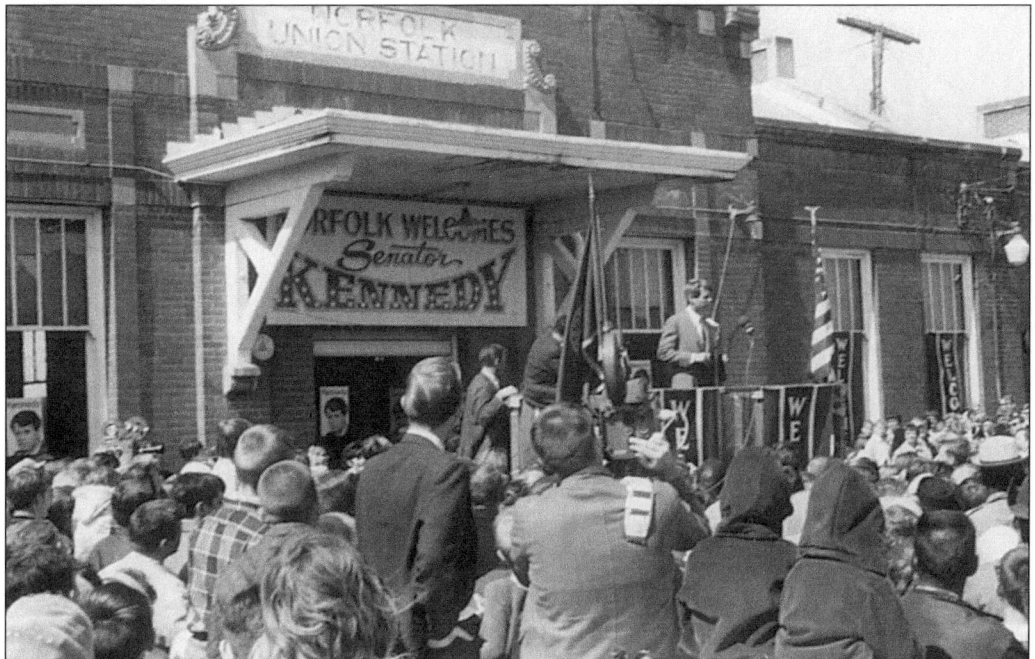

U.S. Senator Robert Kennedy made a stop in Norfolk on April 20, 1968, during his campaign for president. Hundreds of Northeast Nebraskans came that day to see Kennedy who stopped at several sites in Norfolk. Here Kennedy speaks to a crowd in front of Norfolk's Union Station, 120 North 5th Street. Kennedy was assassinated less than two months later while campaigning in California.

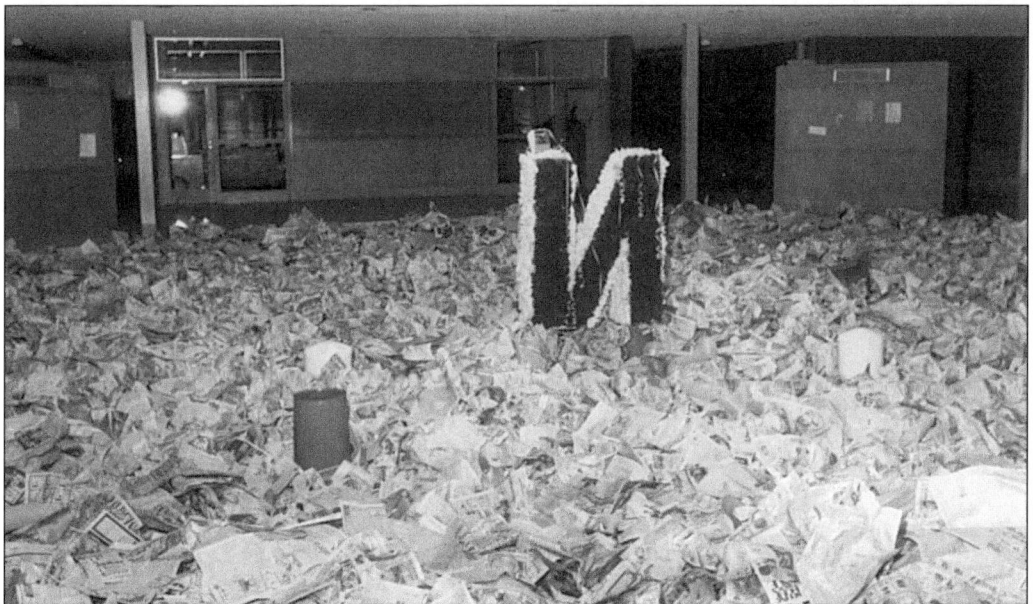

On May 16, 1969, Roger Maxwell, principal at Norfolk High School, arrived at the school to find the forum filled with crumpled newspapers and balloons. No one took the credit—or the blame—for the prank. However, it was the last day of class for the seniors, who were nice enough to clean up the mess.

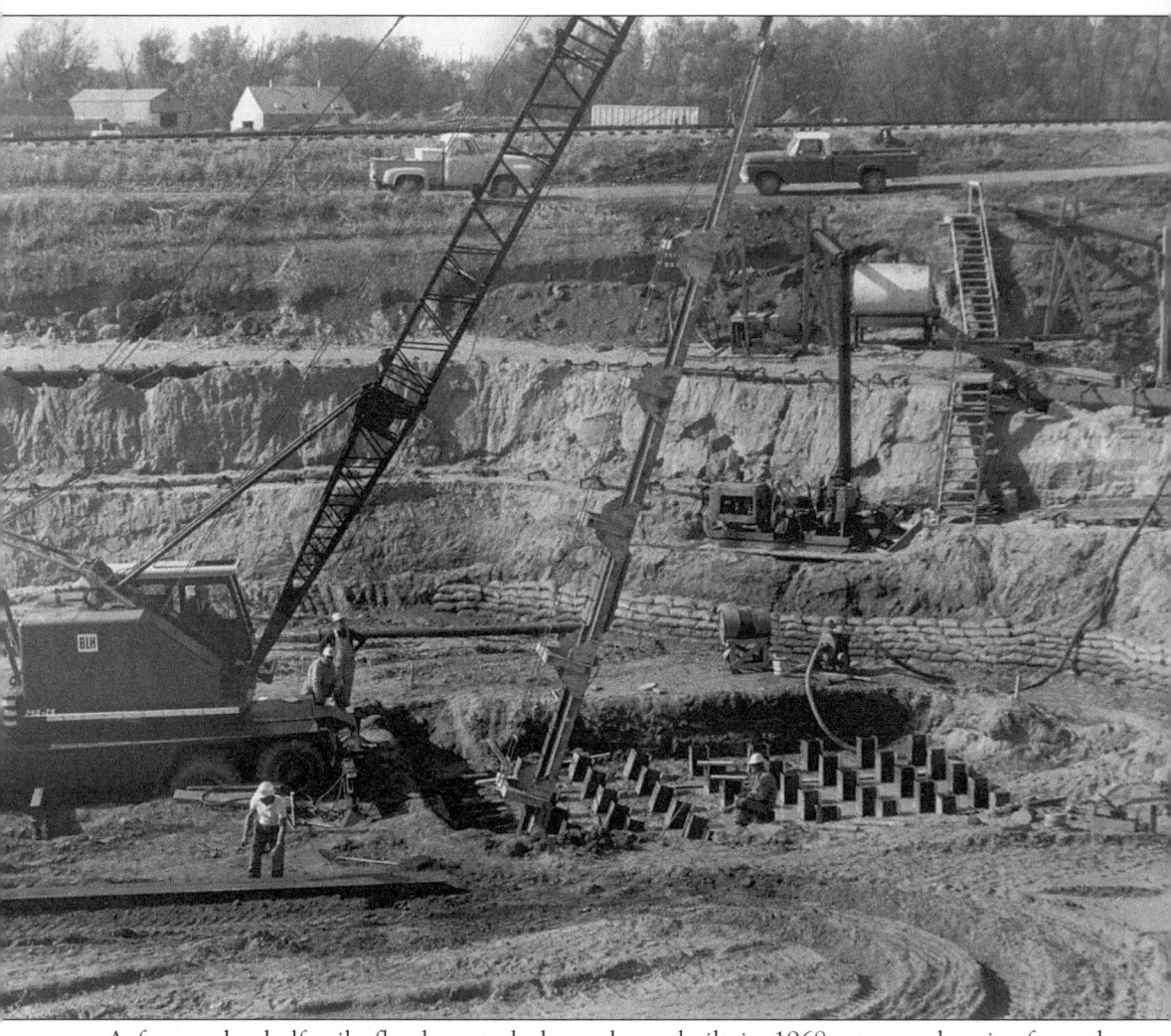

A four and a half mile flood control channel was built in 1968 to save the city from the damaging flood waters that plagued it during its first one hundred years. Before the project was completed, Norfolk experienced six major floods and eleven minor floods because of waters from the Northfork of the Elkhorn River. It has been said that no other capital construction project in the city's history has done more to save property. Because of the flood control, north-central and eastern Norfolk were able to develop without fear of flood damage. Here, workers install pilings for a drop structure and railroad bridge, just north of Benjamin Avenue and east of 1st Street.

Five

LOOKING AHEAD: 1970–2000

"The heritage of the past is the seed that brings forth the harvest of the future."

—Unknown

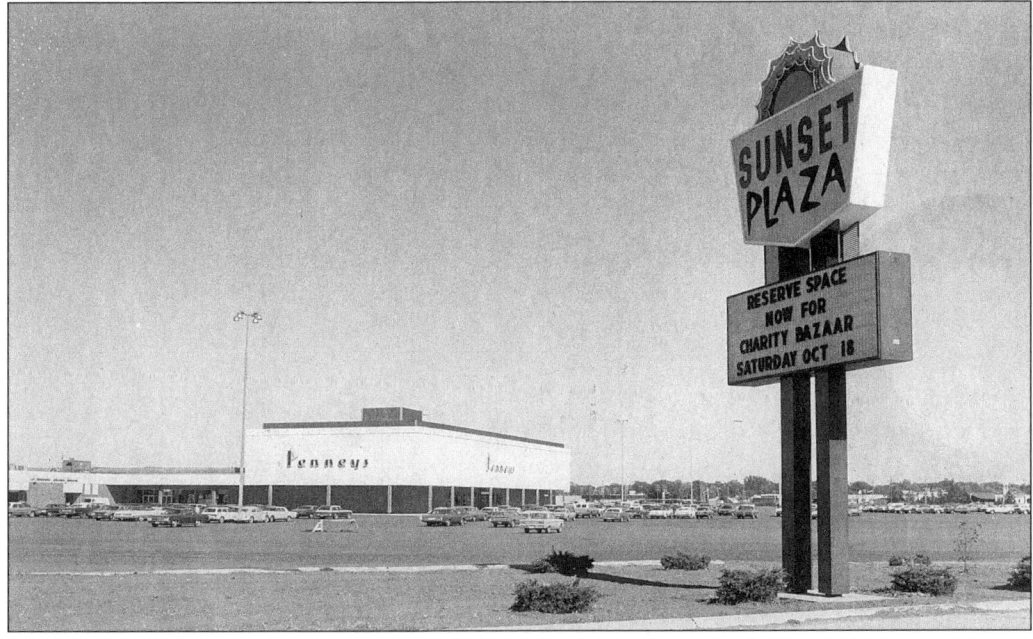

Norfolk has always been the retail trade center of Northeast Nebraska with an attractive downtown area that offered almost anything consumers needed. By the late 1960s, the retail center was starting to shift to the outskirts of town. The Sunset Plaza was Norfolk's first shopping mall. Its opening in 1968 spurred growth in southwest Norfolk.

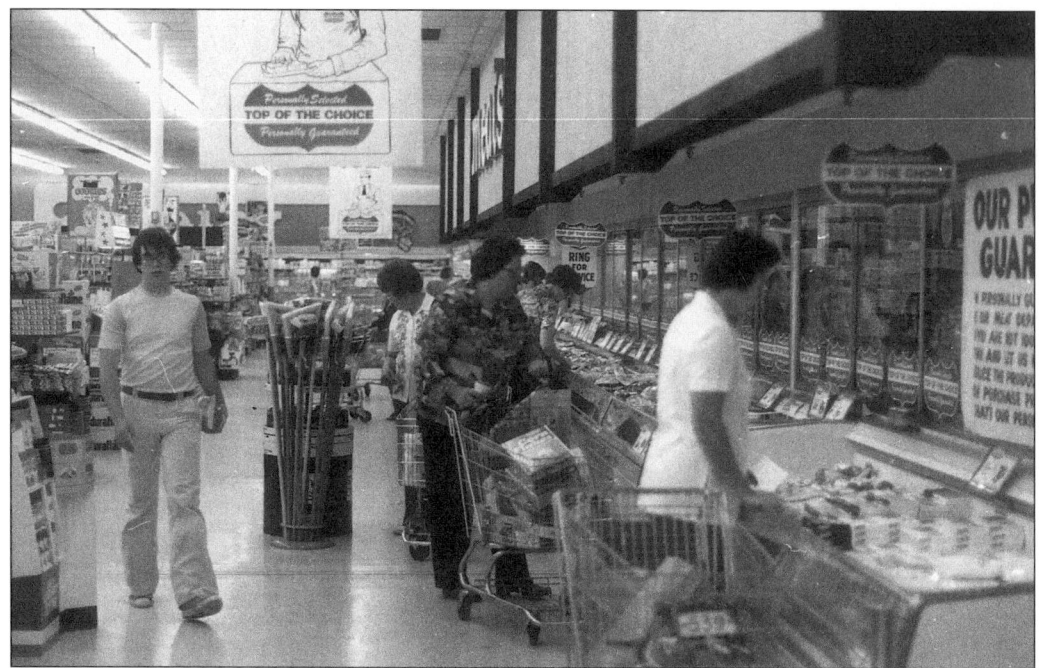

Shoppers walk the aisles of the Hinky Dinky Grocery Store, once located at the Sunset Plaza. The photo was taken in 1977.

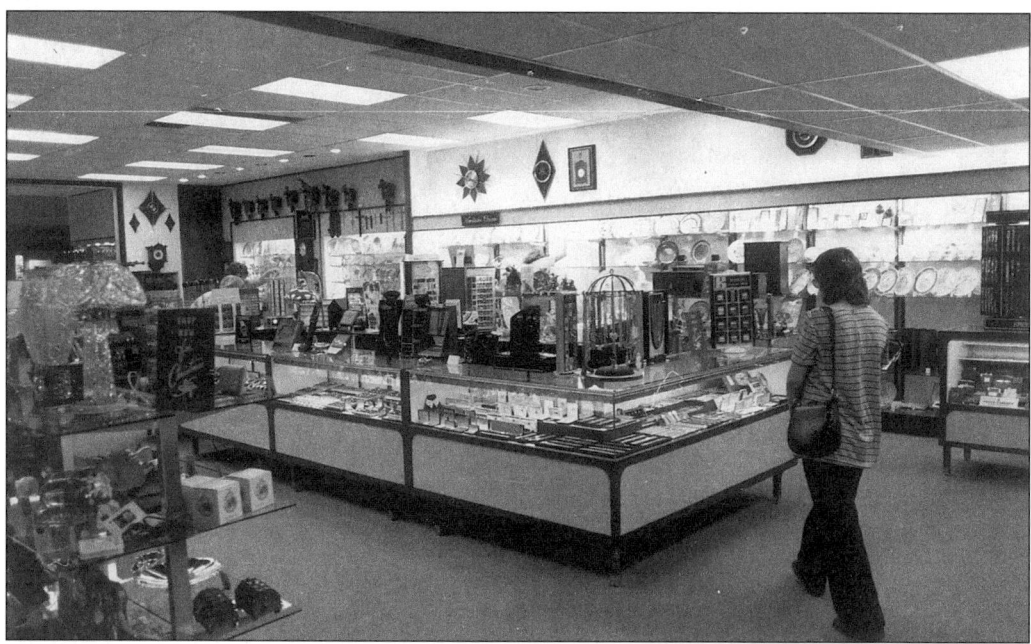

Brodkey's Jewelry Store at the Sunset Plaza is shown here in 1977. Brodkey's is one of the few original tenants remaining at the Plaza, which has expanded greatly in the 1990s. Although Norfolk still has a vital downtown area, some shoppers like the idea of being able to shop a variety of stores while staying inside, out of the weather.

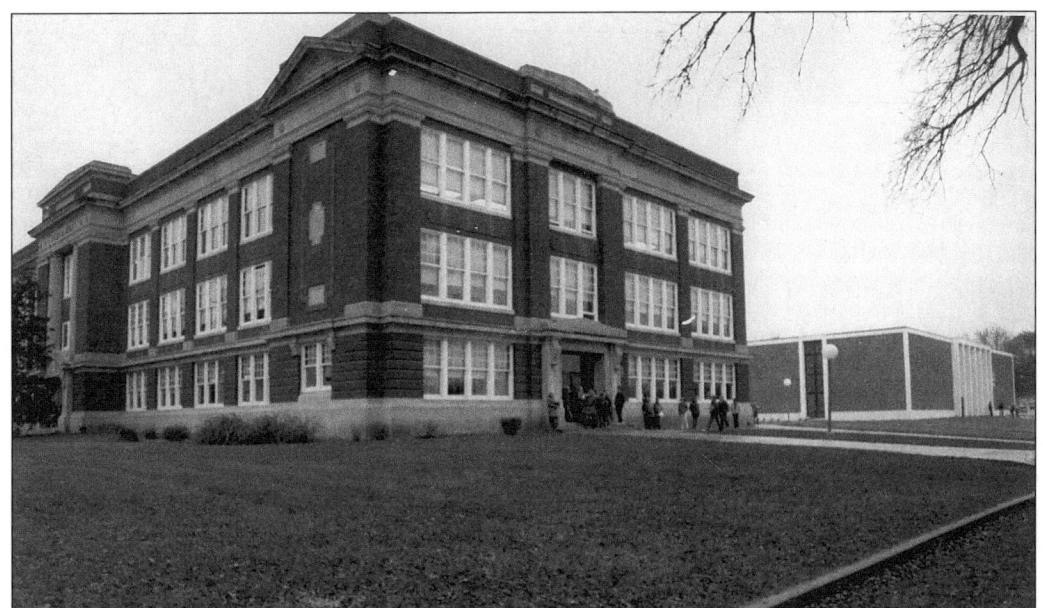

This building at 510 Pasewalk Avenue was originally constructed as a high school. It has served as Norfolk Junior High School since 1968. The addition, which can be seen behind the old building, was built in 1971 to accommodate Norfolk's growing student population. Even with the addition, Norfolk outgrew this building. In 1995, classes for 7th graders were moved to the new Norfolk Middle School at 1221 North 1st Street.

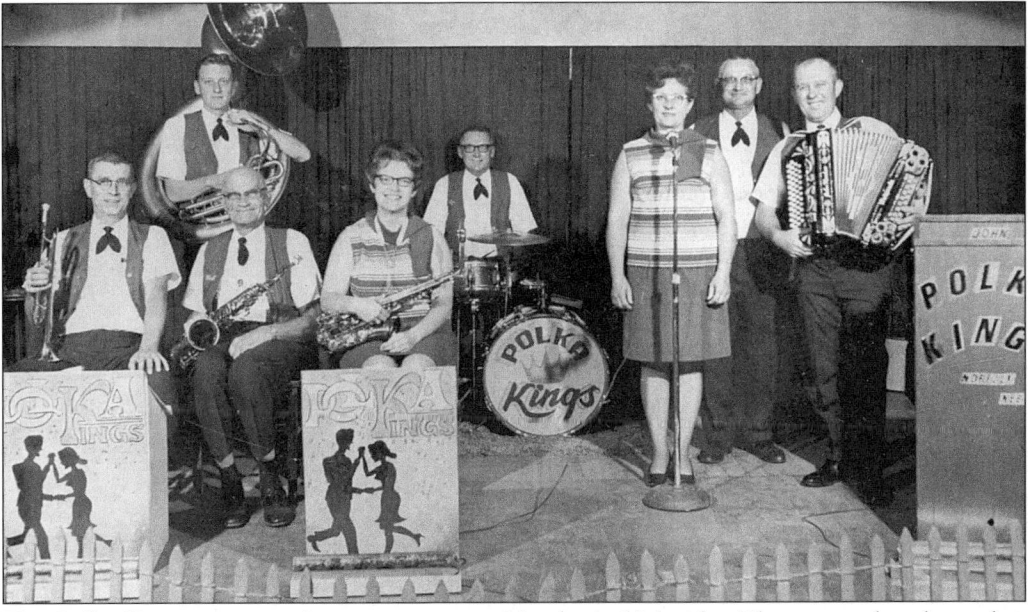

The Polka Kings were popular entertainers in Northeast Nebraska. The group played together for 20 years at the Riverside Ballroom in Norfolk as well as towns throughout the area and one overseas engagement. They are, from left to right, as follows: (front row) Paul Johnston, trumpet; Herb Greckel, saxophone; Carolyn Pavlik, saxophone; Clara Pavlik, vocalist; John Dufek, accordion; (back row) Rudolph Pavlik Jr., tuba; Arvey Pavlik, drums; and Otto Schulz, bus driver.

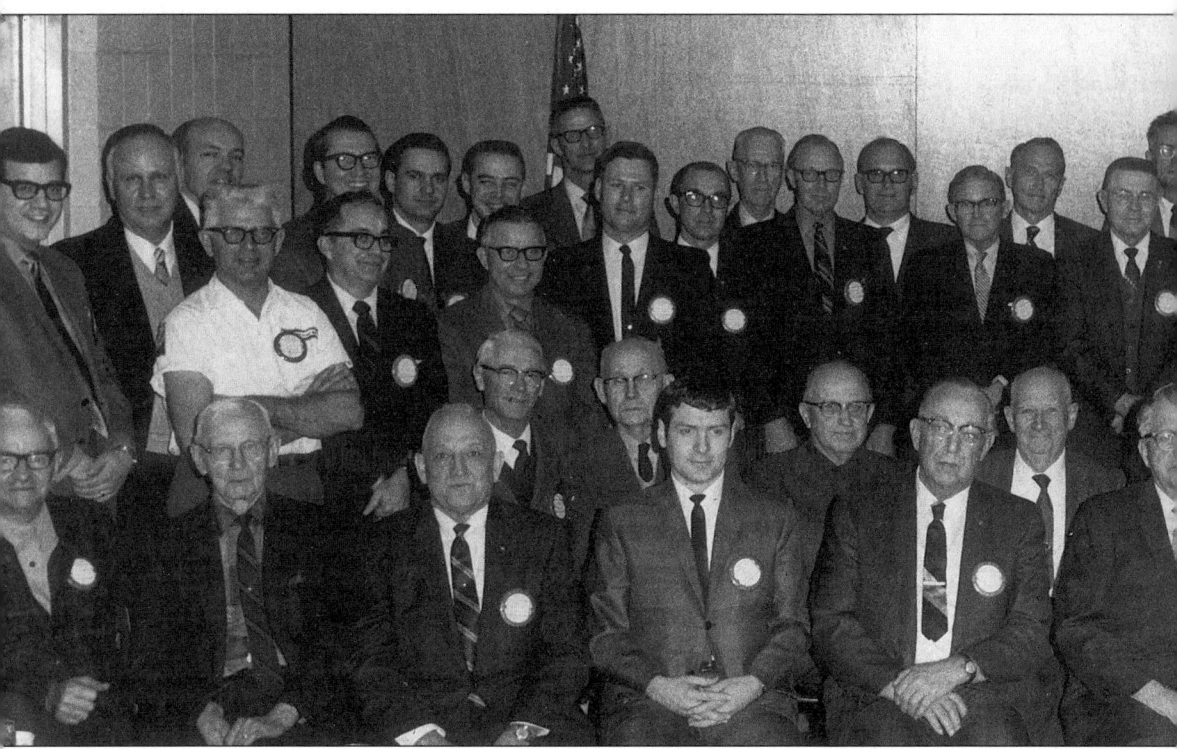

The 50th anniversary of Norfolk's Noon Rotary Club was celebrated February 1, 1970. Here members pose for a photograph. Some of them are identified. They are, seated, from left to right: Foy Clark, Paul Wetzel, Wally Truex, Clyde Wells, unidentified, Rich Authier, Jack Kruger, unidentified, Glenn Davis, M.B. Olsen, unidentified, Ed Horn, Bob Carlisle, Jim Gillette, Charlie Ahlman, Dick Newlun, Emil Reutzel, Henry M. Kuhn, C. William Christian, Bob Adkins, and Harold Milliken. Standing, from left to right, are unidentified, unidentified,

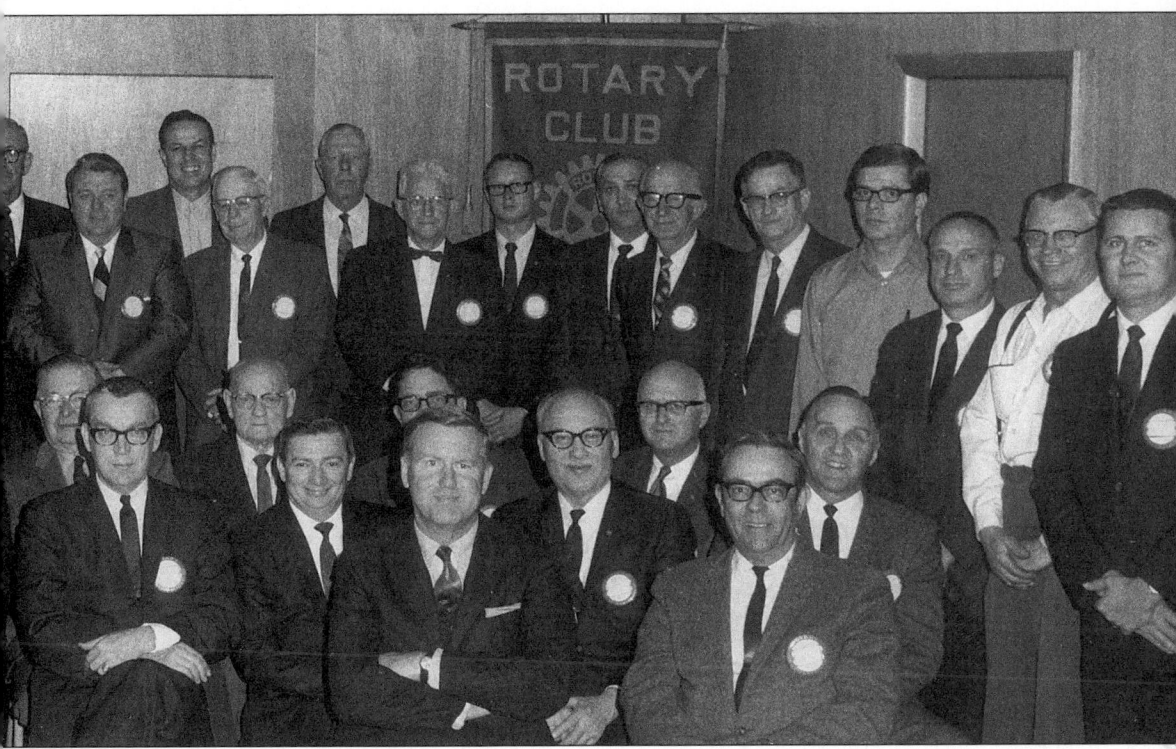

Rev. Grayden Wilson, Mel Hayes, Roger Maxwell, Everet Simpson, unidentified, James Jones, unidentified, Wes Sohl, Laurence Tighe, Merle Jansen, Ralph Walker, Ed Hamm, Charles Howser, Dr. George Salter, Bob Thomas, A.J. Pendergast, Lysle Park, Ike Goldsberry, Stan Thornton, Glenn Shaneyfelt, Charles Crawford, Leonard Ross, Ed Hale, unidentified, Jim Prchal, Otto Burkhardt, Harold Alexander, Roger Kruger, Les Chaffin, Gene Palmer, and Gene Sock.

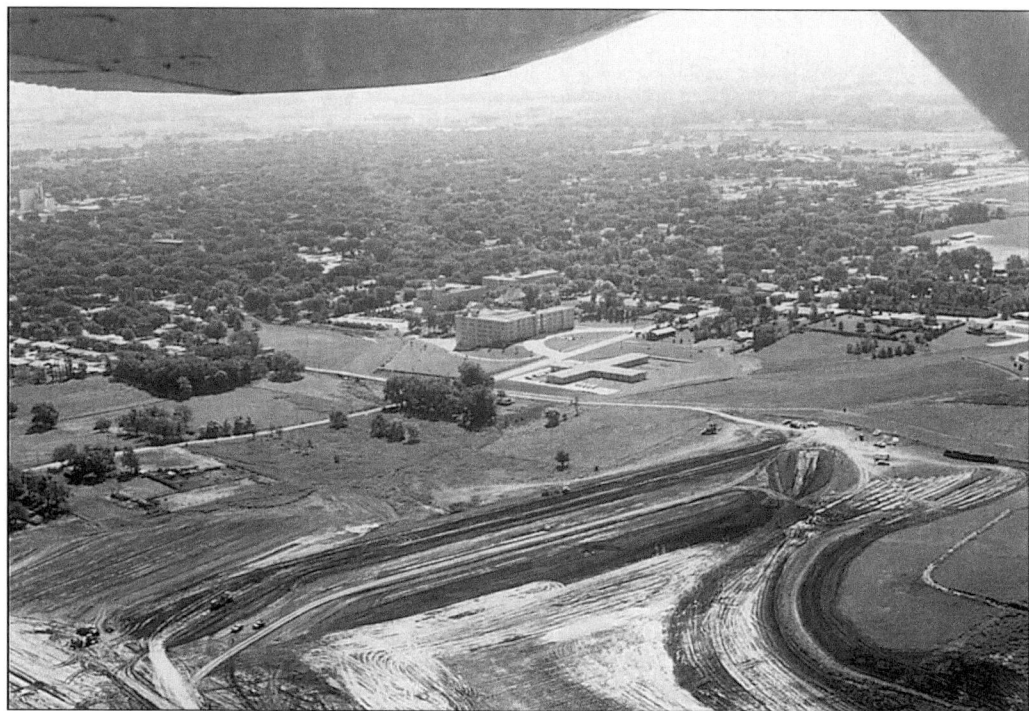

This photo shows beginning construction work on a dam that would create Skyview Lake, a by-product of the major flood control project initiated after the flood of 1962. Before the dam was built in 1971, runoff from Corporation Gulch watershed washed downstream, posing a flood threat to many residents of southwest Norfolk.

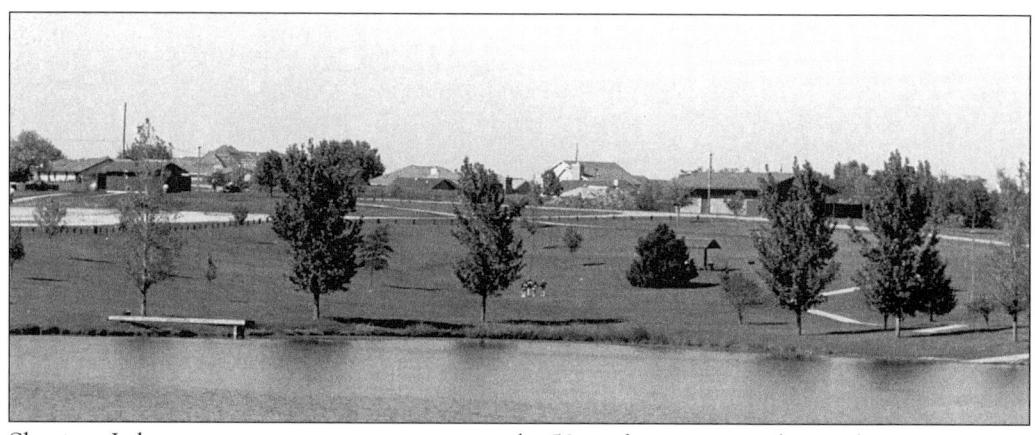

Skyview Lake now encompasses approximately 50 surface acres with another 90 acres of adjoining parkland. The park features picnic shelters, a playground, and a paved walking path. The park is a popular spot for fishing and recreation. It is now home to Norfolk's annual fireworks display.

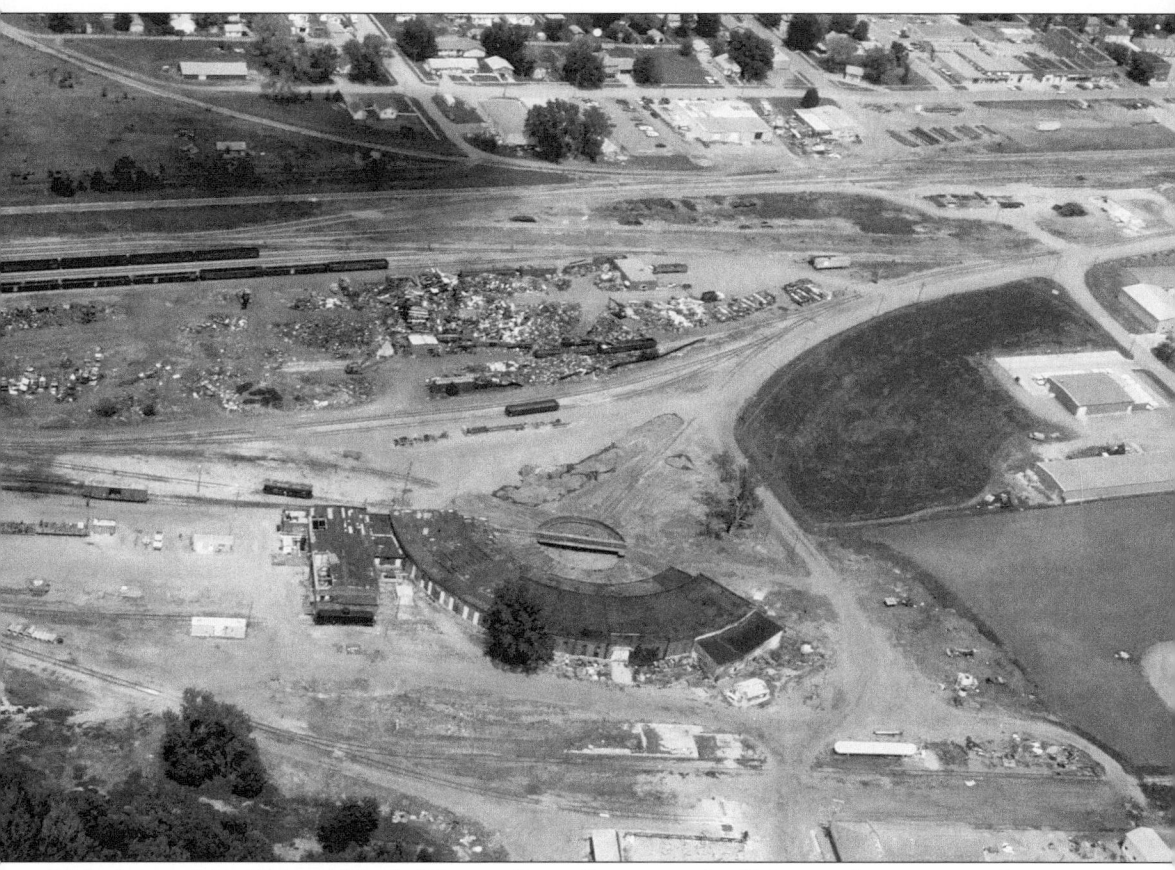

This photo of the Chicago North Western Roundhouse south of Monroe Avenue was taken in 1993, shortly before it was torn down. Roundhouses were maintenance facilities where trains were repaired. Engines could be turned around on the turntable north of the roundhouse.

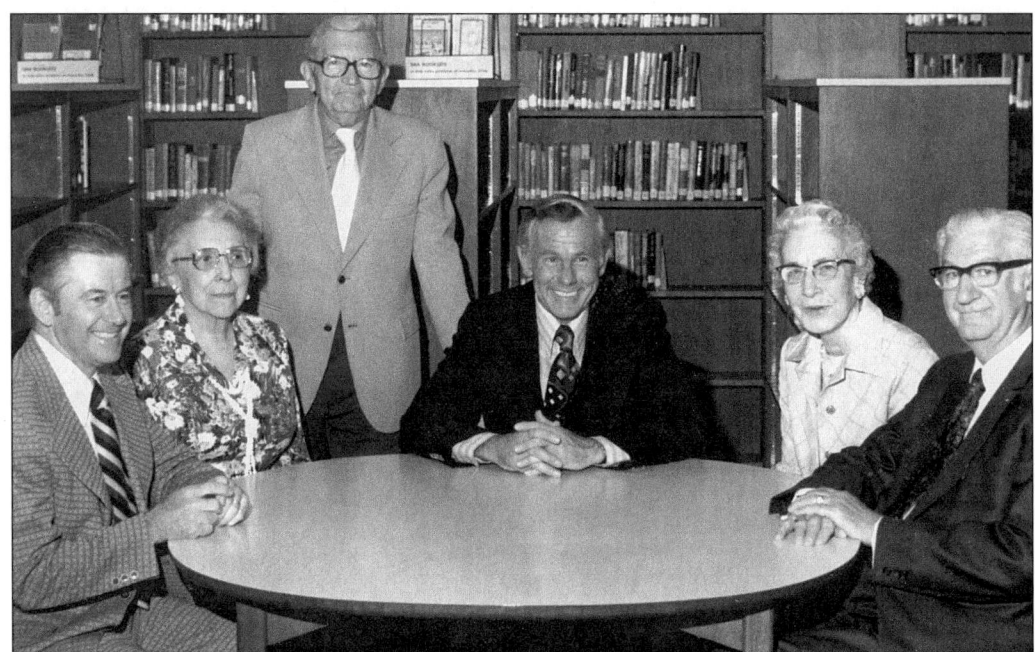

Johnny Carson sits in the library at Norfolk High School. Carson attended Norfolk Public Schools and graduated in 1943. In May of 1976, he gave the commencement address at Norfolk High School. Here he is shown with his teachers Fred Egley, physical education; Fay Gordon, penmanship; Principal Ted Skillstad; Jennie Walker, algebra; and Dr. Allen P. Burkhardt, Superintendent of Schools.

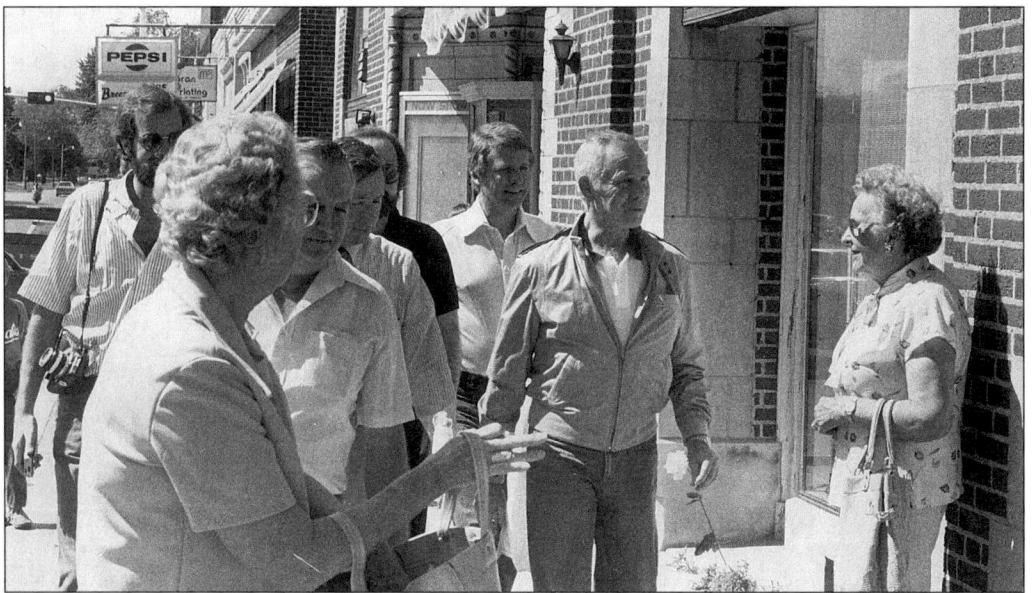

Johnny Carson moved to Norfolk with his family in 1933. The longtime host of NBC's *Tonight Show* returned to Norfolk in October of 1981 to film a television special entitled *Johnny Goes Home*. During filming of the special, Carson visited several sites that were familiar to him, including the house where he lived as a child, the schools he attended, and the Granada Theater, where he once worked.

106

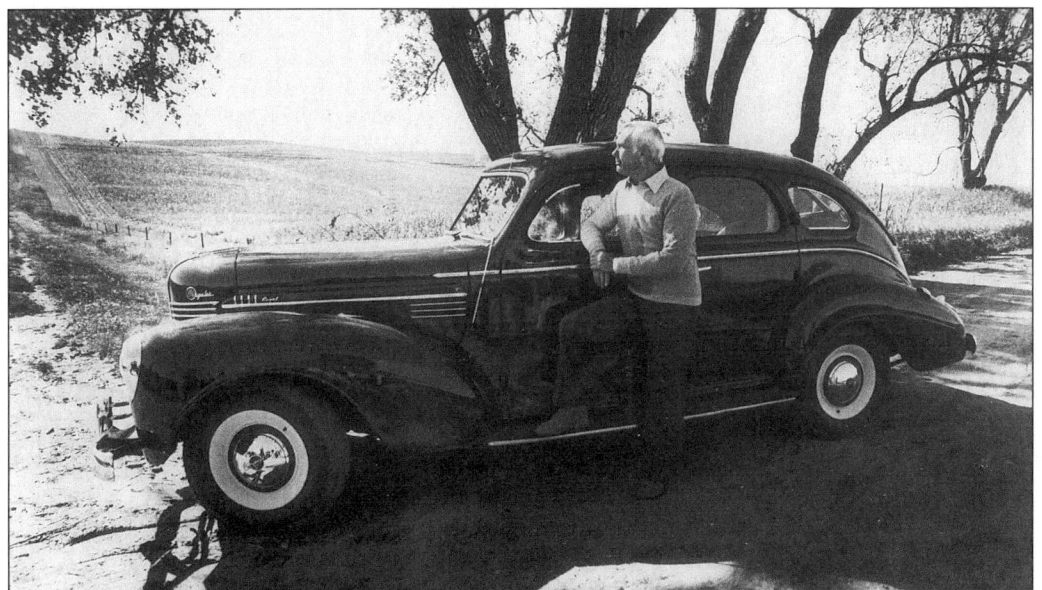

H-e-e-e-r's Johnny, Norfolk's most famous former resident. Carson enjoyed using his father's 1939 Chrysler Royal to tour Norfolk while filming a television special in 1981. Carson's father, H.L. "Kit" Carson, was a manager for the Nebraska Light and Power Company.

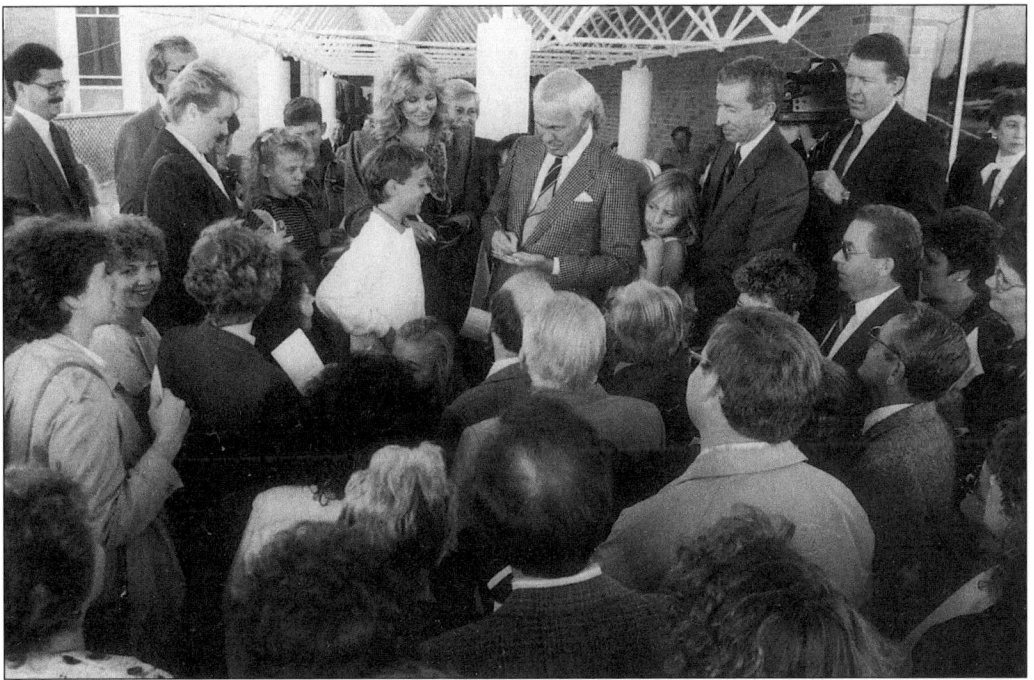

Johnny Carson signs autographs while in Norfolk for the dedication of the new Carson Radiation Center in 1988. It was named in honor of his parents, Kit and Ruth Carson. Carson has made many sizable donations to Norfolk, including the radiation center, the Elkhorn Valley Museum and Research Center, The Johnny Carson Theatre, The Lifelong Learning Center, The Norfolk Arts Center, and the Norfolk Senior Citizen Center.

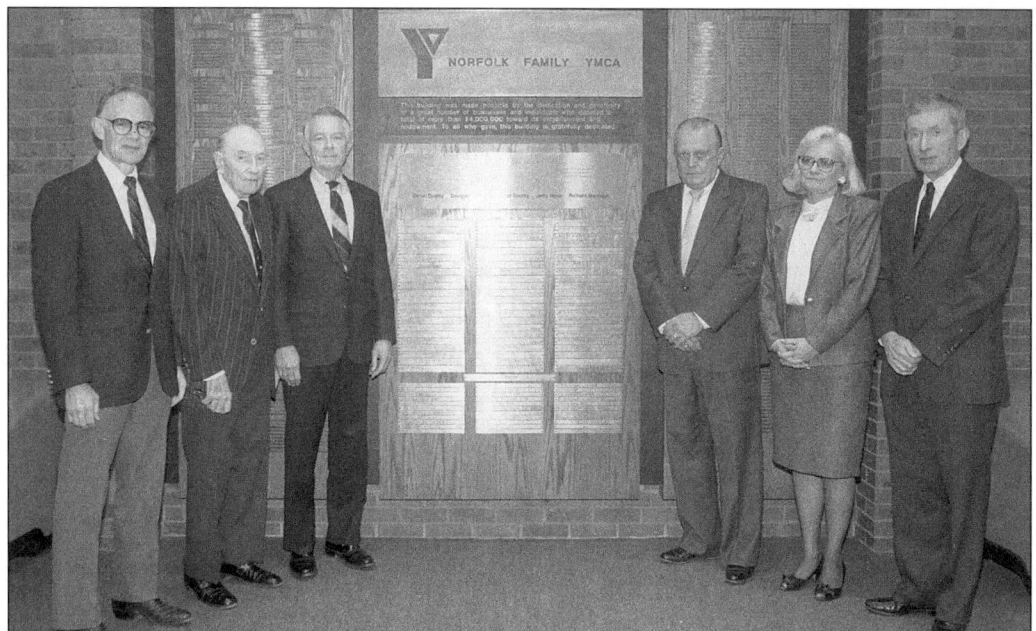

Norfolk opened a new Family YMCA at 301 Benjamin Avenue in 1979. Here the major benefactors, who together gave $2,000,000 to the building project, stand by a plaque in their honor. They are, from left to right, Doug Dudley, Darrel D. Dudley, George Dudley, Richard Morrison Jr., and Judy Rook, who represent their father Richard Morrison, and Jerry Huse.

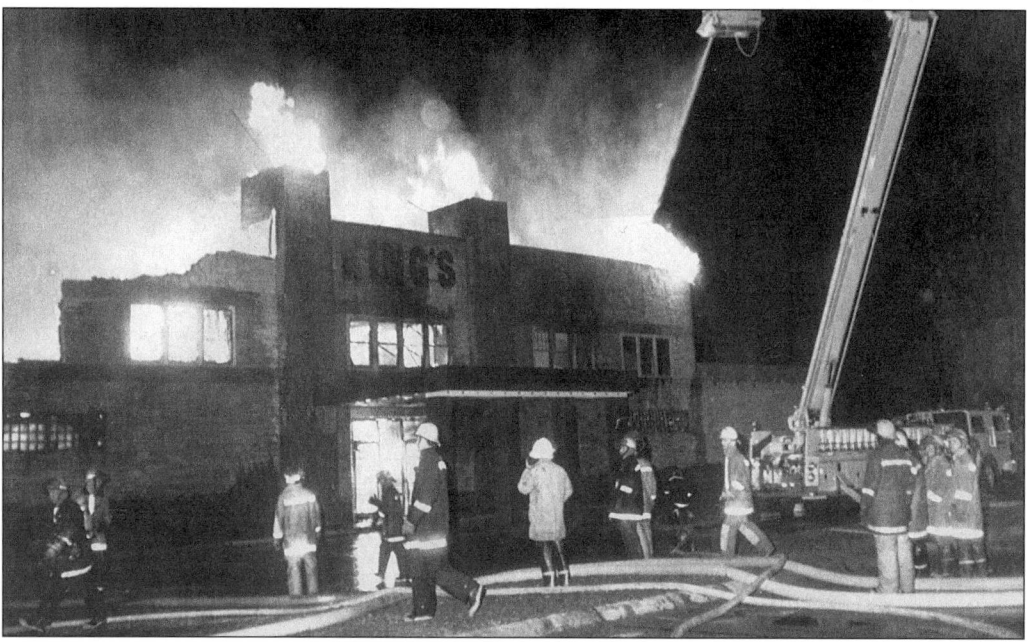

Flames shoot in all directions from King's Ballroom on April 3, 1986. Approximately 130 firefighters fought the blaze that destroyed the building that had been a Norfolk landmark for almost 70 years. The ballroom was destroyed by fire shortly after it was built in 1917 and by flood in 1944. Both times it was rebuilt. This time, however, marked the end of King's Ballroom.

Flags line the sidewalk leading to the Norfolk Veterans Home in this 1978 photo taken on Veterans Day. At the time this photo was taken, the Veterans Home, which has been in Norfolk since 1963, was located on the campus of the Norfolk Regional Center. However, it moved to a new facility in 2001.

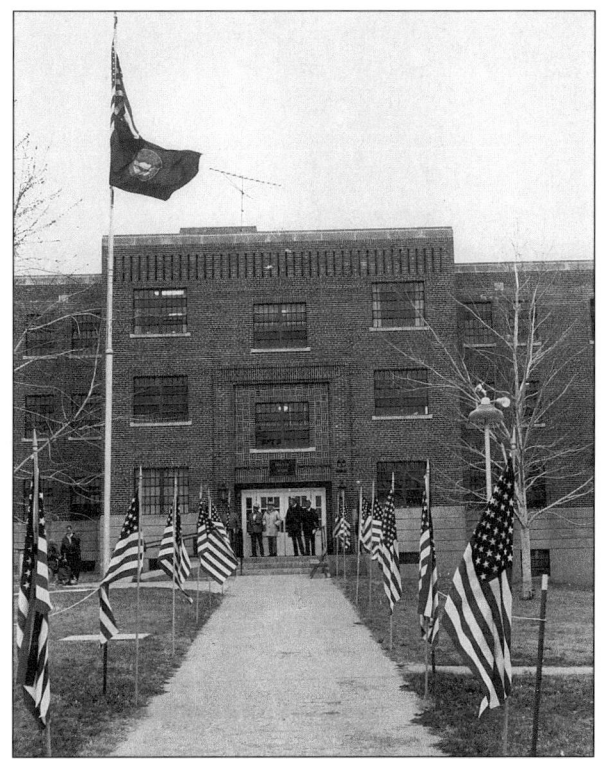

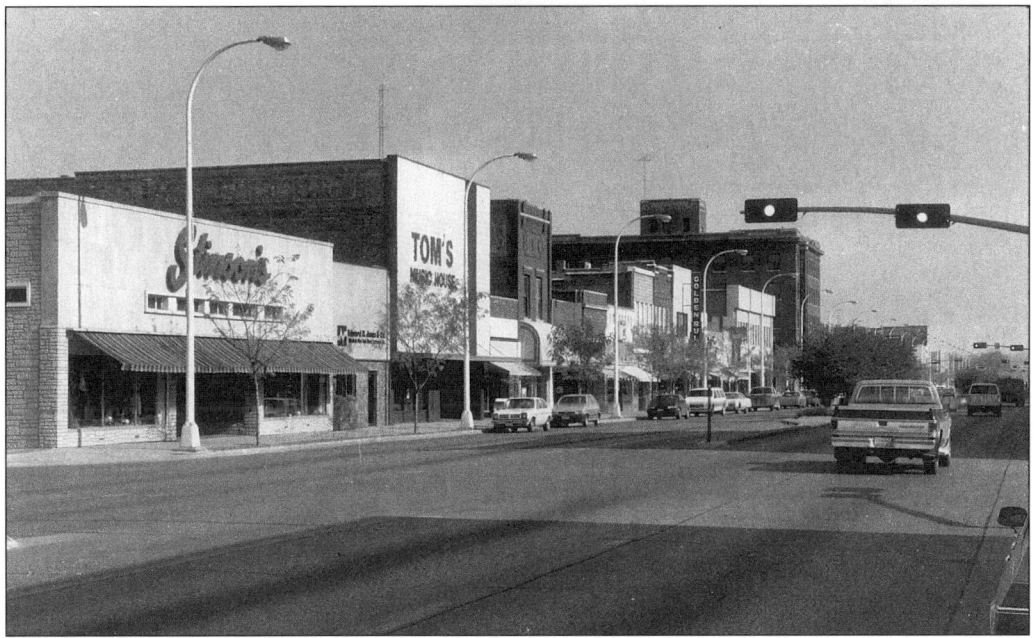

Norfolk Avenue continues to change. Here it is in 1988, when Stinson's Department Store, Tom's Music House, and the Golden Rule were still popular shopping spots. Now, all three have closed and the buildings are home to new retail shops and offices. One of Norfolk's most important landmarks—Hotel Madison, now called The Kensington—rises above the other buildings to the right of the photograph.

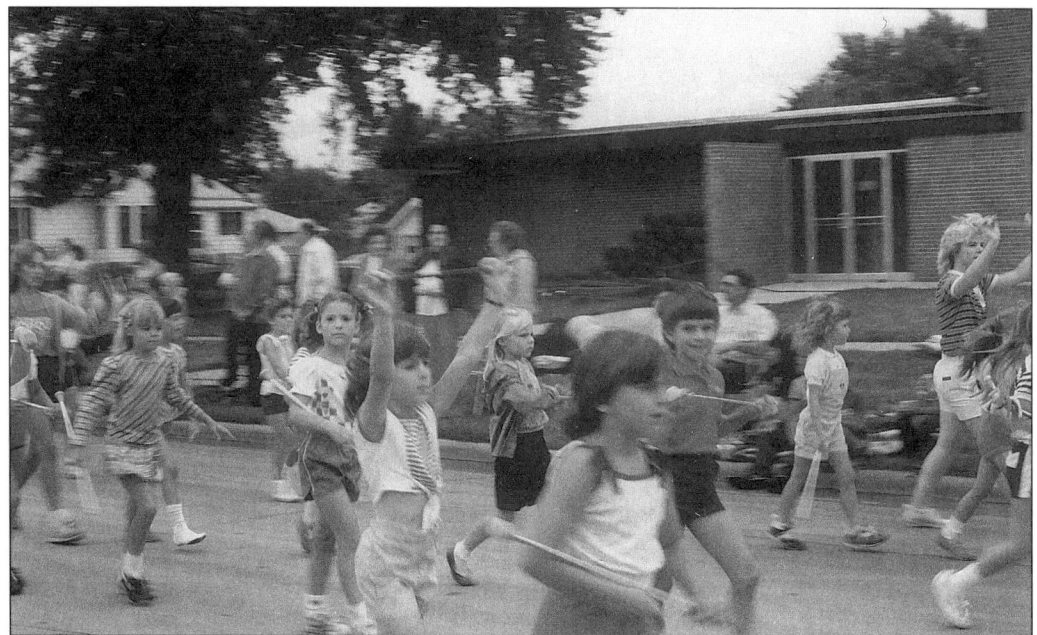

What would the 4th of July be without a parade? In this 1984 photo, students who participated in the city's baton twirling class strut their stuff during the city's annual 4th of July celebration. The parade, a Norfolk tradition, is just one of the city's 4th of July activities. Others include a pie and ice cream social, concerts, and the fireworks show at Skyview Lake.

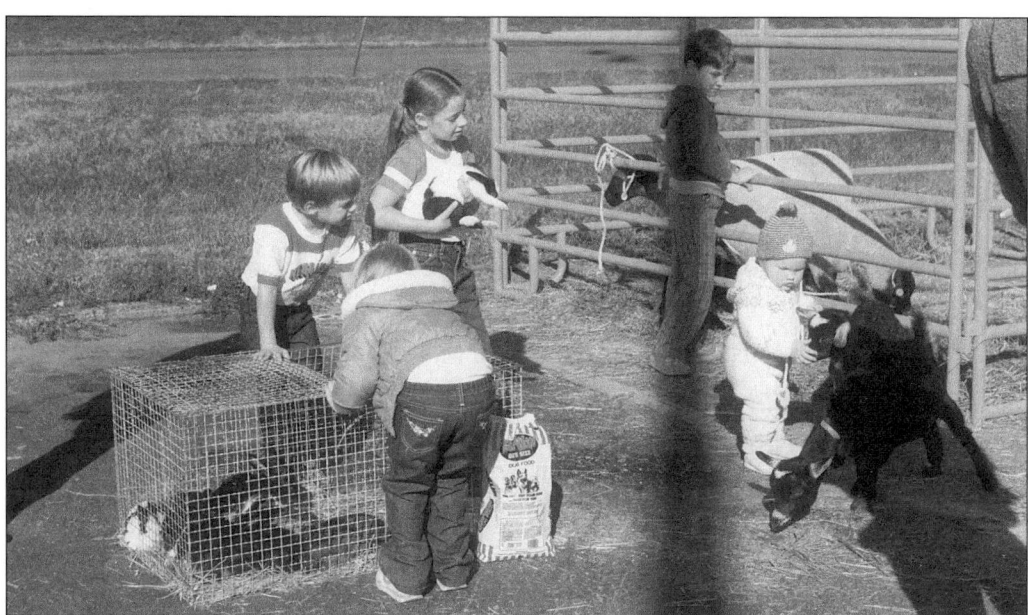

Every fall since 1980, Norfolk has hosted the LaVitsef Time Celebration. If you're wondering where the name came from, it's festival spelled backwards. The name may be backwards, but the festival isn't. The four-day event has something for everyone, including a marching band competition, parade, ice cream social, concerts, and even a pet show. Here, youngsters visit the pet show at the Sunset Plaza in 1984.

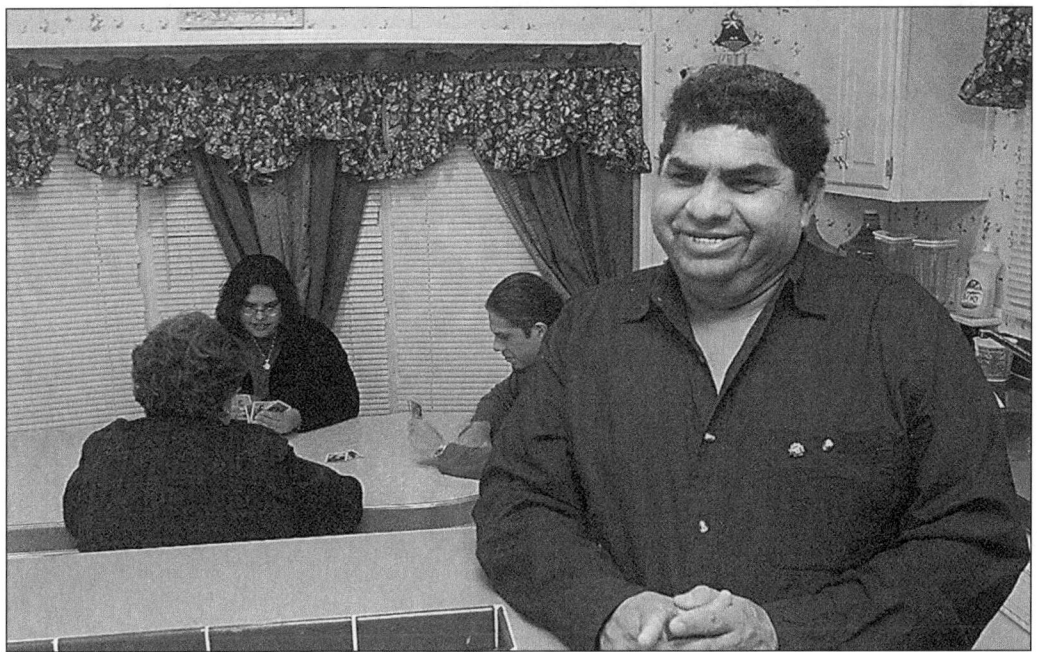

Isac Cartela stands in the kitchen of his home while his wife, Maria, and children, Nelly and Alberto, play cards in the background. Cartela and his family represent the large population of Hispanics who have made Norfolk their home in recent years. Most of them have come here seeking better opportunities, and many have succeeded in opening restaurants and shops.

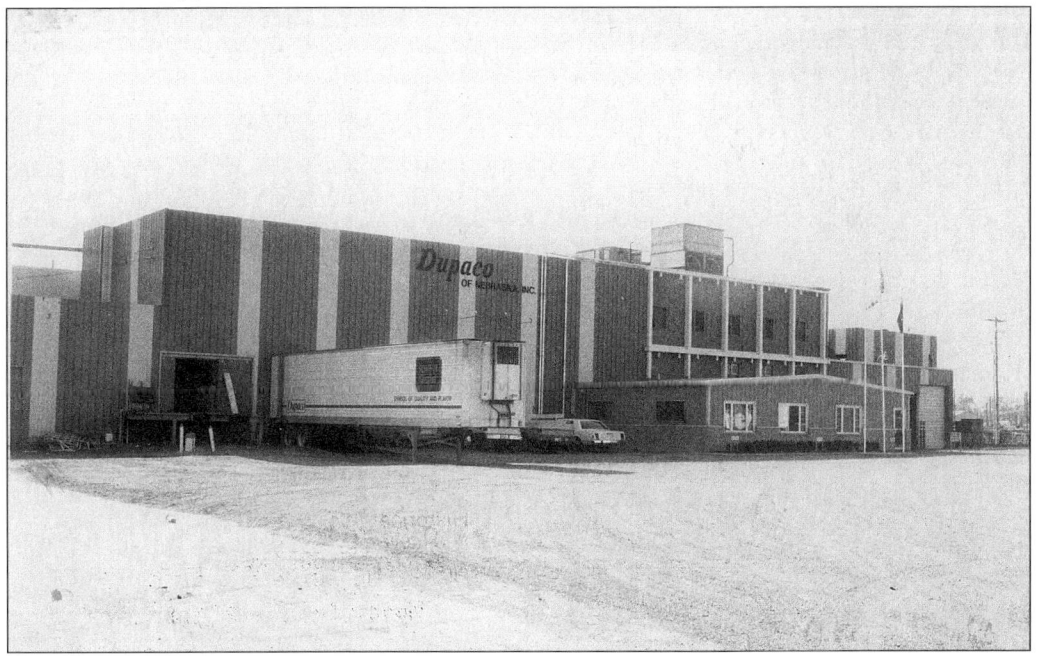

Dupaco of Nebraska, Inc. opened in 1987 as the newest meat packing plant in the Norfolk area. The plants have attracted workers from all over the country and Mexico. The population of the city has continued to diversify. The growth of such industries has led Norfolk to become the state's fourth largest retail center.

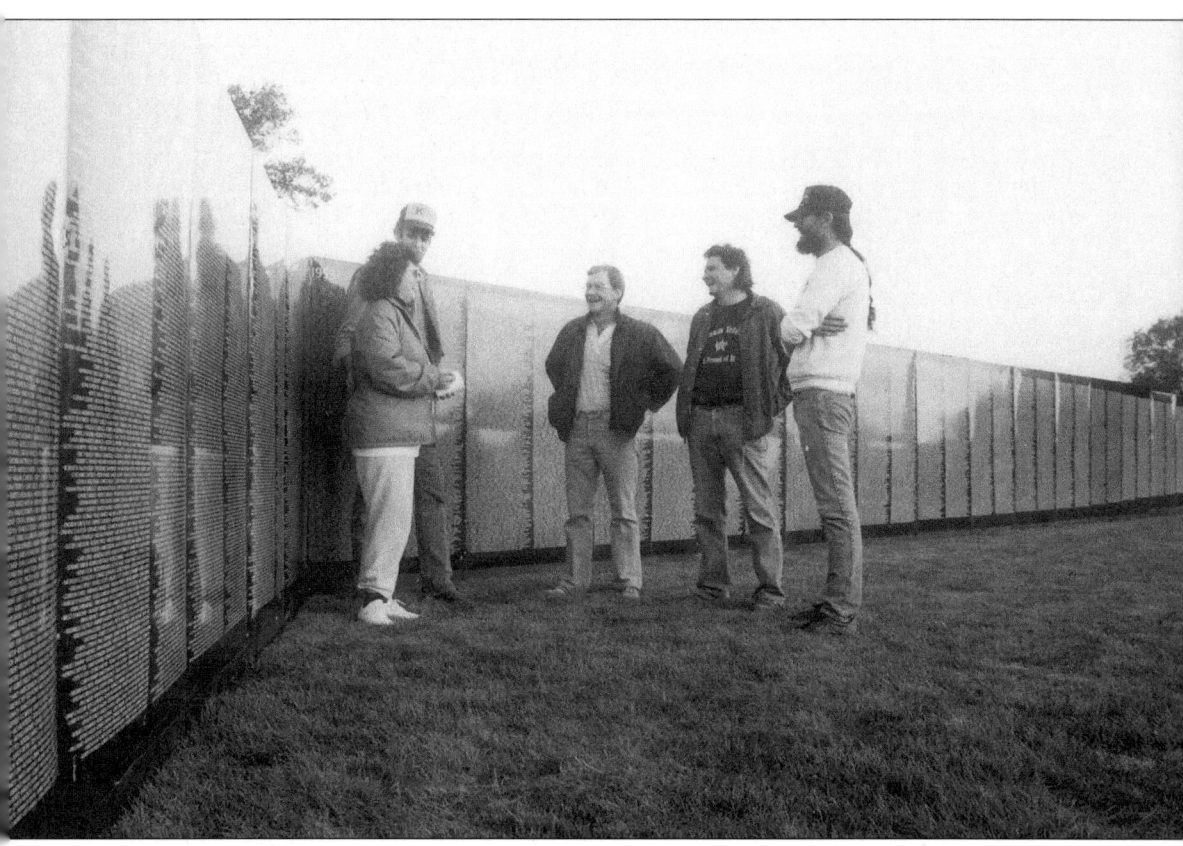

A replica of the Vietnam Veterans Memorial Wall was in Norfolk in the fall of 1988. The memorial was designed to honor the veterans who died as a result of their service during the Vietnam War. Genie and Denny Larson, Bruce Bounds, and Ted Laible, all of Norfolk, visit with John Devitt of San Jose, California, after setting up the Moving Wall at Memorial Field. Devitt created the half-sized replica, which toured the country. Its appearance in Norfolk was sponsored by American Legion Post 16 and VFW Post 1644. As of 1988, nine Norfolkans had their names engraved on the wall: Jerry Allen, Dennis Anderson, Jerome Chandler, Roger Hundt, Jerold Meisinger, Thomas Scheurich, Steven Strube, Claude Van Andel, and Michael Wemhoff.

Mary Voss, left, president of the Elkhorn Valley Historical Society, visits with Dorothy Verges LaBarre and Mayor Carl Maltas. The date was June 15, 1992, and the occasion was the dedication of Verges Park and its historical marker. Mrs. LaBarre's father, Dr. C.J. Verges, developed the park back in the early 1900s. The Nebraska State Historical Society marker explains the park's history; it is the only such marker in Norfolk.

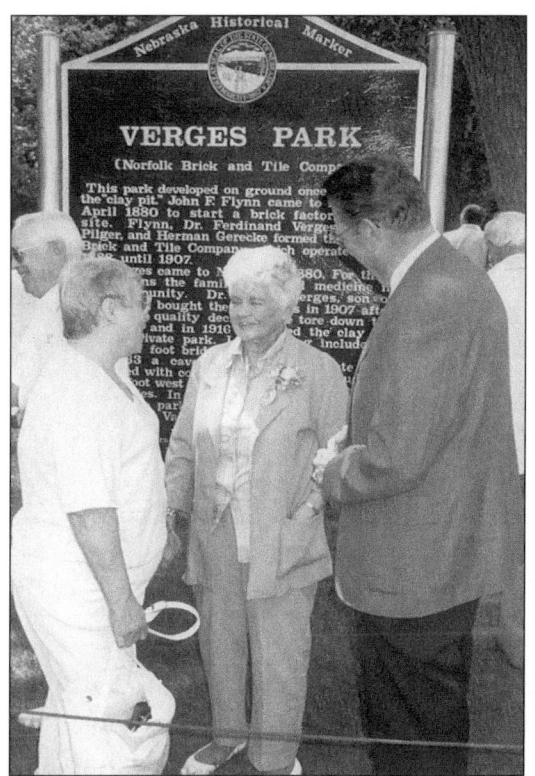

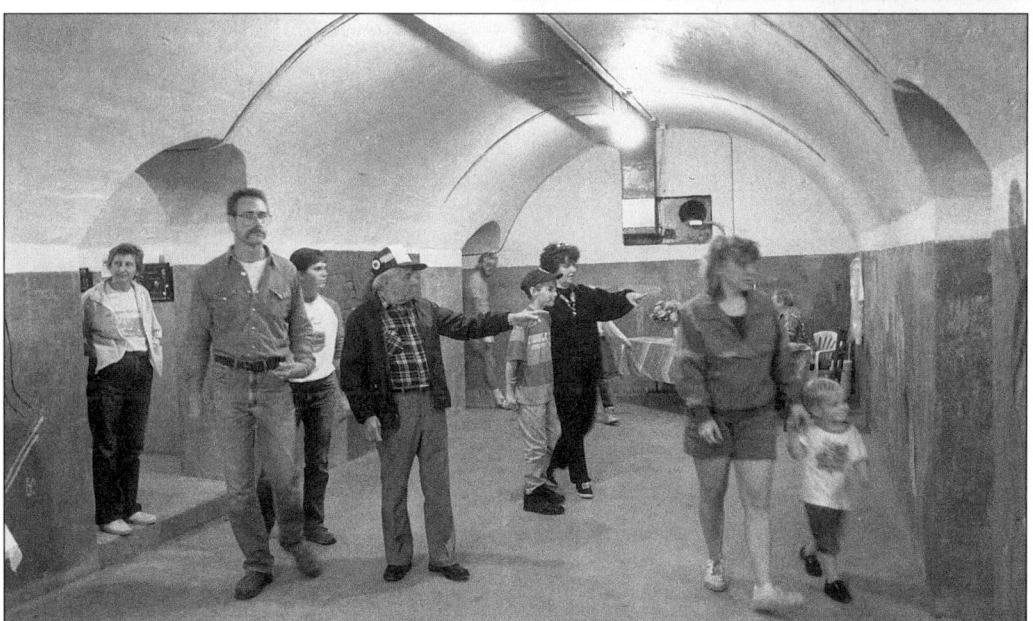

Visitors stroll through the cave at Verges Park. The cave was dug by Val Verges, the son of the park's founder, Dr. C.J. Verges. Val was just a young boy when he started his task, so his father had some of his hired men help finish the project. It eventually was used for meetings and social events. The park is now owned by the Elkhorn Valley Historical Society, and the cave is opened for special tours and holidays.

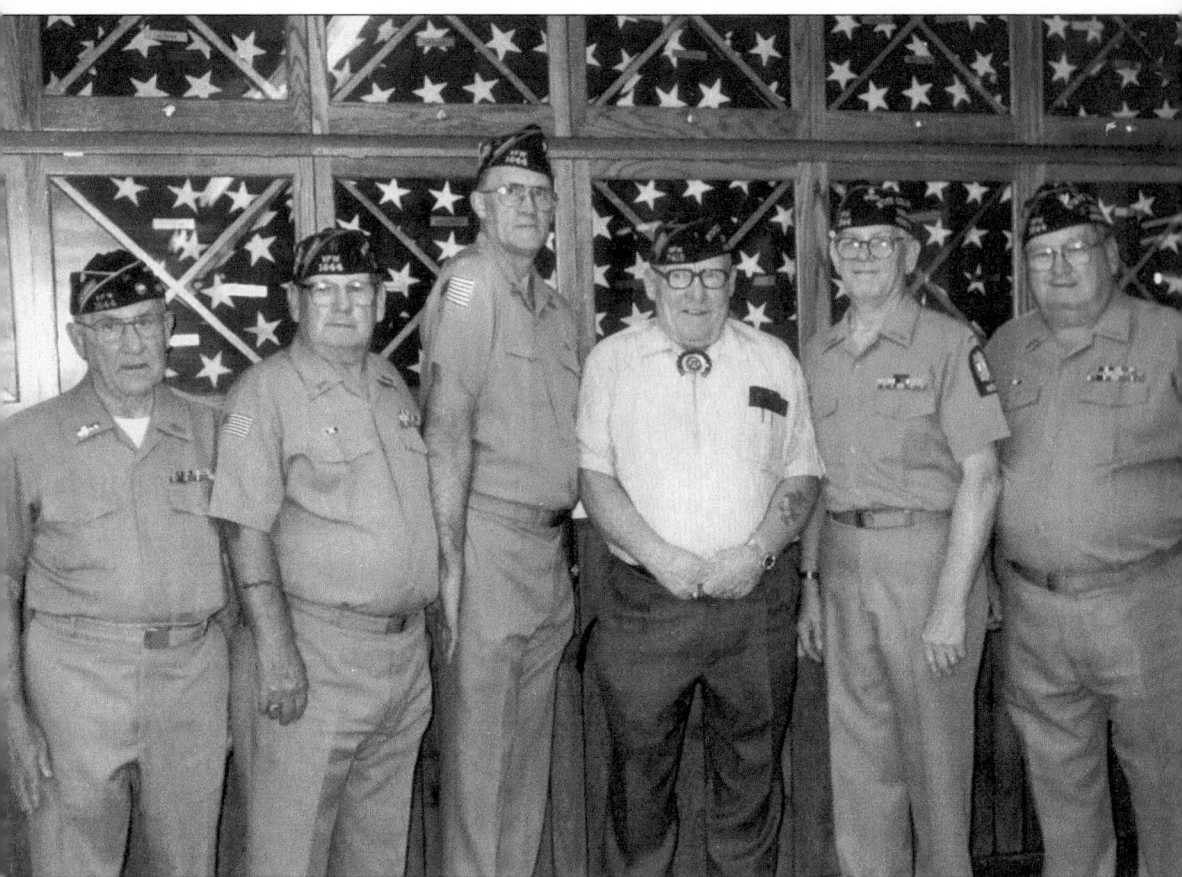

Members of the VFW State Color Guard in 1994 were, from left to right, Elmer Gall, Melvin Jones, John Fehrs, Commander Max West, George Real, and Marvin Jones. They are standing in front of a memorial flag display in the Winter-Munson VFW Post #1644, which is located at the corner of Braasch Avenue and 4th Street. The memorial flags are on permanent loan from the families of deceased veterans.

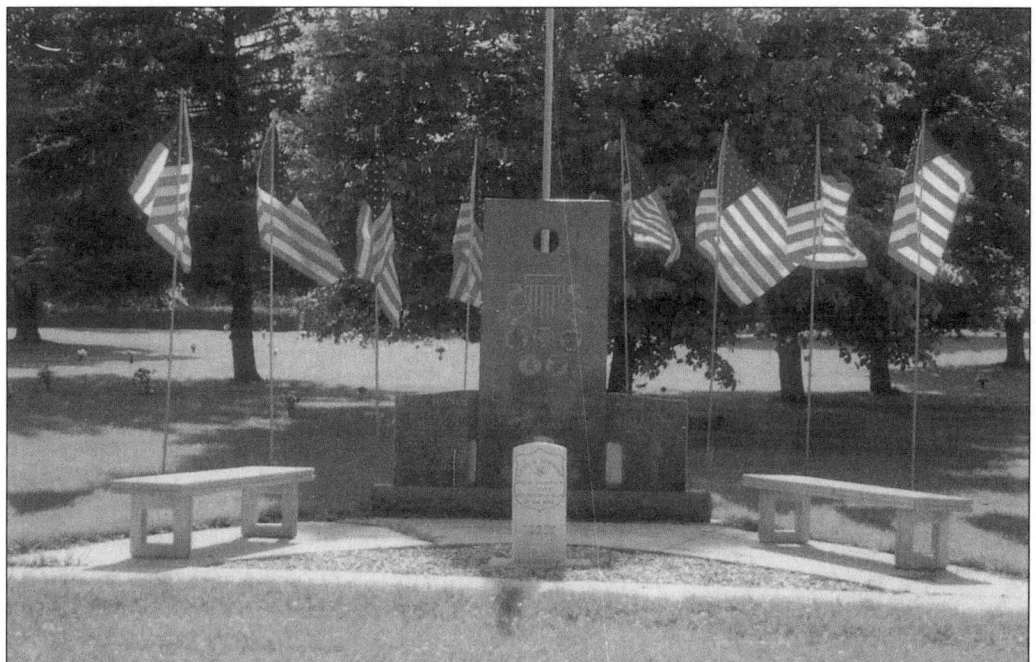

The Vietnam-Korean Memorial at Prospect Hill Cemetery was completed in 1983 to honor the local residents who gave their lives in the Vietnam and Korean Wars. The project was a joint effort between the Veterans of Foreign Wars, Disabled American Veterans, and the American Legion.

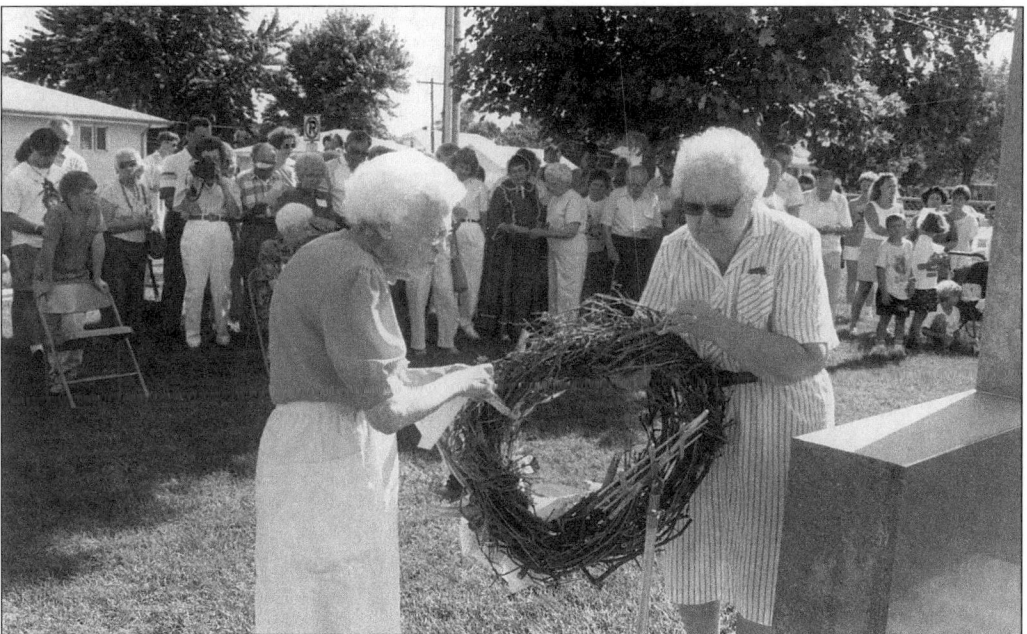

Emma Dommer, left, and Mrs. Harvey Kuester place a wreath on July 13, 1991, at the Pioneer Monument in Liberty Bell Park, 700 Georgia Avenue. Both of their grandfathers were part of the first group of settlers to come to the area. Mrs. Dommer is the granddaughter of Carl Uecker, and Mrs. Kuester is the granddaughter of Wilhelm Klug.

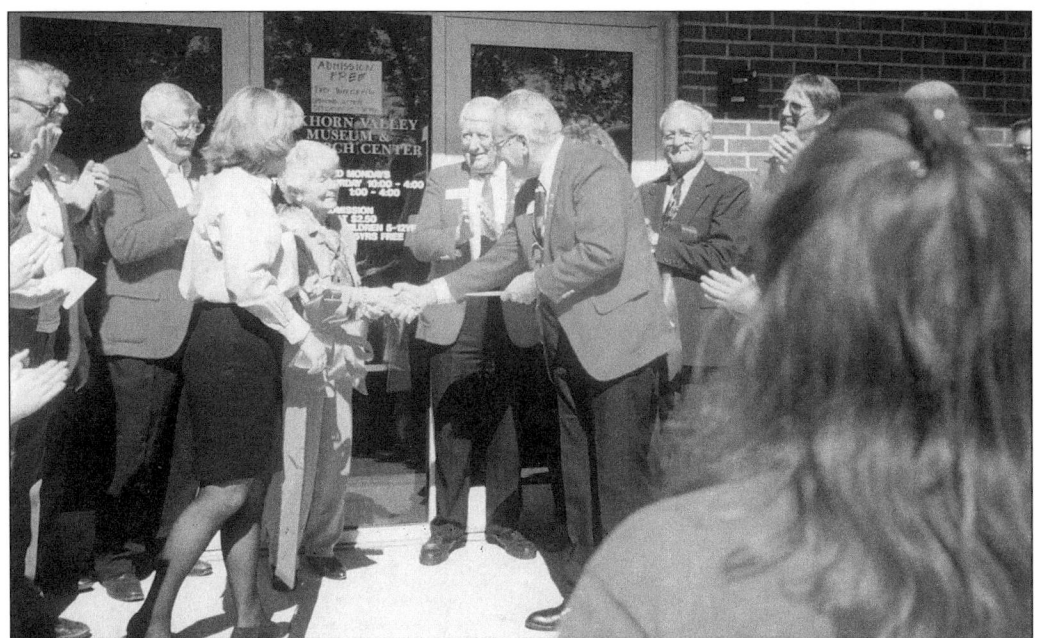

Mayor Harley Rector shakes hands with Dorothy Verges LaBarre at the dedication of the Elkhorn Valley Museum and Research Center on September 27, 1997. Deb Arenz, the museum's first director, looks on. The museum's opening was the culmination of years of work by the Elkhorn Valley Historical Society, which started in 1958. Robert Carlisle was the organization's founding president.

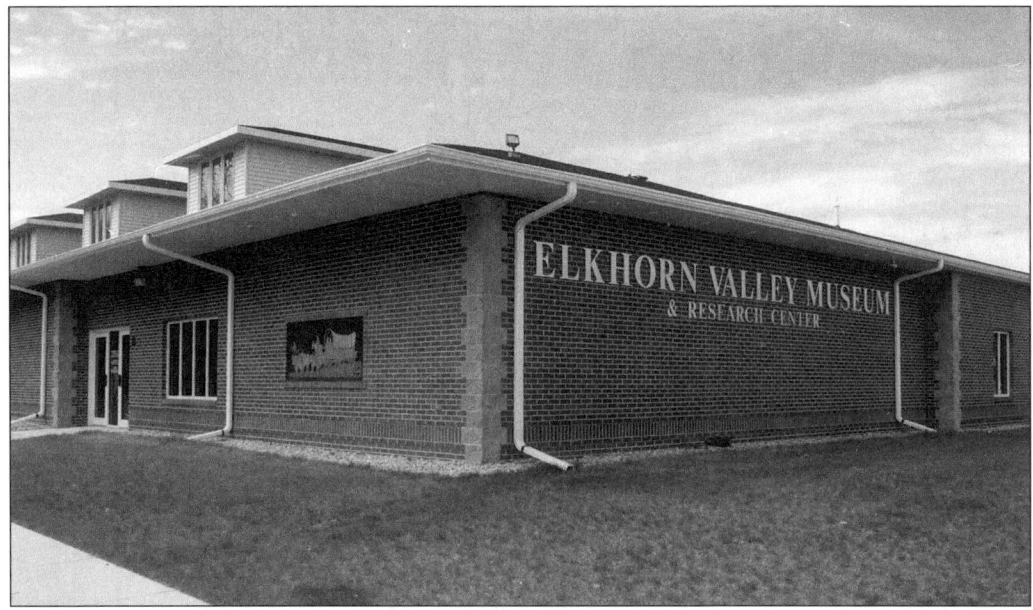

The Elkhorn Valley Museum and Research Center not only showcases the history of the area, but it also offers resource materials available for persons doing historical research. The museum offers several galleries, one of which houses exhibits that change periodically. The museum would not be possible without the generous support of the people of Norfolk and those who have ties to Northeast Nebraska.

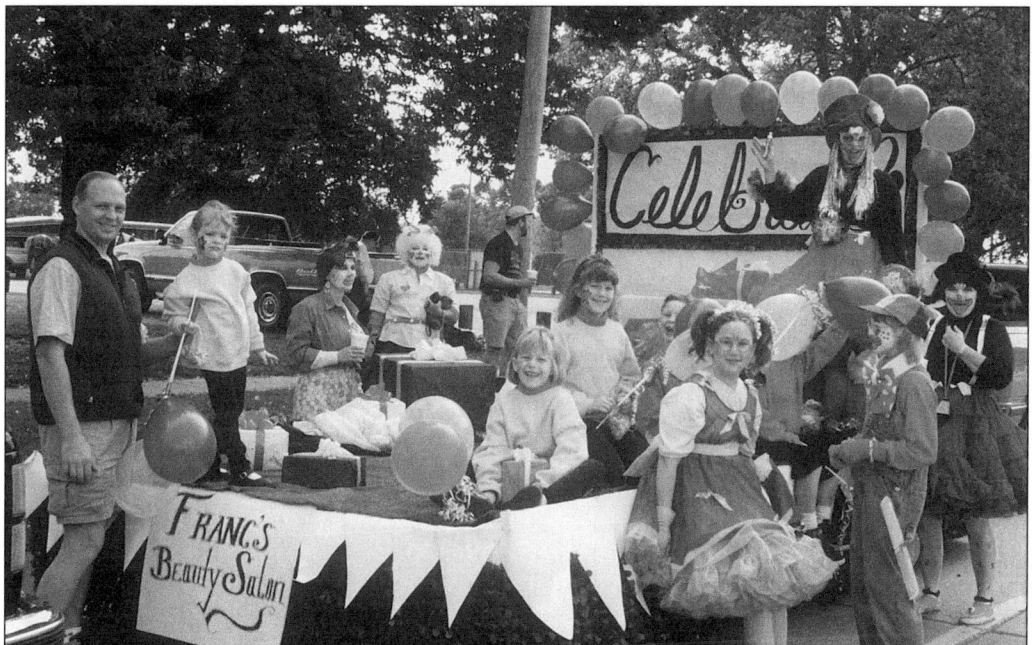

In this 1997 photo, children and adults representing Franc's Beauty Salon prepare to ride a float in the annual LaVitsef Parade. The annual parade is Norfolk's largest. It features the Outstanding Citizen from all of the surrounding towns as well as the winners of the Community Service Award, the Golden Award, and the LaVitsef Sweetheart.

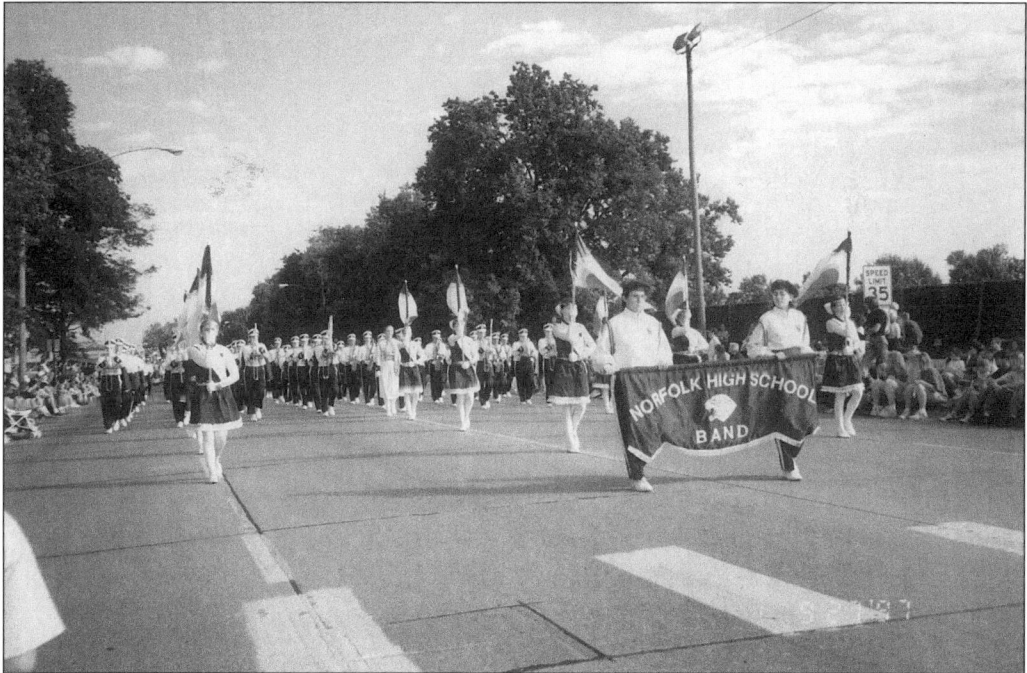

The Norfolk High School band marches in the 1997 LaVitsef Parade. It normally includes about 20 high school marching bands, which participate in a band competition after the parade.

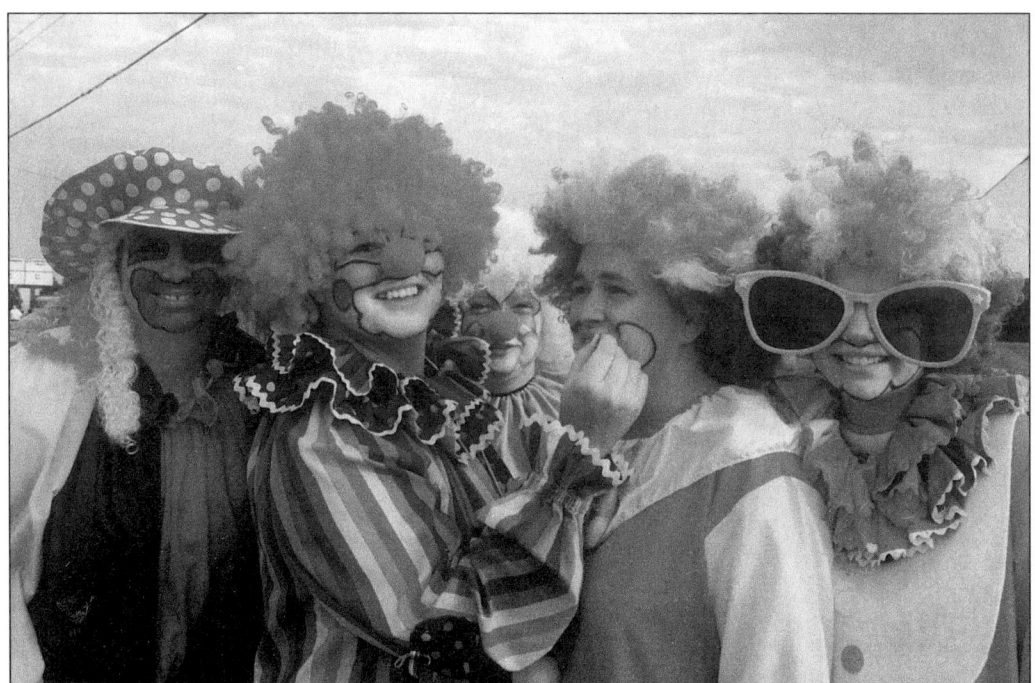

It was time to celebrate in September of 1997 when these clowns were preparing for the annual LaVitsef Parade. Many other special events take place throughout the city on the last full weekend in September.

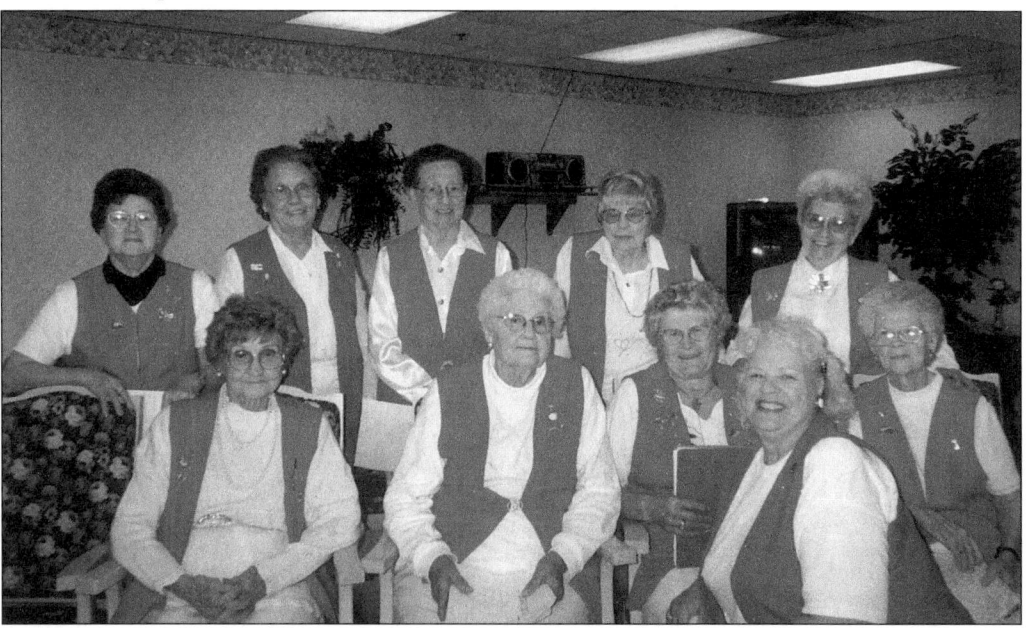

Members of the Norfolk Senior Citizen Center Choraleers are, from left to right, Doris Petersen, Irene Faubel, Martha Bohn, Corinne Waugh, Elnora Remmich, Verna Dohren, Ruth Dolezal, Elaine Wachter, Arlene Schurr, and Elsa Staley. The Senior Citizen Center is a hub of activity for seniors who go there for meals and other activities. The facility is also available for banquets and receptions.

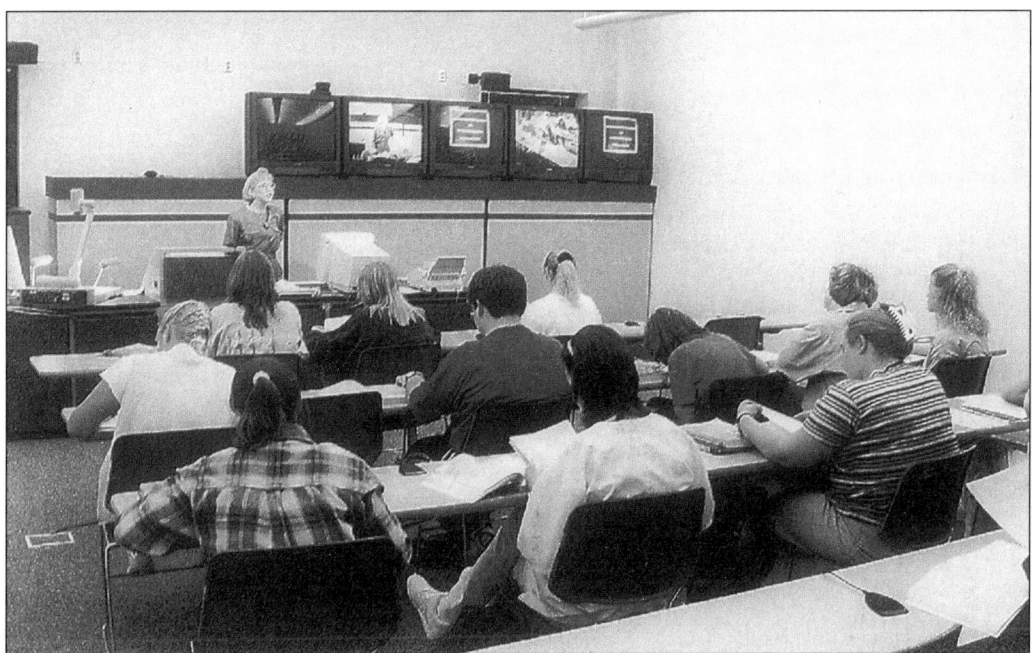

The Lifelong Learning Center, dedicated in March of 1998, is on the campus of Northeast Community College. The 20,000 square foot educational building includes two distance learning classrooms, a computer center, three standard classrooms, and a divisible conference center that can accommodate up to seven hundred people.

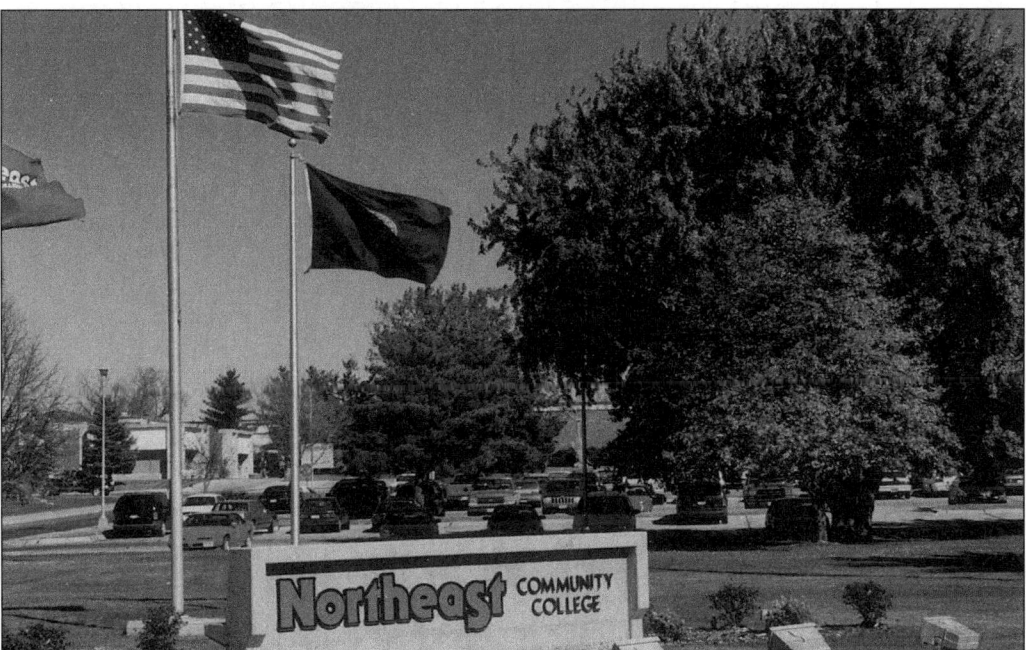

Northeast Community College at 801 East Benjamin Avenue provides technical degrees, diplomas, and associate degrees in the liberal arts. The school offers programs as diverse as truck driving, secretarial science, and utility lineman. The school is often a stepping-stone for students wishing to transfer their credits to a four-year institution.

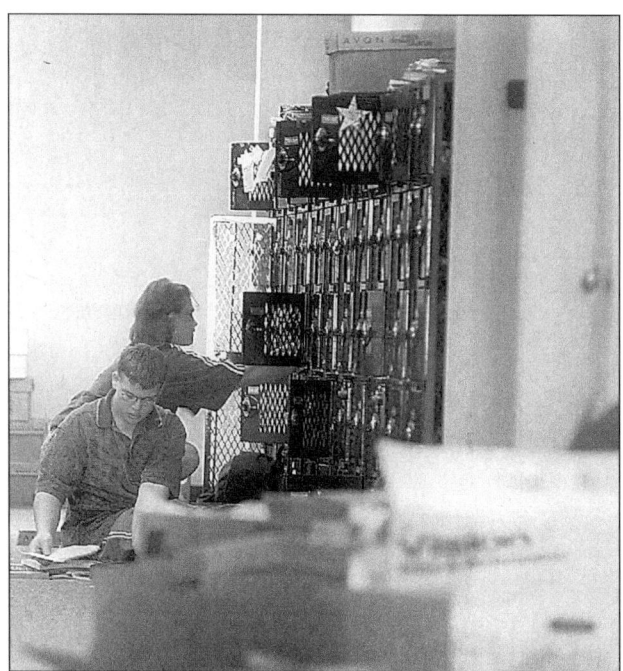

Justin Novotny and Sarah Bethards unpack books from boxes on March 16, 1999, which was their first day of school at the new Lutheran High Northeast. The school, supported by area Missouri Synod Lutheran Churches, had been at several different sites in Norfolk before funds were raised and the new facility was built at 2010 North 37th Street. The first class of LHNE graduated in May of 2000.

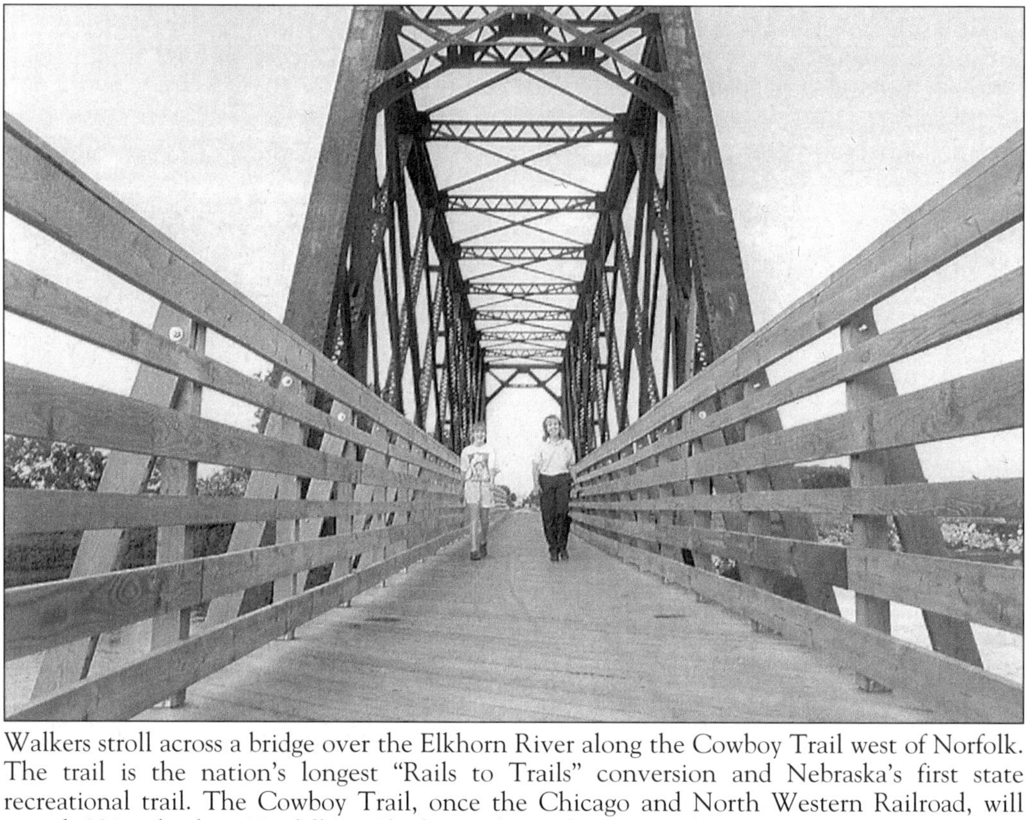

Walkers stroll across a bridge over the Elkhorn River along the Cowboy Trail west of Norfolk. The trail is the nation's longest "Rails to Trails" conversion and Nebraska's first state recreational trail. The Cowboy Trail, once the Chicago and North Western Railroad, will stretch 321 miles from Norfolk to Chadron. The trail was named one of 50 Millennium Legacy Trails by the White House's Millennium Initiative Council.

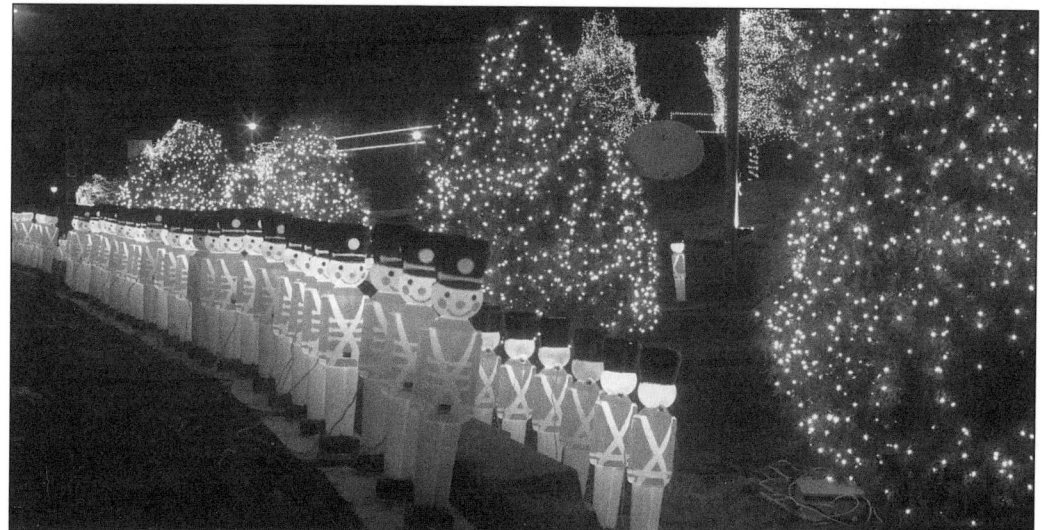

Norfolkans and their visitors are delighted each year by the community's Holiday Rhapsody of Lights. The display includes animated figures and over 500,000 lights. It is now located at Northeast Community College. The display was originally at the home of its creators, John and Connie Day. Here, lighted soldiers stand at attention along the sidewalk.

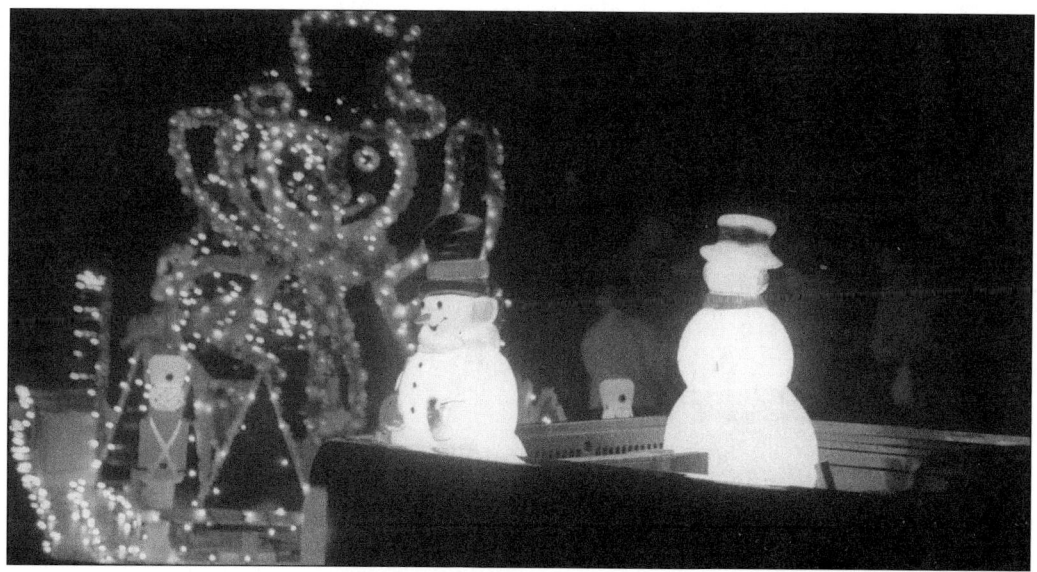

The first Holiday Rhapsody of Lights Festival was in 1998. The purpose of the festival, which normally includes an artisans fair, parade, concert, and other activities, is to raise money to support the Holiday Rhapsody of Lights display. In this photo, a lighted float makes its way down the parade route.

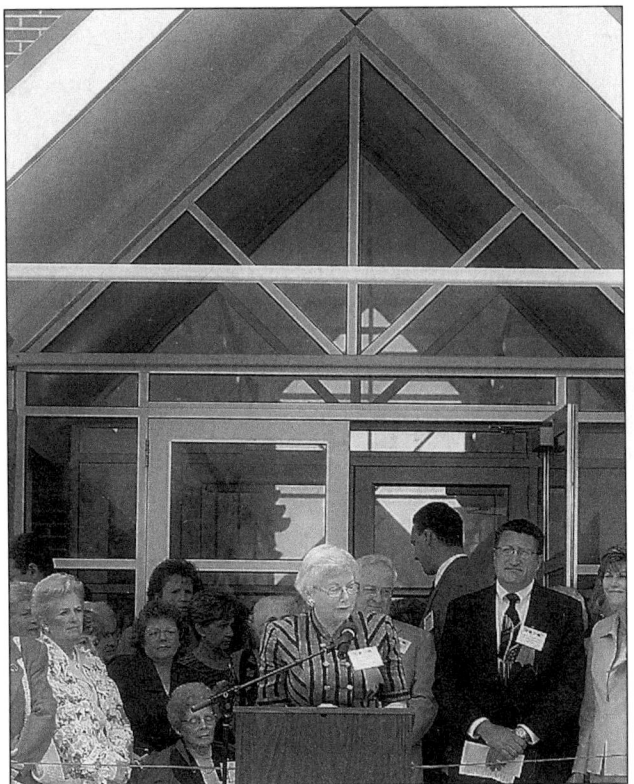

Norfolk, with its modern museum, theater, library, senior citizen center, and arts center is quickly becoming known as the cultural center of Nebraska. At no time was that more evident than on June 5, 2000, when the new Norfolk Arts Center was dedicated. Here Marilyn Mitchell, president of the Norfolk Arts Center Board of Directors, speaks during the dedication ceremony.

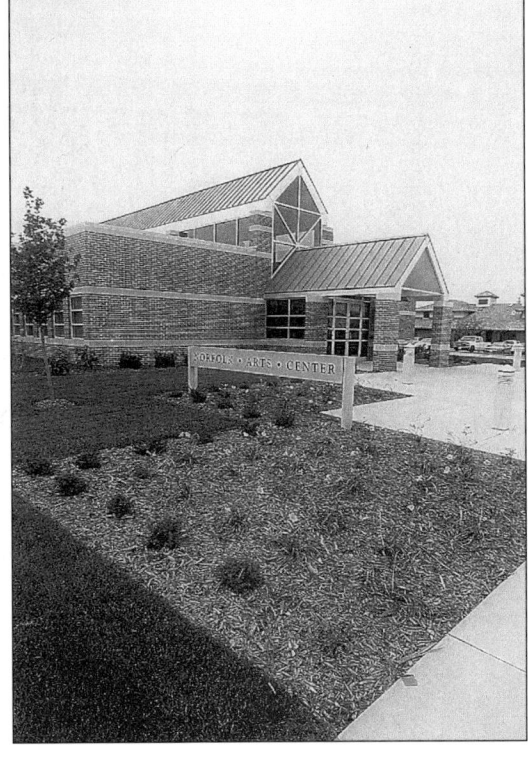

This $1.7 million structure at 305 North 5th Street is the center's third location. The Norfolk Arts Center began in 1978 in the old Carnegie Library building at 803 Norfolk Avenue. By 1994, board members realized the need for a new facility, and a major fund drive was organized. The center includes a gallery, classrooms, a meeting room, and kitchen. A unique feature is the adjacent sculpture garden.

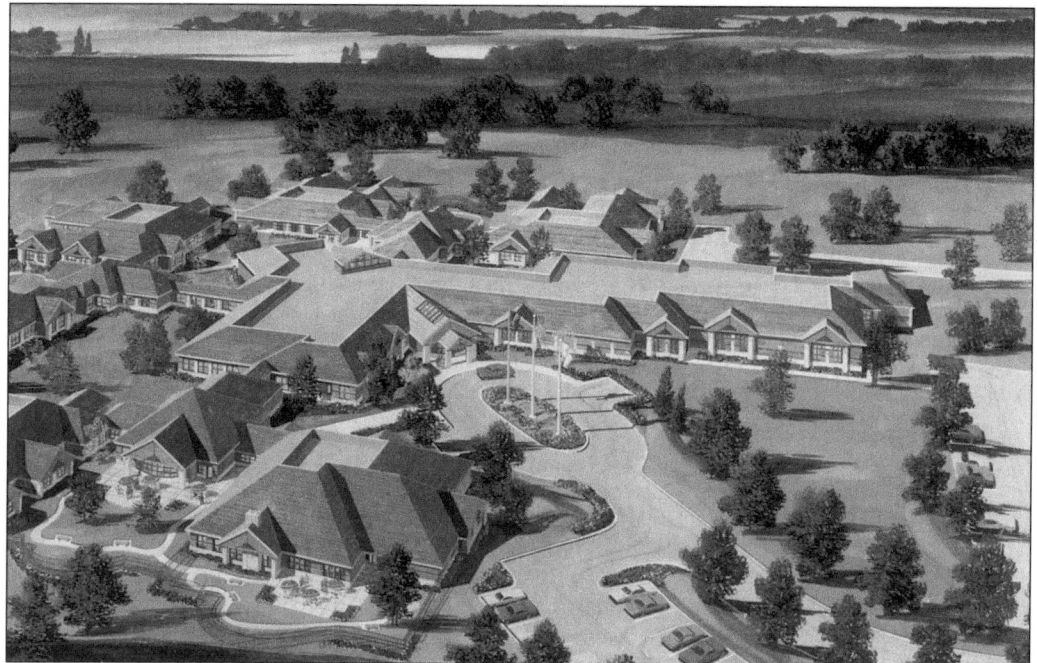

This artist's drawing depicts the $16 million Norfolk Veterans Home that will open in 2001. Before moving into this facility, the Veterans Home was located on the campus of the Norfolk Regional Center in buildings that were built in 1936 and 1948. Ground was broken in January of 1998 for the 159-bed nursing care facility that is located on 19 acres of land on East Benjamin Avenue.

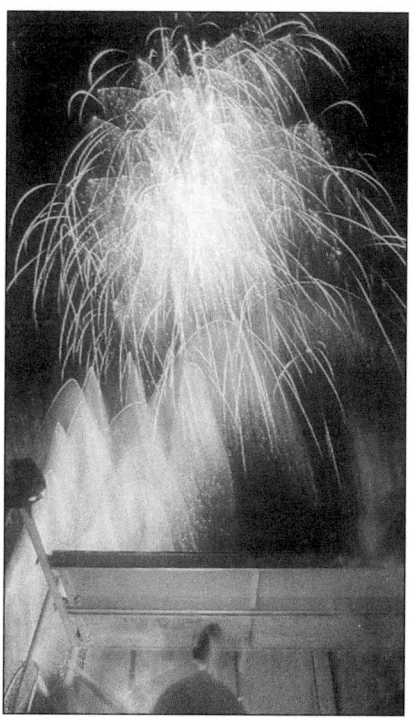

Norfolk certainly has had plenty of reasons to celebrate the last 135 years. If people like Herman Gerecke, Charles Mathewson, and August Raasch could see the town they helped found, they would marvel at what a modern city it has become. The once dirt streets are now paved—not with gold—but with the sweat and determination of a people who were brave enough to carve life out of what was once a wild prairie. Their spirit lives on in the generations that followed. They too plowed their dreams into the rich Nebraska soil where they blossomed and spread their seeds to those who followed. Yes, there have been plenty of reasons to celebrate, and there will be plenty more because Norfolk's future is as bright as these fireworks lighting up the July 2000 sky.

INDEX